D isability Rights UK

Holidays 2012

in the British Isles
A guide for disabled people

Holidays in the British Isles 2012
A guide for disabled people

ISBN 978-0-956777-0-0
© Radar Promotions Ltd 2012

Published by Radar Promotions Ltd for
Disability Rights UK.
Registered Charity No. 1138585

Design: © Anderson Fraser Partnership, London

Disability Rights UK
12 City Forum, 250 City Road, London EC1V 8AF
Tel: 020 7250 3222
Fax: 020 7250 0212
www.disabilityrightsuk.org

Editor:
Mark Shrimpton

Author:
Katie Grant, Raincharm Communications Ltd

Contributors:
Elizabeth Alabaster
Sarah Cosby
Ian Greaves
Jessica Smith, Michelle Stannard, Anna Whelan
and Kayla Whiting from Poached Creative
John Stanford

Production:
Anderson Fraser: Deb Kamofsky, Paul McKenzie
and Humphrey Weightman

Photographs:
VisitBritain/Pawel Libera
Jersey Tourism Image Library
Paul McKenzie

Thanks to:
The tourist boards of the Channel Islands,
England, the Isle of Man, Scotland and Wales
for their information and co-operation.

Special thanks to VisitEngland for providing
information about their register of
accommodation that meets the standards of
the National Accessible Scheme and for
granting us free use of the photographs in
VisitBritain Images.

Holidays 2012

in the British Isles
A guide for disabled people

You can find more detailed descriptions of these regions and the areas they include on page 12.

Contents

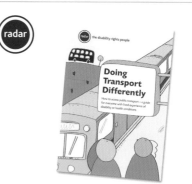

Preface

My name is Liz Sayce. I am the former Chief Executive of Radar and the new Chief Executive of Disability Rights UK. On the 1st January 2012, we joined forces with the National Centre for Independent Living and Disability Alliance to form Disability Rights UK. Joining forces has allowed us to offer a wider range of services and deliver more campaigns with and on behalf of disabled people. We aim to be the largest national pan-disability organisation led by disabled people.

We are in the great position of being able to build on the previous work of Radar with our new partners at Disability Alliance and the National Centre for Independent Living at a time when we really need a strong and sustainable organisation led by disabled people to push for positive change.

Everyone needs a holiday and disabled people are no exception. Going on holiday can make all the difference to how we function and feel in ourselves. With more opportunities to pay for holidays and take control using self-directed support, we can be far more independent and take control of our lives. With many exciting events happening here in the UK in 2012 such as the London 2012 Olympic and Paralympics and the Queen's Diamond Jubilee, we hope that this Guide helps to give you the confidence and inspiration you need to take a holiday. As VisitEngland's 'Holidays at home are GREAT' campaign is currently trying to highlight, in the tough economic times we are living in, taking a holiday in the UK and experiencing the beauty we have on our doorstep can still give you the break you need. We hope you enjoy reading the Guide and happy holidays!

Liz Sayce OBE
Chief Executive
Disability Rights UK

About Disability Rights UK

Radar is now Disability Rights UK. On 1st January 2012, the Royal Association for Disability Rights became part of Disability Rights UK, a new charity formed through our coming together with Disability Alliance and the National Centre for Independent Living. We aim to be the largest, national pan-disability organisation in the UK led by disabled people – with over 700 members consisting of both individuals and organisations.

Our vision is a society where everyone with lived experience of disability or health conditions can participate equally as full citizens.

Our objectives are:
- To mobilise disabled people's leadership and control – in our own lives, our organisations and society;
- To achieve independent living in practice;
- To break the link between disability and poverty;
- To put disability equality and human rights into practice across society.

It has never been more important to have a strong organisation that stands up for disabled people's rights and supports disabled people's organisations nationally. We bring proposals and solutions to help assert the rights of disabled people and encourage social change. We campaign on policy issues with the full participation of disabled people and provide expert advice and resources for disabled people and the organisations that support you.

To find out more about who we are and what we do, visit our website or contact us at:

12 City Forum, 250 City Road, London EC1V 8AF.
Telephone 020 7250 3222
Fax: 020 7250 0212
Email: reception@disabilityrightsuk.org
Website: www.disabilityrightsuk.org

Introduction

Welcome to the Holiday Guide 2012; a book that has regularly been produced for disabled people for over 35 years. Written by and for disabled people, this is an essential read for you and the people who support you to help find out more about accessible and inclusive holiday experiences. Whether it's a day trip out or an adventure holiday, you can use this guide as a support tool and resource to help plan your time away.

Taking a break and going on holiday can be a great experience and essential to your health and wellbeing. It can give you and the people who support you, a well-earned rest and the chance to travel to new places and have new experiences. But, if you have a disability or long-term health condition, you may need to plan carefully to make sure you get the most from your break.

We have compiled this Guide to help you prepare for a holiday and find the information you might need to make sure that your destination and accommodation is suitable. We've included a selection of places to stay and things to do when you get there. There's practical information about how to plan and book a holiday plus a range of resources that might be helpful when travelling around.

Since we started producing a holiday guide over 30 years ago, there have been substantial improvements in the regulations and legislation affecting the provision of accessible accommodation and the other services needed by disabled guests. There are many people within the tourist industry who have a real interest in catering for disabled guests and this number is growing all the time.

Advances in technology have transformed the travel industry. Online resources now provide a wealth of ever-changing options and an increasing amount of information for people with specific needs. Tourism for All UK, Open Britain and DisabledGo are just a few of the organisations providing a wealth of information through their websites and publications.

There is a whole world out there at your fingertips. Take your time to find the information you need and then shop around for bargains. Finding out as much as you can before you go, can really pay off.

We hope you have a wonderful time wherever you go and whatever you do. We know that accessible and inclusive holidays are much more of a reality than they were in the past. We hope our Guide will help you to find the holiday or trip away you always wanted.

We would like to thank John Stanford, who compiled earlier editions of this Guide and everyone who has supported the Guide through advertising.

We welcome feedback on this and all our publications. We have made every effort to ensure that the information in this Guide is correct and up to date. But if you notice an error or can provide more up to date information please email your comments and suggestions to feedback@disabilityrightsuk.org.

Happy holidays!

Finding your way around this Guide

The book is divided into two parts. Part 1 provides general advice and guidance to help you organise your trip and includes a list of organisations and resources you may find useful. Part 2 offers you an armchair tour around the British Isles, to help you decide where you might want to go and let you know about some of the local resources available to you in each region.

1: Advice and guidance

Organising your trip
This section helps you think about choosing a destination, understand how accommodation is graded and assessed and finally, book your holiday.

Getting there and travelling around
This section offers advice to help with travel planning, public transport, motoring and parking.

While you're away
This section includes ideas for how you might spend your leisure time while you are away. It includes details of activity holiday organisers and lists useful organisations and resources. An important part of freedom while you're away, is knowing where to find public toilets that are accessible and meet your needs. So this section also includes a chapter on the Radar National Key Scheme and details of our guide to accessible toilets in the United Kingdom.

Useful resources
This section includes contacts and publications that may be useful wherever you choose to go in the British Isles. It includes organisations involved with tourism and holiday provision, national equipment and vehicle hire companies and a range of publications and websites.

2: Around the British Isles

About each region
A region-by-region tour, including a brief introduction to the area, its scenery and tourist attractions, a map, and a list of local resources including tourist boards, transport, sources of local information and advice, local equipment hire companies and a brief selection of places to stay. You will find a range of accommodation, including properties assessed under VisitEngland's National Accessible Scheme (NAS). An index by region of properties meeting NAS standards can be found at the back of this Guide.

Regions and the areas they include

● **Greater London**
*The London boroughs of Greater London
and a Central London area, (roughly that
within the Congestion Charge area) including
the City of London and parts of Camden,
Islington, Lambeth, Southwark and
Westminster.*

● **South East England**
East Sussex, Kent, Surrey and West Sussex.

● **Southern England**
*Berkshire, Buckinghamshire, Hampshire,
the Isle of Wight and Oxfordshire.*

● **West Country**
*Gloucestershire, Somerset, Wiltshire, Dorset
and the area around Bristol.*

● **Devon & Cornwall**

● **Eastern England**
*Bedfordshire, Cambridgeshire, Essex,
Hertfordshire, Norfolk and Suffolk.*

● **East Midlands**
*Derbyshire, Leicestershire, Lincolnshire,
Northamptonshire and Nottinghamshire
and the southern part of the area that used
to form Humberside.*

● **West Midlands**
*Herefordshire, Shropshire, Staffordshire,
Warwickshire, West Midlands and
Worcestershire.*

● **North West England**
*Cheshire, Cumbria, Greater Manchester,
Lancashire and Merseyside.*

● **Yorkshire**
*North, South and West Yorkshire and the
East Riding of Yorkshire and Kingston-upon-
Hull districts.*

● **North East England**
*Durham, Northumberland and Tyne &
Wear and the Tees Valley.*

● **South East Scotland**
*Edinburgh, Falkirk, the Lothians and the
Scottish Borders.*

● **South West Scotland**
*Ayrshire, Dumfries & Galloway,
Dunbartonshire, Lanarkshire, Renfrewshire
and Glasgow.*

● **East Scotland**
*Aberdeenshire, Angus, Clackmannan, Fife,
Perth & Kinross and Stirling.*

● **Highlands & Islands of Scotland**
*Argyle & Bute, Highlands, Moray, Orkney,
Shetland and the Western Isles.*

● **North Wales**
*Anglesey, Conwy, Denbighshire, Flintshire
and Gwynedd.*

● **Mid & West Wales**
*Carmarthenshire, Ceredigion, Pembrokeshire
and Powys.*

● **South Wales**
*The area that formed the counties of
Glamorgan and Gwent including Cardiff
and Swansea.*

● **Northern Ireland**

● **Republic of Ireland**

● **Channel Islands**

● **Isle of Man**

These regions do not necessarily correspond to official administrative areas but were originally devised for the convenience of Radar National Key Scheme keyholders.

Freespace - inclusive design

Planning your holiday

Holiday brochures often say little about what is available for people with a disability or health condition. However, many providers of holiday-related services do have facilities available and some are very committed to providing a comfortable and welcoming experience. So how do you choose where to go and where to stay?

What type of holiday?

Whether you are thinking of a city break to shop and visit art galleries, a peaceful relaxing rest in the countryside or a fun-filled time at the seaside, there will be many destinations in the British Isles to choose from.

Finding inspiration

Holiday brochures and travel magazines are a great source of holiday ideas. Have a look at the travel sections of national newspapers or their online versions. Lots of people write travel and holiday blogs on the internet. For interesting travel tips and ideas, try the Lonely Planet blog or TravelPod. You could also look at disabledtravelers.com a resource dedicated to accessible travel information and ideas.

Where to go?

Finding information

Find out as much you can about the area you are thinking of visiting. This Guide provides an overview about each region around the British Isles and lists me of the places you can visit when you get there, but it is worth doing more research. Take a look at the suggested websites and publications.

You can get help, advice and ideas from tourist information centres and travel companies. Call in to speak to them in person or get in touch by email or telephone.

Where to stay?

Do you want to be pampered in a five-star hotel, self-cater in a countryside cottage, have fun in a holiday park or are you looking for a respite break?

Your questions will be similar. What kind of accommodation shall I stay in? How do I look at the choices? How will I know that it is the quality I expected? Will it have the facilities or nearby resources that I want? How can I find out whether it will meet my requirements if I have an accessibility need?

Would you like a hotel with a swimming pool? In an area where you can go bird-watching? Holiday providers, guidebooks and tourist boards use slightly different symbols to represent facilities at premises or leisure facilities. They should let you see at a glance whether the hotel has the general facilities you want.

Grading systems for accommodation quality are quite consistent. When you find accommodation of the right quality – within your price range – check the facilities carefully directly with the provider. Some places will have all the facilities you are looking for. Others may appear less well equipped

but if you talk to them in advance, they may be able to arrange for the support or equipment you need.

Remember you can only do so much by email. Talking to the people who run the accommodation can be helpful. It is always worth asking what they can do to help you out. A large hotel chain may have someone specifically responsible for accessibility.

Ask as many questions as you need and find out as much as you can about the accommodation before you book. When you have decided, try to book accommodation well in advance.

Finding accommodation

So how do you find the right kind of accommodation of the right quality – that will also meet your accessibility needs? You have the right and should ask hotels to provide you with their 'Access Statement'. You can research online or look for hotels that have been assessed under the National Accessible Scheme.

Checking accessibility

Accessible accommodation can be enjoyed by everyone, including people with access needs. This includes people with hearing and visual impairments, wheelchair users, older and less mobile people and people with pushchairs.

Some hotels include accessibility information on their websites. You can find details via national and local tourist board websites or at:

- www.openbritain.net
- www.disabledgo.com

Look for symbols which show that the accommodation has been assessed or audited. Check that the information is still up to date by contacting the hotel directly and ask about their facilities and rooms specifically designed for disabled people.

Ask for their Access Statement:
This is an explanation of how access and facilities for disabled people have been addressed in their particular accommodation.

If you are considering booking, it's a good idea to make the request by letter or email as you will then have a written record that you asked them about these facilities and services. The last thing you want to do is arrive and find out that the person on duty has no record of the things you need.

If you have mobility problems you may want to ask for a room on the lowest floor so that you aren't dependent on lifts in case of an emergency. Every place that offers accommodation should have a clear plan of action and clear instructions about what to do if there is a fire or another emergency when you need to get out safely.

If you use a wheelchair, let the hotel know how wide it is. Ask them to confirm door widths and make sure there is space to move your wheelchair around comfortably. If the room has a roll-in shower, ask if they have an adapted shower wheelchair you can use.

Assessing accessibility

ENGLAND
National Accessible Scheme (NAS)

VisitEngland rates the accessibility of visitor accommodation throughout England. Their standards cover mobility, visual and hearing impairments.

Accommodation that has been assessed as meeting NAS standards can display one or more of the symbols below. You can find out more on the VisitEngland website at: Ⓦ www.visitengland.com/accessforall

MOBILITY IMPAIRMENT LOGOS

Older and less mobile guests
If you can climb a flight of stairs, but banisters or grip handles would make this easier, look out for this logo.

Part-time wheelchair users
If you have problems walking or can walk a maximum of 3 steps, or need to use a wheelchair some of the time, look out for this logo.

Independent wheelchair users
Similar to the international logo for independent wheelchair users. If you're a wheelchair user and travel independently, look out for this logo.

Assisted wheelchair users
If you're a wheelchair user and travel with a friend or family member who helps you with everyday tasks, this logo applies to you.

Access Exceptional
Achieves the standards above for either independent wheelchair users or assisted wheelchair users and fulfils additional, more demanding requirements with reference to the British Standard BS 8300.

VISUAL IMPAIRMENT LOGOS

Visually impaired guests (1)
If you have difficulty reading small print, are registered blind, have poor sight or a visual impairment, accommodation with this logo is suitable for you.

Visually impaired guests (2)
An exceptional level of facilities and services that would be suitable for anyone with a visual impairment from mild sight loss to having no sight at all.

HEARING IMPAIRMENT LOGOS

Hearing impaired guests (1)
If you have a slight hearing difficulty, are deaf, wear a hearing aid or have a hearing impairment, look out for accommodation displaying this logo.

Hearing impaired guests (2)
An exceptional level of facilities and services that would be suitable for anyone with a hearing impairment from mild hearing loss to profound deafness.

SCOTLAND
Accessibility categories

As part of the VisitScotland grading scheme, properties are inspected and graded by Quality Advisors using criteria drawn up in co-operation with wheelchair users. Where a property holds one of the awards above, at least one bedroom in a hotel, guesthouse, B&B or hostel is accessible to the level given.

They are awarded one or more of the following gradings:

Category 1: Wheelchair access without assistance. Accessible to a wheelchair user travelling independently.

Category 2: Wheelchair access with assistance. Accessible to a wheelchair user travelling with assistance.

Category 3: Access for those with mobility impairment. Accessible to a wheelchair user able to walk a few paces and up a maximum of three steps.

You can find detailed descriptions of each category at:

Ⓦ www.visitscotland.com/guide/ where-to-stay/accessible-scotland/ accessibility-categories

And search facilities to locate appropriate accommodation at:

Ⓦ www.visitscotland.com/guide/ where-to-stay

Ⓦ www.visitscotland/accommodation/ accessible-scotland

WALES

You can search for accommodation according to mobility, hearing or visual impairment in the Accommodation search on Accessible Wales.

Ⓦ www.visitwales.co.uk

REPUBLIC OF IRELAND

By law, to comply with the Disability Act, Fáilte Ireland must make its buildings, services and information accessible to people with disabilities. The Fáilte Ireland Access Officer can be contacted to arrange help or information for people with disabilities to access the services and information it provides.

Ⓣ 01 8847781

Ⓔ accessibility@failteireland.ie

LONDON

Direct Enquiries has carried out access audits of selected hotels around the UK. Their resource is particularly helpful for hotels in London. They use a system with 18 basic and 11 additional disabled access symbols to represent specific access resources.

Find out more at:

Ⓦ www.directenquiries.com

Ⓦ www.inclusivelondon.com/ disabledaccess.aspx

Inclusive London is an online nationwide access register to buildings, venues and services. Inclusive London's listings are compiled from Access Audits, guided telephone access assessments and information supplied by the businesses listed and user-contributed information.

Ⓦ www.visitlondon.com/ accommodation/accessible

Assessing quality

STAR RATINGS

National assessing bodies – the AA, VisitEngland, VisitScotland, Visit Wales, the Northern Ireland Tourist Board, and Fáilte Ireland (the all-Ireland tourist board) – rate accommodation. They aim to make reliable, impartial and consistent assessments.

The assessing bodies work to very similar criteria and award a number of stars from one to five, to reflect facilities and overall quality. The more stars awarded – the higher the level of quality. If you see a quality assessment logo displayed next to your chosen accommodation, it means an official assessor has visited and given it a rating.

How is accommodation graded?

The star rating system covers all kinds of accommodation:

- Hotel, country house hotel, small hotel, town house hotel and metro hotel;
- Guest house, B&B, farmhouse, inn, restaurant with rooms;
- Self-catering, campus accommodation, serviced apartments;
- Touring park, campsite, caravan park, timber lodge or chalet.

Different types of accommodation offer different facilities so each type of accommodation is assessed in different ways and different criteria apply according to the market's expectation of that kind of accommodation.

For details about quality assessments in Britain, visit the relevant websites for each country you are thinking of visiting. You can also find details of accommodation definitions and quality ratings at:

AA

- www.theaa.com/travel/ accommodation_restaurants_ grading.html

England

- www.qualityintourism.com

Scotland

- www.visitscotland.com/ quality-assurance

Wales

- www.visitwales.co.uk/ holiday-accommodation-in-wales/ grading-visit-wales-tourist-accommodation-grading-scheme

Northern Ireland

- www.discovernorthern ireland.com/Accommodation-Rating-System-A1592

The Republic of Ireland

- www.discoverireland.ie/shamrock
- www.discoverireland.ie/ Where-To-Stay/Accommodation-Guide

Some of these sites also have online search and booking systems to help you identify and contact accommodation with the specific facilities you would like.

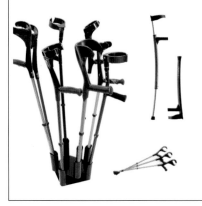

AWARD SCHEMES

England

VisitEngland gives awards to hotels and guest accommodation (Gold only for Self-Catering and the Rose award for Caravan Parks) that provide exceptional quality in all areas.

 Gold award: This award is given to Hotels, Guest Accommodation and Self-Catering properties. It reflects a very high level of quality. Properties achieving the Gold award have exceptional levels of quality, comfort and cleanliness in bedrooms and bathrooms, and outstanding levels of customer care and food.

 Silver award: This award is given to Hotels and Guest Accommodation. It reflects a high level of quality, comfort and cleanliness in bedrooms and bathrooms with very good levels of customer care and food provision.

 Rose award: Caravan Holiday Homes for hire that are of a high standard are recognised by the Rose award. These can only be found sited on 4 or 5 star Holiday Parks. The equivalent in Scotland is the Thistle award.

 Breakfast award: Sponsored by Kellogg's, this award recognises those hotels and B&Bs that offer their guests a quality and choice of breakfast, service and hospitality that exceeds what would be expected at their star rating.

Scotland

 Gold award: In Scotland the Gold award recognises serviced accommodation which consistently achieves the highest levels of excellence within their VisitScotland star grading. Scotlands equivalent of England's Rose award is the Thistle award.

Wales

 Gold award: Recognises outstanding quality, exceptional comfort and unfailing hospitality.

JUST IN CASE
YOU'RE TRAVELLING ABROAD...

INSURANCE

TRANSPORT

FCO TRAVEL ADVICE
know before you go
fco.gov.uk/travel

WHEELCHAIR ACCESS

HEALTH AND MEDICATION

CAR HIRE

- Ensure you have comprehensive travel insurance which takes into account your personal circumstances and medical history
- Research your destination and the facilities and support available there
- Check our travel advice at www.fco.gov.uk/travel for the latest in-country situation
- Check which vaccinations and health precautions you may need by visiting your GP or by visiting www.fitfortravel.nhs.uk
- Check if you need permission to take your prescribed medicines with you. Take your prescription with you and ensure you have enough to cover emergencies
- For more information and to order our free Disabled Travellers leaflet go to www.fco.gov.uk/publications or call 08444 777 399.

Disabled travellers

Foreign & Commonwealth Office

Foreign & Commonwealth Office

radar the disability rights people

Ways to book

You can book your holiday in a number of ways. You can use a travel agent, a tour operator, go direct to an accommodation or travel provider directly or book online, although there may be limits to booking accessible accommodation via mainstream websites.

Booking through an agent

Some tour operators and holiday services specialise in holidays for disabled people. Whether you choose a specialist or go to a general provider, it is sensible to book holidays through travel agents or tour operators that are members of the Association of British Travel Agents (ABTA). Their booking conditions will meet ABTA's code of conduct. And, if the company runs into financial difficulties ABTA can help you to get money back. They also run an arbitration scheme to deal with complaints about their members.

Association of British Travel Agents (ABTA)
30 Park Street, London SE1 9EQ.
📞 0901 201 5050 (Consumer affairs)
🌐 www.abta.com

Booking on the internet

The internet has changed the process of booking travel and holidays and it is a good way to compare prices and find last-minute deals. To get the best deals you may need to be flexible about dates and/or the place you want to go. If you have specific requirements, you will need to balance these against costs. To get the best deal, you will need to do plenty of research so leave yourself good time.

There are lots of websites that can help, with some specialising in flights and others in accommodation. Booking flights and hotels separately can save money, but bundles or package deals are often cheaper.

Travel
Specialist websites like Skyscanner or Cheapflights.co.uk are useful for flights. Recently, Kayak.com has emerged as an up-and-coming favourite but a quick Google search will bring up lots of alternatives. It is worth trying several as they collate information about available flights in different ways.

Plan rail ticket purchases 12 weeks before your travel date. This is usually when advance tickets (generally the cheapest fares) become available.

TheTrainline offers an email alert system which lets you know when advance tickets for a specific journey come on sale.

Hotels

Once you've arranged your travel, you will need a place to stay. You can book online through websites like Hotels.com, LateRooms and Trivago. Once you've located some suitable accommodation, you can sort results in terms of price, star rating or criteria such as distance from the airport or city centre.

Take the time to look carefully at what is included in the price. Sometimes the total booking price doesn't cover breakfast, towels, VAT or internet use.

Packages

While some websites specialise in either travel or accommodation, others focus on package deals. Examples include lastminute.com, Expedia and TravelSupermarket.com, but most holiday sites – including those specialising in flights, hotels or travel to particular regions – now offer holiday options as a bundle. This is more common with flights abroad but it can also work with UK destinations and holidays too. Planning your whole trip on one website can often save you money. Explore all of the different options available to you if you're looking for a bargain.

> **Top Tip**: When comparing holidays, look carefully at what the price includes. Paying less for something that doesn't meet your requirements might be a false economy. Read the full terms and conditions before booking. There are sometimes extra costs, which could see you paying more than you thought.

FINDING THE BEST DEAL

Comparison websites are useful when you know where you want to go and have specific dates for travel in mind. If you're someone who's always on the lookout for a fantastic holiday deal, the web has other very handy resources:

The travel agent's website: The cheapest holidays are sometimes available directly from travel agents. For example, Thomson and MyTravel put their latest offers in a special section of the site. Bookmarking them on your computer and checking back regularly could be one way to find a great deal.

Travelzoo: When you sign-up for free at Travelzoo, you'll receive a weekly email newsletter filled with the site's current most popular holiday deals. To take advantage of a deal, you'll need to purchase an online voucher, which can later be redeemed once you've decided when to travel.

Review websites: Booking a last-minute holiday can be risky but it doesn't always have to be the case. It is always worth looking at user reviews on websites such as TripAdvisor. If you can, send in your own reviews of places you have stayed and the services you have received as a disabled person.

Booking directly

If you prefer, you can telephone or email to book directly with your chosen accommodation or holiday provider.

Describe any facilities or adjustments you need when you make the booking. If you need help to get to and from the place you are staying, then make sure you tell the provider when you book.

It is helpful to confirm by email so you can write down everything you need. If you book with a travel agent, they should let you contact a venue directly, particularly if you need to find out about equipment or support.

Your disability or health condition
You will need to decide how much you want to say about this when you make enquiries and bookings. The more information you can give the better, but the decision about how much you disclose is up to you. You might want to keep things private or ask them to be discreet.

Some accommodation providers might assume things about you if you are disabled. But remember that it is never OK for anyone to discriminate against you because of your disability or health condition.

Before you go

There are key things everyone should check before going away on holiday. If you are disabled, there may be other things you might need to organise before you go.

Key things to check

The list below will give you some ideas of the things you may wish to check before setting off on your holiday:

- Double check that all your holiday arrangements are in place;
- Make a list of any extra equipment you might need to take with you;
- If you need medicines, take more than you may need and take a written prescription for more, in case you lose them or run out. If you have to go through any security checks, it is helpful to have documentation that explains what your medicines are.

INSURANCE

Everyone should get insurance before they travel. You never know if your trip might get cancelled or you might be ill and not able to go. If you have no insurance, then there is little you can do to get your money back.

Make sure you get appropriate insurance for your type of holiday. You might need a specific type of insurance, particularly if you are travelling or going on an activity holiday. If you already have a policy, check what it says before you go. You might need to get in touch with them and change it.

Your rights as a disabled person

All companies have a legal duty to make sure that they do not treat you, as a disabled customer, in a less favourable way than they would treat other customers. The Equality Act (2010) places duties on service providers, which includes insurance and travel companies providing services within the UK. For example, a company must not refuse to provide a service to a disabled person that they offer to other members of the public unless this can be justified (see below). And, they must not provide the service on terms or standards that are worse than those they would give to any other consumer.

However, the law does allow insurers to apply special conditions or extra charges to disabled people in certain circumstances. They can charge a disabled person a higher premium, if they can show that a disabled person is at a greater risk and therefore more likely to make a claim.

An insurance company can only justify a difference of treatment of a disabled person if:

- the decision is based on information which is relevant to the assessment of the risk being insured;
- the information (such as statistical data, or a medical report) is from a source on which it is reasonable to rely;
- the less favourable treatment is reasonable when this information and all other relevant factors are taken into account.

It is worth checking whether any standard policy offered by a travel company meets your individual situation, including that of any equipment that has to be taken. Some voluntary organisations can assist their members, or people with the condition with which they are concerned, to obtain appropriate insurance cover which would otherwise be difficult.

Some companies with insurance packages designed specifically for disabled people are:

All Clear Travel Insurance

All Clear House, 1 Redwing Court, Ashton Road, Romford, Essex RM3 8QQ.
- 0845 250 5350
- www.allcleartravel.co.uk

Chartwell Insurance

Chartwell Insurance Services, East Winch Hall, East Winch, King's Lynn, Norfolk PE32 1HN.
- 0844 888 5222
- info@chartwellinsurance.co.uk
- www.chartwellinsurance.co.uk

En Route Insurance

5th Floor, Cavendish House, Breeds Place, Hastings, East Sussex TN34 3AA.
- 0800 783 7245
- info@enrouteinsurance.co.uk
- www.enrouteinsurance.co.uk

Fogg Travel Insurance Services Ltd

Crow Hill Drive, Mansfield, Nottinghamshire NG19 7AE.
- 01623 631331
- sales@fogginsure.co.uk
- www.fogginsure.co.uk

Free Spirit

P J Hayman & Company Ltd, Stansted House, Rowlands Castle, Hampshire PO9 6DX.
- 0845 230 5000
- freespirit@pjhayman.com
- www.free-spirit.com

Travelbility

J & M Insurance Services, Peregrine House, Bakers Lane, Epping CM16 5DQ.
- 0845 338 1638
- www.jmi.co.uk

Rights & wrongs

You've done your research, arranged the facilities you need and completed all your checks. You should have a hassle-free and successful holiday. But sometimes, despite best-laid plans, things go wrong. A holiday provider might not understand your needs or the standard of accommodation you expected. Here we explain your rights as a disabled person, the treatment you should expect and what to do if something does go wrong.

Your rights

THE LAW
Under the Equality Act 2010, service providers in the UK must make 'reasonable adjustments' to make sure disabled people are not discriminated against.

Service providers include organisations that provide:
- holiday accommodation
- tourist attractions
- restaurants and places to eat
- transport and ways to get around

They cannot refuse to serve you or provide a lower standard of service because of your disability.

You cannot be treated unfavourably because of something connected with your disability, unless they can show, in a reasonable way, why they cannot change things for you.

What is a reasonable adjustment?
When disabled people want to access or use a service, the provider has to make 'reasonable adjustments' to any aspect of their service that would put a disabled person at a substantial disadvantage compared to non-disabled people.

Under the Equality Act 2010, service providers only need to make changes that are 'reasonable'. These might include simple changes to layout, improved signage and information and staff training to improve accessibility to disabled customers. It might be something as simple as changing check out times to accommodate your needs.

It's about what is practical in each service provider's individual situation and what resources they may have. They will not be required to make changes that are impractical or beyond their means.

DISABILITY RIGHTS HANDBOOK

37th Edition
April 2012 - April 2013

A guide to benefits and services for all disabled people, their families, carers and advisers

NEW EDITION

Disability Rights UK

As comprehensive as ever

- How the benefit system works and how to make a claim
- Benefits for people with an illness, injury or disability including Attendance Allowance, Disability Living Allowance and Employment & Support Allowance
- Benefits for carers, young people and children and those looking for work, or in retirement
- Benefits for people on a low income, including the Social Fund, Tax Credits and help with rent and Council Tax
- Benefits for people injured at work or serving in the Armed Forces
- Challenging benefit decisions; how to appeal
- Care services: getting them and paying for them

New this year

- Expanded guidance on the work capability assessment and extra information on completion of the ESA50 questionnaire
- What to expect from the Government's Welfare Reforms

Welfare benefits and tax credits – are you keeping up to date?

Disabled people could be the hardest hit in the latest overhaul of the benefits system. The Government's £18 billion programme of welfare cuts is already having a significant impact and further changes are in the pipeline. In this period of unprecedented change, keeping up with the new rules is more crucial than ever before.

Stay informed – know your rights

The 'Handbook' provides information and guidance on benefits and services for people with experience of disability or health conditions. Fully updated for 2012, our user-friendly guide presents this complex information in a concise, straightforward and jargon-free way.

37th Edition out May 2012

Prices held – no increase on last year!

Disability Rights Handbook 2012-2013
£28.50 inc P&P (£14.00 for people claiming benefits)

Order online at www.disabilityrightsuk.org

Do you provide advice to disabled people? How will this year's changes affect your clients? Without up-to-date information, your advice could be inaccurate and your service compromised.

Do you have a disability or health condition? 10 million people miss out on £6 billion in disability benefits each year. Understand your rights and responsibilities or your benefits could be at risk.

Do you care for a disabled person or someone with a long-term condition? You may qualify for financial help. Have you thought about claiming but don't know where to start?

Written in plain English by benefits specialists and legally referenced, the 'Handbook' has the answers you need to help ensure the quality of your advice or claim what's due.

Keep your Handbook up to date all year

Join Disability Rights UK and we'll keep you up to date throughout the year with 'Disability and Welfare Rights Updates', our bi-monthly PDF magazine.

Join online at www.disabilityrightsuk.org

Disability Rights UK was formed through the merger of Disability Alliance, Radar and National Centre for Independent Living.

Disability Rights UK

Reasonable adjustments include:

- using large print for registration and guest information;
- ensuring that at least one copy of the fixed menu is in Braille;
- providing phones with large buttons;
- providing portable vibrating alarms for guests who will not be able to hear an audible fire alarm;
- where a low reception desk is not available, providing an alternative low desk for wheelchair users.

In the UK, information produced by travel agents, tour operators, airports and airlines should be clear and simple to use. They should also take reasonable steps to make sure that their information services are accessible to disabled people. It should be available in accessible formats, such as Braille, large print or on audiotape but you may need to ask specifically and give them time to provide it.

Your responsibilities

Remember that service providers may have conditions they ask you to meet in order that they can provide you with appropriate facilities or support. Meeting their requirements is a good way to help them meet yours.

Communicating your needs
Make sure you explain your particular requirements clearly, particularly if your impairment or condition is not obvious

or if you are booking by phone, post or over the internet. Don't expect staff at travel agents, travel offices or airports automatically to know or understand your needs.

If you are in a hotel or guesthouse and it will take you longer than most people to get ready in the morning, ask if you can check out slightly later. Sometimes just asking will prompt a hotel to offer an 'adjustment' that can make all the difference to the comfort of your stay.

Your feedback after your holiday
We are often encouraged to give feedback about a holiday or accommodation. Giving your comments to the holiday provider, making comments online and also to Disability Rights UK can reward good providers with positive marketing and encourage poor providers to improve.

What if things go wrong?

Good service providers know that making their services more accessible will benefit disabled people and could result in recommendations and return visits. If a problem arises, try to deal with it in a way that encourages them to treat you the same as any customer whose business they want to keep.

Try to sort things out amicably at the time they happen: Often problems can be solved if you tell the provider straight away.

Experiencing discrimination or a provider refusing to make adjustments for your needs: If this happens then you have legal rights under the Equality Act (2010) which requires service providers not to discriminate and to make adjustments that are reasonable. Reminding a holiday provider of this can prompt them to be more flexible and sort things out for you. If you think you may experience discrimination you should get in touch with the Equality and Human Rights Commission (EHRC) – you can find their contact details at the end of this Guide in the Useful Resources section.

Complaints to do with where you are staying that are not to do with disability: If general standards in the accommodation are not what you were expecting then you should complain. Holiday providers should have a way for you to do this. For example, you might need to go to the tourist body that runs the provider or to the organisation awarding the rating.

Complain as soon as possible after discovering the problem. If the problem arose while you were on holiday it will help if you can show you complained at the time. Write to the holiday or accommodation provider you are complaining to, even if you made the complaint in person or by phone.

If your complaint is not resolved or you need some help making the complaint, contact your local Citizens Advice Bureau if you are in England or Wales. Citizens Advice produce a factsheet on making a complaint about your holiday (dowloadable from their website).

Or find out if the tour operator or agent you booked with is a member of a trade association such as the Association of British Travel Agents (ABTA). ABTA have some useful publications about complaints in the 'Consumer Zone' of their website. They also operate an arbitration and conciliation service to resolve disputes but you will have to pay a fee for this. If your accommodation or holiday provider is not a member of ABTA, contact Consumer Direct.

Association of British Travel Agents
30 Park Street, London SE1 9EQ.
☎ 0901 2015050
🌐 www.abta.com

Citizens Advice
☎ 08444 772020 (For Wales)
   08444 111444 (For England)
🌐 www.adviceguide.org.uk

Consumer Direct
☎ 08454 040506
For a Welsh-speaking adviser:
☎ 08454 040505
Consumer Direct is the government-funded consumer advice service. It offers information and advice on problems with goods and services, energy and post.

Public transport

In the past, public transport was developed with little or no regard to the needs of disabled people. Thankfully this has changed – particularly as transport regulations under various pieces of both UK and EC law come into effect. However, progress still needs to be made both geographically and between various forms of transport.

Travel planning

It makes sense to plan your journey in advance. If you think you might need assistance at any point in the journey, let the people running the services know about what help or support you might need.

In most of England, county and unitary councils have responsibilities for public transport and have a Public Transport Information Officer. Some publish specific information for disabled passengers. Elsewhere, in larger towns and cities, this responsibility is carried out by Passenger Transport Executives (PTEs) and in London, by Transport for London. Contact details for these organisations are listed below.

> Some of this information based on Disability Rights UK's self-help guide *'If only I'd known that ...'* – an information-packed guide to services, welfare rights and facilities, it covers all ages from childhood to later years.

Centro/Network West Midlands
Centro House, 16 Summer Lane, Birmingham B19 3SD.
- ☎ 0121 200 2700
  Textphone 0121 214 2787
- ⓦ www.cento.org

GMPTE
2 Piccadilly Place, Manchester M1 3BG.
- ☎ 0871 200 2233
- ⓦ www.gmpte.com

MerseyTravel
24 Hatton Garden, Liverpool L3 2AN.
- ☎ 0151 227 5181
  Textphone 0151 330 1087
- ⓦ www.merseytravel.gov.uk

Metro
Wellington House, 40-50 Wellington Street, Leeds LS1 2DE.
- ☎ 0113 251 7272
- ⓦ www.wymetro.com

Nexus

Grainger Chambers, Hood Street,
Newcastle upon Tyne NE1 6JQ.
- 📞 0191 202 0747
   Textphone 0191 202 0501
- 🌐 www.nexus.org.uk

South Yorkshire PTE

11 Broad Street West, Sheffield S1 2BQ.
- 📞 01709 515151
- 🌐 www.sypte.co.uk

Transport for London

Travel Information, 55 Broadway,
London SW1H 0BD.
- 📞 020 7222 1234
   Textphone 020 7918 3015
- 📧 travinfo@tfl.gov.uk
- 🌐 www.tfl.gov.uk

In Northern Ireland, rail and bus
services are overseen by:

Translink

Central Station, Belfast BT1 3PB.
- 📞 028 9066 6630
   Textphone 028 9035 4007
- 🌐 www.translink.co.uk

In Scotland, the national transport
agency liaises with Regional Transport
Partnerships and has a range of
executive functions including
administering fare concessions and the
Blue Badge scheme.

Transport Scotland

Buchanan House, 58 Portdundas Road,
Glasgow G4 0HF.
- 📞 0141 272 7100
- 🌐 www.transportscotland.gov.uk

> Published by Radar and now sold by
> Disability Rights UK, 'Doing Transport
> Differently' lets people with any kind
> of disability – learning difficulties,
> mental health conditions, visual
> impairments, hearing impairments,
> wheelchair users, mobility
> impairments and more – know what
> kind of access is out there, how to
> plan your journeys, and what to do if
> things go wrong. The guide is written
> by and for disabled people and is
> full of travellers' experiences of using
> trains, buses, coaches, undergrounds,
> light railways, ferries and more. To
> download your free copy go to
> www.radar.org.uk/publications/
> doing-transport-differently

In Wales transport planning is
undertaken by four Regional Transport
Consortia:

For South East Wales
SEWTA
- 🌐 www.sewta.gov.uk
For South West Wales
SWWITCH
- 🌐 www.swwitch.net
For North East Wales
Taith
- 🌐 www.taith.gov.uk

For Mid Wales
TraCC
Ⓦ www.tracc.gov.uk

Nationally, general information on transport services and timetables is available through:

Traveline
Ⓣ 0870 608 2608
   Textphone 0870 241 2216
Ⓦ www.traveline.org.uk

You can also find information at:

www.transportdirect.info
A transport planning website that includes options for using all types of public transport and private motoring for point-to-point journeys in Great Britain.

www.dptac.gov.uk/door-to-door
A regularly updated source of information for disabled people about all forms of transport.

> **Ricability** is an independent consumer research charity offering free, practical and unbiased reports for older and disabled people. Ricability published a report called *'Wheels Within Wheels'* – a guide to using a wheelchair on public transport. To find out more, visit www.ricability.org.uk or write to: Unit G03, Wenlock Business Centre, 50-56 Wharf Road, London N1 7EU. Telephone 020 7427 2460 Textphone 020 7427 2469.

TRAVEL TRAINING
In some areas, travel training is available to help disabled people use accessible buses and other forms of public transport independently.

This sort of training can help you gain confidence, particularly if you are more used to using special transport.

TRAVEL IN LONDON
Public transport in London is becoming more accessible, with buses, taxis, the Docklands Light Railway and London Tramlink all providing accessible services. In addition many private hire (minicab) firms operate wheelchair accessible vehicles.

If you are older or disabled and public transport is not always accessible to you, assisted transport services may be the answer. You can find out more about assisted travel options including Dial-a-Ride, Taxicard and Capital Call, as well as community transport schemes on the Transport for London website:
Ⓦ www.tfl.gov.uk

You can use assisted travel to go shopping, visit friends or family, go to the library, or for other recreational purposes. However, you cannot use these services for work or hospital appointments. You can read more about things to do in London in the London section of this guide.

London 2012

London 2012 is aiming for a 'public transport' Olympic Games, so plenty of options have been made available to help you get to events across London and the UK. This includes making it easier for disabled people to get to and from the Games.

2012 Games coach services: Dedicated direct coach services will be provided to a variety of 2012 Games venues from a range of locations outside the M25.

2012 Games shuttle services: London 2012 will provide shuttle services from some recommended stations that are more than a short walk away from the London 2012 or co-host city venue entrance.

2012 Games park-and-ride: Secure park-and-ride sites will be provided at convenient locations near to a variety of London 2012 venues.

London Underground: All London 2012 venues within London can be reached by the 'Tube', with the exception of ExCeL, Greenwich Park and Woolwich Arsenal.

Docklands Light Railway (DLR): The DLR serves London 2012 venues at the Olympic Park, ExCeL, Greenwich Park and The Royal Artillery Barracks.

London Overground: London Overground serves London 2012 venues in the Olympic Park on the Richmond/Clapham Junction to Stratford line.

London's buses: London has an extensive bus network and there are routes and stops close to all London 2012 venues.

National rail: Great Britain is well-served by an extensive rail network, which connects London and all the co-host cities. Special 2012 Games train tickets are available for travel between 18 July and 14 September 2012.

River services: A number of London 2012 sporting venues are accessible by river. These include Greenwich Park, North Greenwich Arena, The Royal Artillery Barracks, Horse Guards Parade and Eton Dorney.

Taxi and private hire vehicles: There will be taxi and private hire vehicle drop-off areas as close to the London 2012 or co-host city venue entrance as possible.

Cycling: All London 2012 venues are accessible by bike and will have free, secure, managed cycle parking.

Walking: Many London 2012 Games venues are easily accessible by foot, particularly those in central London. You can download a map of accessible stations in the UK, a map of accessible stations in the South East or the London map which all show levels of step-free facilities and staff assistance at stations from:

Ⓦ www.london2012.com/visiting/
getting-to-the-games/

If you require assistance when making your National Rail journey, you will need to book this when you buy your train tickets or once you have received your Games Travelcard.

To book rail tickets and assistance visit the London 2012 Games Train Ticket booking website:

Ⓦ www.nationalrailgamestravel.co.uk

The number of spaces available to wheelchair users on each train is limited, so it is important that you book your space in advance. Most trains can accommodate wheelchairs that are up to 70cm wide and 120cm long. There are a small number of older trains that can only currently carry wheelchairs that have a maximum width of 67cm.

The maximum combined weight of a person and their wheelchair that can be carried varies from 230kg to 300kg.

You can plan a journey to any of the venues. You can do this by going to travel.london2012.com

Air travel

Under new European law, if you are disabled or have difficulty moving around you can receive assistance when you fly to and from Europe, including domestic flights.

You do not need to be permanently or physically disabled to benefit from this service. In fact, anyone who has difficulty moving around, for example, because of their disability, age or a temporary injury, can receive help when they fly.

Remember that air travel is an international industry. This means that if you fly outside of the UK then you may encounter different attitudes and practices towards disability.

Things that can make air travel more complicated for disabled passengers can arise from security requirements, design and safety features of aircraft, the size of airports, and for many people, unfamiliarity with the environment.

Under EC Regulation 1107/206 it is illegal for an airline, travel agent or tour operator to refuse a booking on the grounds of disability or to refuse to allow a disabled person onboard who has a valid ticket or reservation.

Airport managers are required to organise the provision of the services necessary to enable disabled passengers to board, disembark and ensure a safe transit between flights. Each airline is responsible for services onboard its aircraft and should not charge extra for giving support or making an adjustment. This is against the law.

In Britain, if you are refused boarding on the grounds of disability or reduced mobility or do not get the services you have requested and need you should contact the Equality & Human Rights Commission (EHRC). Further details can be found in the Useful Resources section of this Guide. They will advise you on your rights and may have to refer the matter to the Civil Aviation Authority (CAA). The CAA has the power to prosecute. An airline found guilty of discrimination could face an unlimited fine.

Here are some tips from the EHRC that you can use when travelling by plane

1. Before you fly
Consider the kind of assistance you may need, and check the airline's safety rules.

2. Booking your flight
Always tell your airline, travel agent or tour operator at least 48 hours in advance if you need special assistance.

3. Arriving at the airport
Find out in advance about the layout and facilities at your chosen airport.

If you have asked for assistance, then airport staff should be expecting you when you arrive.

4. At the check in desk
Remember to confirm any pre-booked assistance when you check in. Seats with extra legroom are always in demand, so if you need one, explain why.

5. Moving through the airport
Airports must provide free assistance to get disabled and less mobile passengers to their flight.

6. Boarding the flight
Disabled and less mobile passengers will usually be called for boarding first. All staff who deal with customers must have disability awareness training.

7. On board
Airlines must make all reasonable efforts to arrange suitable seating for you. You can take up to two items of mobility equipment onto the aircraft.

8. Leaving the plane
Unless you're in a hurry, you will usually be the last to leave as it's easier to move around in an empty cabin.

GETTING HELP
The EHRC deals with complaints about UK airlines and airports in England, Scotland and Wales. For more advice, please contact the Helpline:

England
☏ 0845 604 6610
Scotland
☏ 0845 604 5510
Wales
☏ 0845 604 8810

Or go to the website
Ⓦ www.equalityhumanrights.com

Assistance for disabled passengers

Airlines generally have established procedures for assisting disabled passengers. Most disabled people, particularly those with permanent and stable conditions, won't require medical clearance before travelling. However, the rules vary between airlines. For certain conditions you will generally need clearance for flying even if you don't normally need treatment. It is important to check when you book what, if any, medical information will be required.

Most airports are accessible and many have introduced facilities and services to make it easier for disabled people to use them. However, many airport terminals are large, complex premises so finding facilities and assistance may be difficult. Some people, who normally manage independently, may need assistance. Airports often have information for disabled people on their website and some publish access guides.

Wheelchair users should be able to use their own wheelchairs until boarding. Other people may be given wheelchair assistance to reach the aircraft door. Depending on the airline and the size of the aircraft there may be an on-board wheelchair to help you transfer to your seat.

You may be able to request a seat in a particular area, say near a toilet or with extra legroom. However, for safety reasons airlines allocate seats beside emergency exits (which do have more space) to people who are perceived as having the necessary dexterity and strength to open the doors.

Most pieces of equipment required by a disabled passenger are carried free of charge. Larger items (including wheelchairs) are carried in the hold, but smaller items can be taken into the cabin.

You should ask the airline about carriage of equipment – particularly if you may need it during the flight and, especially, if you intend on carrying liquid medicine on board.

You may need to ask in advance for any assistance or service that you might need in connection with your flight. Air travel often involves more organisations than other forms of transport, particularly if the flight is by a charter aircraft as part of a holiday package. Usually requested arrangements work out well but when things do go wrong it is often the result of a failure in the communication chain. It is therefore advisable to check that appropriate messages have been passed on. You may need to emphasise the importance of the requests.

> More detailed information is included in 'Your Rights to Fly – What you need to know' issued by the Equality & Human Rights Commission in 2009. The booklet can be downloaded from www.equalityhumanrights.com

FURTHER INFORMATION ON FLYING AND THE LAW
Information from the EHRC

A new law, (EC) 1107/2006, came into effect on 26 July 2008. The law affects the whole of the air travel process, not just the flight itself. It also covers booking your flights, arriving at the airport, checking in, getting on and off the plane and leaving the airport. For more information see our step by step guide on your rights to fly – you can find this on the EHRC website. The regulation applies to tour operators and travel agents as well as to airports and airlines. This means that tour operators and travel agents must pass on your needs to the airlines, and they in turn must inform the airports of the individual services required.

If you have a complaint you can get in touch with the EHRC for advice. They are responsible for dealing with complaints about UK airlines and airports in England, Scotland and Wales and can advise you of your rights and what further action you can take.

Complaints must be made to the EHRC within the statutory limit of six months less one day. Unfortunately, they will not be able to assist you after this stage.

The EHRC provide advice and example letters to send to the appropriate body – be that the travel agent, the airline, the airport or another organisation. If you are not satisfied with the response, they can take the matter further. They will liaise with colleagues in the Department for Transport and the CAA (the airline regulator) and other European Union nations to improve services to disabled and less mobile passengers.

Bus & coach travel

For many years, bus travel was among the least accessible forms of public transport for disabled people. But things are changing. Buses and coaches are becoming increasingly accessible to disabled people, especially wheelchair users.

Regulations now require all new buses to be equipped with lifts or ramps with a level floor to a space to carry a passenger using a wheelchair. They also incorporate features such as colour-contrasted handrails and easy to operate bell-pushes. Older vehicles will however, continue to be in use for some years.

Information on routes normally served by accessible buses should be available from a Public Transport Information Office (PTE) or from the individual bus company. The boarding features of a modern bus generally work well at bus stations or other dedicated bus stands. But there can be problems at roadside bus stops if there isn't a footpath, or if the vehicle does not pull in sufficiently close to the footpath, because of road works or badly parked cars.

There has been slower progress in making scheduled long-distance coach travel accessible to wheelchair users, although since 2005 new coaches are equipped with lifts. The following information is taken from Direct Gov:
Ⓦ www.direct.gov.uk

ACCESSIBILITY OF BUSES AND COACHES
New buses and coaches designed to carry more than 22 passengers on local or scheduled services must comply with Public Service Vehicles Accessibility Regulations (PSVAR).

All buses and coaches, both old and new, need to comply with the PSVAR by the following dates:
- 1 January 2017 – all buses must comply with the accessibility regulations;
- 1 January 2020 – all coaches must comply with the accessibility regulations.

Regulations for England, Scotland and Wales
The PSVAR ensure public service vehicles are accessible to disabled people. They are the responsibility of the Department for Transport's Buses and Taxis Division.

You can read more about PSVAR on the Direct Gov website.

Regulations for Northern Ireland
Northern Ireland has separate regulations; the Department for Regional Development is responsible for these.

FREE OFF-PEAK TRAVEL
Eligible older and disabled people are entitled to free off-peak travel on local buses anywhere in England. Similar concessions are available across Wales, Scotland and Northern Ireland.

If you're eligible for a free bus pass, you can use it anywhere in England during 'off-peak' times. Off-peak is:
- between 9.30 am and 11.00 pm Monday to Friday;
- all day at weekends and on public holidays.

How to get free off-peak travel

If you live in England, you will be entitled to a bus pass giving free off-peak travel on local buses when you reach 'eligible age'. If you were born after 5 April 1950, the age you become eligible is tied to changes in the State Pension age for women. This affects both men and women.

You're eligible for a disabled person's pass if you live in England and are 'eligible disabled'. This means you:
- are blind or partially sighted;
- are profoundly or severely deaf;
- are without speech;
- have a disability, or have suffered an injury, which has a substantial and long-term effect on your ability to walk;
- do not have arms or have long-term loss of the use of both arms;
- have a learning disability.

You're also eligible disabled if your application for a driving licence would be refused under section 92 of the Road Traffic Act 1988 (physical fitness). However, you won't be eligible if you were refused because of persistent misuse of drugs or alcohol.

Services outside England

The England bus pass only covers travel in England. It does not give you free bus travel in Wales, Scotland or Northern Ireland. If you live outside England, you'll need to apply for a different pass from your local council.

Wheelchairs on buses and coaches

By 1 January 2017 most wheelchair users will be able to travel on buses. And most wheelchair users will be able to travel on coaches by 1 January 2020. But you may find you can't if:
- your chair is very heavy or very big (taking up a space – when you are in it – of more than 700 mm wide or 1200 mm long)
- you need to travel with your legs fully extended or the backrest reclined

Before you travel: Make sure that your wheelchair is in a safe condition to travel. This means making sure that it is properly maintained and in good condition. If you have a power assisted chair you must ensure that the battery is secure. If your chair has adjustable kerb climbers, you should check that they are set not to catch on the ramp.

The transport operator has the right to refuse to let you travel if they believe that your wheelchair is not in a safe condition.

It is important to check whether your wheelchair can be carried by the bus or coach operator before you travel.

Further advice on taking a wheelchair on public transport can be found on the Ricability website:

Ⓦ www.ricability.org.uk

While you are travelling: You must make sure your wheelchair brakes are on. If you use a power assisted wheelchair then you should make sure the power is switched off.

By January 2017, there will be a designated space for wheelchair users on buses, and on coaches by 1 January 2020. Buses and coaches will require:

- a forward facing wheelchair space fitted with a wheelchair restraint system;
- wheelchair user restraint.

On buses designed to carry standing passengers the wheelchair space may be a rearward facing protected area. This will be fitted with a padded head and back restraint. The area will also have a vertical stanchion or retractable arm to prevent the wheelchair from slewing into the gangway.

Mobility Scooters

You should contact your local operator to find out whether or not your scooter is transportable on their buses and coaches before you travel.

COACH AND STATION FACILITIES

If you need assistance at the coach station, contact either the station or the coach company before you travel. Let them know what you will need.

Assistance from coach drivers and other staff

Bus and coach drivers are required by law to provide reasonable assistance to disabled people. In particular, to help them get on and off the bus or coach. This does not extend to physically lifting passengers or heavy mobility equipment. If you need help to get on and off a coach, you should make a request when you book your ticket.

Induction loops

Many ticket office windows have induction loops to help people who have a hearing aid. These windows are clearly marked. Phones at many stations are also fitted with devices to help people who have a hearing aid.

Support and assistance dogs

You can take support and assistance dogs into station buffets and restaurants, and onto coaches.

Accessible toilets

Many coach stations have accessible toilets. Some operate under the National Key Scheme (NKS), which enables disabled people to use accessible public toilets independently with their own Radar key. You can buy a Radar key from Disability Rights UK from:

☎ 0207 250 3222
Ⓦ www.radar-shop.org.uk

Some coaches have toilets on board. If you can't access the toilet on a long-distance coach journey, if for instance, the toilet is situated down some steps the driver should stop at coach stations so that you can use the toilets. You can find out more about accessible toilets later on in this section.

BUS AND COACH COMPANIES

Goldline, the express coach service between towns and cities in Northern Ireland, uses wheelchair accessible coaches on many of its services.

Megabus has some vehicles with a wheelchair lift. Wheelchair users should phone to make a booking so that a bus with a lift or ramp is made available.
☎ 0141 332 9841.

National Express has introduced a new vehicle in which a lift is incorporated at the main entrance and which has a space for a passenger using a wheelchair. This type of vehicle should be in use across their network during 2012. On other services, folded manual wheelchairs can be carried and if you give advance notice, you can get help to manage the entrance steps.

National Express Disabled Persons Travel Helpline
☎ 08717 818179
Textphone 0121 455 9986

Ⓔ dpth@nationalexpress.com
Ⓦ www.nationalexpress.com

Oxford Tube, which runs regular, scheduled services between Oxford and London, has introduced 26 new low floor buses each of which has one space for a passenger using a wheelchair.
☎ 01865 772250
Ⓦ www.oxfordtube.com

Scottish Citylink has wheelchair accessible coaches on its regular service between Edinburgh and Glasgow and its services, run in partnership with Megabus, between Glasgow and London.
☎ 0870 550 5050
Ⓦ www.citylink.co.uk

Victoria Coach Station – This is both the terminus for most coach services in and out of London and an important place at which connections can be made. There is a mobility lounge where disabled people can wait and from which assistance can be provided. To book assistance call:
☎ 020 7027 2520
Ⓦ www.tfl.gov.uk

> Information on firms with accessible coaches available for private hire, for group trips and other purposes, should be available from a Public Transport Information Office or PTE.

Door-to-door and community transport

Some localities have special transport schemes for people who are not able to use public transport. They include: 'dial-a-ride' and 'ring-and-ride'. This sort of service allows you to book an adapted vehicle to carry you on a door-to-door journey.

Demand for these services is likely to exceed the resources available so you may find a variety of restrictions in place, for example limits on the number of journeys you can book in any given period and travel may be restricted to a particular administrative area.

More general Community Transport schemes exist where no public transport is available, often, but not exclusively in rural areas. Vehicles used for community transport will often be accessible to disabled passengers.

Special transport schemes are locally run according to local priorities. You should be able to get information on what's available in your area from the relevant Public Transport Information Office. You can also find out about community transport schemes at www.a2binfo.net

Community Transport Association UK (CTA UK)
Highbank, Halton Street, Hyde, Cheshire SK14 2NY.
☏ 0870 774 3586
Ⓦ www.ctauk.org
CTA UK gives advice and support on establishing and improving community transport schemes and provides training.

British Red Cross
44 Moorfields, London EC2Y 9AL.
☏ 0844 871 1111
Textphone 020 7562 2050
Ⓦ www.redcross.org.uk
British Red Cross branches offer a transport service for people who cannot get about easily or use public transport. It helps people to get to medical appointments, go shopping or just to get out of the house. Call or visit the website for details of local Red Cross Branches.

Travelling by sea

Information on ferry operators between the British mainland and the Isle of Wight, the Scottish islands, the Channel Islands, Isle of Man and Ireland is given in the appropriate Regional sections of this Guide. If any assistance may be required the ferry company should be notified in advance.

Price concessions on car ferries are often available to disabled people, and to members of one of the organisations for disabled motorists.

FERRY TRAVEL

Large, modern ships used on international journeys may be accessible with lifts between decks, toilets designed for disabled people and adapted cabins. Much simpler vessels on estuary crossings with open car decks generally have few special facilities and may not be accessible.

If you are planning to travel by ferry, you need to remember that in tidal waters, the gradient of any boarding ramp will vary according to the tide. This is the case even in places like London, quite a long way from the sea. At low tide, ramps may be very steep.

If you need assistance or information, get in touch with the ferry operator in advance. Contact details and other information can be obtained from the public transport information points or motoring organisations.

Travelling by sea

Services on ferries and ships vary considerably, even across the UK, so it is important to plan ahead and ensure all sections of your journey are accessible to you. Section 8 also contains some useful information. Port facilities and services (including booking facilities) in the UK should be accessible to disabled people. However, there is currently no legislation requiring operators of passenger vessels to do the same. Despite this, many ferry and cruise operators provide access to their services for disabled people.

Access to sea travel

DPTAC has published Access to Sea Travel – Information for Disabled People and Persons with Reduced Mobility. This document can be downloaded from the DPTAC website:

🌐 dptac.independent.gov.uk/pubs/ seatravel/index.htm

Or you can get a printed copy direct from DPTAC.

Directgov has also published information on overseas travel by sea. You can read this by going to:

🌐 www.direct.gov.uk/en/ DisabledPeople/TravelHolidays AndBreaks/GettingThere/ DG_4017236

Making a complaint about sea services

For information on how to make a complaint about a port or ship service, see the DPTAC document Access to Sea Travel (for details, see above).

Directgov has also published information on how to make a complaint about boat services on inland waterways in Britain: www. direct.gov.uk/en/TravelAndTransport/ Boatingandtravellingbywater/ RiversAndWaterways/DG_10035954.

Rail travel

Since 1998, all new trains have had to incorporate access features for disabled people, including spaces for passengers using manual wheelchairs, appropriate toilets and signage. Many trains introduced before that date also have spaces for passengers using wheelchairs. Very few trains can accommodate the larger makes of scooters. Older trains are gradually being phased out but some are still in use.

Accessibility for disabled passengers at train stations is variable. There has been an active process of adapting premises, but effort has been concentrated on larger stations and those where modernisation was already planned. Many smaller stations still have steps to one or more platforms.

PLANNING YOUR JOURNEY
It is worth looking at options to take through-services across major population centres rather than changing trains. Information on services and disruptions can be obtained from:

National Train Enquiries
- 📞 08457 484950
  Textphone 0845 605 0600
- 🌐 www.nationalrail.co.uk

The National Rail website also has 'Stations Made Easy' pages showing the layout of stations. This can be useful in planning a journey through a station you are not familiar with.

Despite continuing improvements, many disabled passengers may still need help at some points of their rail journey. If you think you may need assistance, it helps to give as much advance notice as possible.

If you will be travelling on more than one train line, you should address any requests for information and assistance to the Train Operating company responsible for the first leg of your journey:

Arriva Trains Wales
- 📞 0845 300 3005
  Textphone 0845 605 0600

C2C
- 📞 Telephone 01702 357640
  (also Textphone)

Chiltern Railways
- 📞 0845 600 5165
  Textphone 0845 707 8051

Cross Country
- 📞 0844 811 0125
  Textphone 0844 811 0126

East Coast

T 0845 722 5225
Textphone 0845 120 2067

East Midlands Trains

T 0845 712 5678
Textphone 0845 707 8051

First Capital Connect

T 0800 058 2844
Textphone 0800 975 1052

First Great Western

T 0800 197 1329
Textphone 0800 294 9209

First Hull Trains

T 0845 071 0222
Textphone 0845 678 6867

First ScotRail

T 0800 912 2901

First TransPennine

T 0800 107 2149
Textphone 0800 107 2061

Grand Central Railway

T 0844 811 0072
Textphone 0845 305 6815

Heathrow Express

T 0845 600 1515

London Midland

T 0800 092 4260
Textphone 08944 811 0134

London Overground

T 0870 601 4867

Merseyrail

T Telephone 0800 027 7347
(also Textphone)

National Express East Anglia

T 0800 028 2878
Textphone 0845 606 7245

Northern Rail

T 0808 156 1606
Textphone 0845 604 5608

SouthEastern

T 0800 783 4524
Textphone 0800 783 4548

South West Trains

T 0800 528 2100
Textphone 0800 692 0792

Southern

T 0800 138 1016
Textphone 0800 138 1018

Virgin Trains

T 0845 744 3366
Textphone 0845 744 3367

The **Disabled Persons Railcard** gives a third off many rail fares for the cardholder and an adult travelling companion. The Scheme celebrated its 30th anniversary in 2011. A list of qualifying criteria and an application form are in the 'Rail travel made easy' leaflet, available from Travel Centres and staffed stations. It takes up to two weeks to obtain a new or renewed railcard, so applications should be made ahead of any planned journeys. A one-year railcard currently costs £20 and a three-year card is available for £54. A Disabled Persons Railcard application helpline is available on: Telephone 0845 605 0525 (7am to 10pm, Monday to Sunday); Textphone 0845 601 0132; email disability@atoc.org or see www.disabledpersons-railcard.co.uk. Application forms should be sent to: Disabled Persons Railcard Office, PO Box 11631, Laurencekirk AB30 9AA.

Passenger Focus

Freepost (RRRE-ETTC-LEET), PO Box 4257, Manchester M60 3AR.

📞 0300 123 2350

✉ info@passengerfocus.org.uk

🌐 www.passengerfocus.org.uk

Passenger Focus is the national watchdog for passengers. It can assist with complaints about rail travel where a response from an initial approach to the train operator has been unsatisfactory.

Mainline trains

On mainline (intercity, suburban and cross-country) trains there is a space designed for wheelchair users to travel in safety and comfort. You must always use this space and should apply your brakes when the train is moving. If you use a powered wheelchair, you should make sure that the power is switched off when travelling.

All intercity train services and most other mainline services are wheelchair accessible. Access to the train is provided by a ramp kept either at the station or on the train. Wheelchair accessible sleeper cabins are available on overnight trains between London and Scotland but not on those between London and the West of England.

Local and regional services

Most trains can accommodate wheelchair users and new trains also have facilities to assist sensory impaired people. For example, public

information systems that are both visual and audible. To arrange a train journey in the UK, contact National Rail Enquiries:

📞 0845 7484 950

Textphone 0845 6050 600

National rail and the Disabled People's Protection Policy

Rail companies must produce a Disabled People's Protection Policy (DPPP). The DPPP explains how the company helps disabled passengers to use their stations and trains. You can get copies of a company's DPPP direct from the company.

Traintaxi

You can use Traintaxi to find out if accessible taxis are available at a station. Traintaxi lists up to three local taxi or cab firms serving each station. You can find out more about taxis later in this section.

Cross-channel services

THE CHANNEL TUNNEL

As an alternative to ferries or planes, the Channel Tunnel offers a useful route to continental Europe. Two services exist:

Eurostar

Eurostar operates train services from London St Pancras International, Ebbsfleet and Ashford to Brussels, Lille and Paris. They offer a limited number of reduced rate tickets for passengers using wheelchairs and their companion. As spaces are limited, it is worth booking well in advance. Assistance is available on request at check-in; you are asked to arrive as early as possible.

📞 0870 518 6186
🌐 www.eurostar.com

Eurotunnel

Eurotunnel operates vehicle-carrying shuttle trains between Folkestone and Calais. Disabled drivers or disabled passengers are asked to make themselves known at check-in so that they can park at the front of the shuttle. A maximum of five vehicles carrying disabled drivers or passengers (who may need assistance in an emergency evacuation) can be carried in any shuttle. Terminals are accessible and have toilets for disabled people. There is no need for people to get out of their vehicles if they do not wish to. Information is available from:

Eurotunnel Customer Relations Department

📞 0800 0969 992
🌐 www.eurotunnel.co.uk

Taxis

In London, all licensed taxis must be able to carry a passenger using a standard wheelchair. So all 'London black cabs' manufactured since 1989 have to have space to carry a passenger using a manual wheelchair and either carry or be equipped with a ramp.

Black cabs also feature a hidden step up to the cab which the driver can simply swing out from the chassis. In addition, black cabs are fitted with swivel seats that can be rotated through 90 degrees, enabling the passenger to take their seat outside of the taxi and then swivel into the vehicle.

Similar rules have been introduced by local authorities responsible for regulating taxis in other areas. In some areas price concession systems are available to disabled people for journeys by taxi and/or private hire cars. This may be as part of a more general concession scheme or a separate system. On a local basis, other specialist taxi services may exist for disabled people.

A wide range of other cars are used as private hire vehicles and when you make a booking you should check with the operator whether their vehicles meet your accessibility requirements. Private hire vehicles should carry assistance dogs at no extra charge.

The Government is committed to an accessible public transport system in which disabled people have the same opportunities to travel as other members of society. Taxis and private hire vehicles (PHVs) are a vital link in the accessible transport chain and, although disabled people are reported to travel a third less often than the public in general, they use taxis and PHVs on average 67% more often.

You can find out more about accessible taxi and private hire vehicles from local authorities. You can also go to these websites:

- ⓦ www.transportdirect.info or
- ⓦ www.traintaxi.co.uk

Stay Safe with Cabwise Transport for London's Text Service

Text CAB to 60835, and you'll receive two minicab numbers and one taxi (black cab) number straight back to your mobile phone by text. You don't even need to say where you are as your location is plotted using GPS. So save 60835 to your mobile now and it'll be there whenever you need it.

Text charged at 35p per enquiry plus standard text message rate. Roaming rates apply to overseas networks.

Customers on the 3 network need to enter different information. See tfl.gov.uk/cabwise for further details.

> **www.traintaxi.co.uk** is a database giving information on the availability of taxis at stations throughout Britain. It includes telephone numbers for up to three taxi companies for advanced bookings and indicates which ones say they have accessible vehicles. You should check whether the company can meet your requirements when you book.

Stay Safe in London

Unbooked minicabs are illegal. You may be approached by minicab drivers seeking passengers or offering a service; avoid using these as they are unsafe, unlicensed, uninsured and illegal and you put yourself in danger if you use these services.

Booking your minicab with a licensed minicab company guarantees that your trip will be carried out by a licensed driver in a licensed vehicle. It also means that a record is kept of your

53

Practical advice about how to do everyday things differently

Each guide is packed with practical advice and includes real-life stories to inspire people to take control of different aspects of their lives, with maximum choice and independence.

Doing Careers Differently

Whatever your aspirations and wherever you are in your career, this guide will help you both take the first step or plan longer term to make a success of your career while living with a disability or health condition.

Doing IT Differently

Provides information and assistance to allow everyone the opportunity to take advantage and overcome the barriers of Information Technology (IT) and computers regardless of disability.

Doing Work Differently

Explores practical solutions to real questions related to work and provides real life examples of how people have started a job, found a new career, or found a way to keep doing their current job if their circumstances change.

Doing Money Differently

Looks at new ways of making, saving and looking after your money. It is a toolkit to help you understand money better and lessen the amount of time you spend thinking and worrying about it.

Download your free copy from: www.radar.org.uk/publications

Telephone: 020 7250 3222
Textphone: 18001 020 7250 3222
Email: radar@radar.org.uk
www.radar.org.uk

 the disability rights people

journey, your driver and the vehicle used. Therefore, in the event of any problems, the driver can be traced.

Only taxis (black cabs) can be stopped by customers and can pick up off the street. Even minicabs lined up outside pubs and clubs are breaking the law if they accept your fare without a booking being made first.

Many clubs have licensed minicab operators inside who can take your booking. Check with staff to see if a minicab service is available.

You can use these two companies to book taxis in London:

Cabwise: text CAB to 60835 (see above for details)

Findaride: find details of licensed private hire and minicab operators in any part of London:

🅦 tfl.gov.uk/findaride

To comment or complain about taxi and private hire services:

🅣 TfL on 0845 300 7000

🅔 tph.coms@tfl.gov.uk

🅦 www.tfl.gov.uk/contactcabs

Trams and underground systems

Trams and other light rail systems developed over recent years in a number of places, including Croydon, Greater Manchester, Nottingham, Sheffield and the West Midlands, have

been designed to be usable by disabled people.

The Tyne Wear Metro and the Docklands Light Railway in East London are fairly accessible to wheelchair users but you may need to be accompanied. Access for disabled passengers is still limited on the older underground systems in London and Glasgow. In London, new developments, such as the Jubilee Line extension between Westminster and Stratford are designed to be accessible.

Transport for London is running a programme to create step-free routes to the platforms and other access improvements at almost 100 stations. You can find up-to-date information on Underground Maps published by Transport for London and available at www.tfl.gov.uk

If Only I'd Known That ...

An information-packed guide to services, welfare rights, facilities and support for anyone with a disability or health condition, this guide includes resources for all ages from childhood to later years.

Available to order online from:
www.disabilityrightsuk.org

Get Motoring

Your guide to everything the disabled motorist needs to know about finding, financing and maintaining a car.

Available from Radar's online shop
www.radar-shop.org.uk

Get Caravanning

A guide to helping you explore caravanning from a disabled person's point of view.

Available from Radar's online shop
www.radar-shop.org.uk

Motoring

For many disabled people, having a car provides one of the main routes to independent mobility. Developments in technology and vehicle design mean that it is increasingly possible to find cars that can be adapted to meet the needs of disabled drivers or passengers. Motoring organisations such as the AA and RAC provide particular services for their disabled members and can give help and advice with things like planning routes and insurance. When you are away from home it is also worth finding out in advance about parking facilities.

Parking

THE BLUE BADGE SCHEME

This scheme provides a national system of on-street parking concessions for people with severe mobility problems.

Having a Blue Badge will help you to park close to your destination, either as the passenger or as the driver. However, the badge is intended for on-street parking only. Off-street car parks, such as those provided in local authority, hospital or supermarket car parks are governed by separate rules. You can get a leaflet to tell you more about where you can and cannot park in the on-street environment. You need to go to www.directgov.uk to find out more about this.

Blue Badges are issued by local councils who are responsible for assessing whether you are eligible. In those parts of England where there are County and District Councils, badges are issued by the County Council.

Blue Badge holders can generally park without charge in areas controlled by parking meters and in pay-and-display bays. They are also exempt from time limits imposed on others and may park for up to three hours on yellow lines, except where loading or other restrictions apply. This time limit does not apply in Scotland. The scheme does not apply in parts of the centre of London where four local authorities (The Royal Borough of Kensington and Chelsea, City of Westminster, City of London and London Borough of Camden) have set up their own, special disabled badge schemes for people that live, work or study in the central area. You can apply direct to these boroughs for details of their own schemes.

Although the Blue Badge Scheme does not apply to off-street parking, it is

often used by local authorities as the basis for concessionary use of car parks and to indicate that designated parking bays in privately-owned parking areas are being used correctly. A Blue Badge does not always entitle you to free parking in off-street car parks, even when they are run by the local council. Always check to find out if you need to pay.

> The **Department for Transport** has produced a guide to concessions that are available to disabled people. You can download this list from their website: www.dft.gov.uk

Outside the EU it will be a matter of local policy whether countries will recognise the Blue Badge. Some countries that have high numbers of tourists may award a short-term badge for the duration of your stay. Always check before you use your badge. If you incur a fine that you don't pay you could be refused entry next time you visit the country.

At the time of writing, the Blue Badge Scheme was under review. Proposals for the future include raising the application cost, involving an independent assessment for applicants, (governed by their local authority), and changing the badge design to prevent fraudulent use. For the latest news, visit www.direct.gov.uk

Blue Badge Helpline
📞 020 4944 2914 or 0161 367 0009
The Community Transport Association provides a specialist advice service on matters related to the Blue Badge.

Blue Badge Network
198 Wolverhampton Street, Dudley
DY1 1DZ
📞 01384 257001
📧 headoffice@
   bluebadgenetwork.org.uk
🌐 www.bluebadgenetwork.org.uk

The Blue Badge Network is a membership organisation aiming to help disabled people and, in particular, to maintain the integrity of the concessionary parking permit.

Blue Badge Nav (BBNav)
BBNav is a satellite navigation system with all the usual functionality as well as offering full coverage of Blue Badge on-street parking bays, car park access and local council parking rules for over 150 major UK cities and towns. To find out more go to:
🌐 www.bbnav.co.uk

DISABILITY MOTORING ORGANISATIONS

Disabled Motorists Federation

☎ 0191 416 3172

🌐 www.dmfed.org.uk

The Disabled Motorists Federation is another national organisation of disabled motorists. It is volunteer-run and can be contacted by phone or via their website.

Mobilise

National Headquarters, Ashwellthorpe, Norwich NR16 1EX.

☎ 01508 489449

✉ enquiries@mobilise.info

🌐 www.mobilise.info

Mobilise is a national charity that campaigns and provides information on all matters related to motoring/ mobility and disabled people.

National Association for Bikers with a Disability (NABD)

Unit 20, The Bridgewater Centre, Robson Avenue, Urmston, Manchester M41 7TE.

☎ 0844 415 4849

✉ office@thenabd.org.uk

🌐 www.nabd.org.uk

NABD caters for disabled people who want to enjoy the freedom of motorcycling. It provides a range of services for its members including advice and help on training, licensing, adaptations and the associated costs and insurance. It has a network of local representatives and produces a quarterly magazine.

Leisure activities

Taking part in leisure activities is one of life's great pleasures. Having a disability or impairment may limit what you do but with the right help, support and equipment we can take part in a wide range of activities. This section of the Guide tells you about some of the things you might like to do while you're away.

Arts

While you are away, you might want to go to a play or a show. The local tourist information service or library should have a list of what is on. You can also get information on taking part in or visiting arts-related activities from a wide range of organisations. Check ahead on the internet before you go or consider an app for your Smartphone, if you have one. These are some of the organisations currently providing information about the arts in the UK:

Arts Council of England
14 Great Peter Street, London SW1P 3NQ.
- 0845 300 6200
  Textphone 020 7973 6564
- enquiries@artscouncil.org.uk
- www.artscouncil.org.uk

The Arts Council of England is responsible for arts funding and development in England and provides information and advice to artists and arts organisations. Elsewhere in UK contact:

Arts Council of Northern Ireland
77 Malone Road, Belfast BT9 6AQ.
- 028 9038 5200
- www.artscouncil-ni.org

Create Scotland
Waverley Gate, 2-4 Waterloo Place, Edinburgh EH1 3EG.
- 0845 603 6000
- www.createscotland.com

Arts Council of Wales
Bute Place, Cardiff CF10 5AL.
- 0845 8734 900
  Textphone 029 2045 1023
- www.artswales.org

Artsline
c/o 21 Pine Court, Wood Lodge Gardens, Bromley BR1 2WA.
- 020 7388 2227 (also Textphone)
- www.artsline.org.uk

An online information service for disabled people on arts and leisure events activities in and around London which includes details on access and provision for disabled people at arts and entertainment venues and events.

Attitude is Everything

54 Chalton Street, London NW1 1HS.

☎ 020 7383 7979

ⓦ www.attitudeiseverything.org.uk

This organisation work with audiences, artists and the music industry to improve deaf and disabled people's access to live music. It promotes a *'Charter of Best Practice'* to venues and festivals throughout the country.

Disability Cultural Projects (DCP)

ⓦ www.disabilityarts.info

DCP Access guide

ⓦ www.artsaccessuk.org

DCP produces EtCetera, a weekly electronic newsletter of opportunities, an events list and an online arts access guide. The website also contains extensive links to disability arts organisations and archived material from the National Disability Arts Forum that closed in 2008.

> **MAGIC Deaf Arts** is a group of 16 major museums and art galleries in London. Each provides events and facilities for deaf and hard of hearing visitors, including specialist tours and sign interpreters at public talks and lectures. Visit their website www.magicdeaf.org.uk for a calendar of events.

The Mayflower Theatre

Empire Lane, Southampton SO15 1AP

☎ 02380 711813

ⓦ www.mayflower.org.uk

The Mayflower Theatre in Southampton offers discounts for disabled people and companions. These discounts are not available for all performances. Other theatres may offer similar discounts but you will have to check with the theatre directly or on the internet before you book your tickets.

Music and the Deaf

The Media Centre, 7 Northumberland Street, Huddersfield HD1 1RL.

☎ 01484 483115

Textphone 01484 483117

ⓦ www.matd.org.uk

Music and the Deaf help deaf people of all ages access music and the performing arts. It provides talks, signed theatre performances and workshops. In West Yorkshire it runs after-school clubs and a Deaf Youth Orchestra. Music and the Deaf also runs training days and collaborative projects with orchestras, opera, theatre and dance companies and is one of the five lead organisations in Sing-up, a project to promote singing in schools.

National Theatre

South Bank, London SE1 9PX.

☎ 020 7452 3000

ⓔ access@nationaltheatre.org.uk

ⓦ www.nationaltheatre.org.uk

The National Theatre aims to be accessible and welcoming to all. Its three auditoriums have allocated wheelchair spaces and assistance dogs are welcome. People with hearing impairments can attend captioned and signed performances. Blind and visually-impaired people can attend audio-described performances and receive synopses notes on CD or cassette. Touch tours and get Braille cast lists are also available. Its access mailing list offers free information on CD, in Braille and large print via email.

Nordoff Robbins

2 Lissenden Gardens, London NW5 1PQ.
📞 020 7267 4496
✉ admin@nordoff-robbins.org.uk
🌐 www.nordoff robbins.org.uk
A national organisation that seeks to use the power of music to transform the lives of children and adults living with illness, disability, trauma or in isolation. Their trained practitioners work in a range of settings including music therapy, music and health projects and community music schemes as well as the organisation's own centres.

Official London Theatre (OLT)

🌐 www.officiallondontheatre.co.uk/access
Official London Theatre want to ensure your trip to the theatre is as fantastic an experience as possible, and have a variety of resources to help.

For extensive venue access information about theatres across London, visit their detailed venue access site made in collaboration with Direct Enquires, an access and disability specialist.

You can download the OLT Venue Access Guide, which includes detailed access information for more than 70 theatres in London. They also have a selection of Access Enabled maps, detailing step-free journeys to many of London's most popular theatres. Visit their website to find out more.

Zinc Arts (formerly Theatre Resource) aims to advance and promote creativity, culture and heritage of disabled people and other socially excluded groups in Essex and Hertfordshire. It arranges a wide range of programmes and events. Contact Zinc Arts, High Street, Chipping Ongar, Essex CM5 0AD. Telephone 01277 365626; Textphone 01277 365003 or visit www.zincarts.org.uk

Shape

Deane House Studios, 27 Greenwood Place, London NW5 1LB.
📞 0845 521 3457
    Textphone 020 7424 7368
🌐 www.shapearts.org.uk
Shape offers a range of activities to

enable disabled people to participate and enjoy arts and cultural activities mainly in the London area. Shape Tickets is a service offering its members tickets, often at reduced prices, at venues throughout London coupled with access assistance and transport if required.

Signed Performances In Theatre (SPIT)

6 Thirlmere Drive, Lymm, Cheshire WA13 9PE.

📞 01925 754231

🌐 www.spit.org.uk

SPIT promotes British Sign Language interpreted performances in mainstream theatre and provides a link between arts organisations and the Deaf community. Its website includes a directory of signed and captioned performances nationwide.

STAGETEXT

1st Floor, 54 Commercial Street, London E1 6LT.

📞 020 7377 0540
   Textphone 020 7247 7801

📧 enquiries@stagetext.org

🌐 www.stagetext.org

Stagetext provides access to the theatre for deaf and hard of hearing people through captioning. The full text, together with character names, sound effects and off-stage noises, is shown on LED displays as the words are spoken or sung. Around 200 productions are captioned each year in over 80 venues across the UK. Information on forthcoming performances is given on its website.

VocalEyes

1st Floor, 54 Commercial Street, London E1 6LT.

📞 020 7375 1043

📧 enquiries@vocaleyes.co.uk

🌐 www.vocaleyes.co.uk

VocalEyes is a national organisation which provides audio description for performances in the theatre and also for museums, galleries and architectural heritage sites. A programme of forthcoming events is published in print, Braille and on tape as well as on their website.

Cinemas

In the past, few cinemas were accessible to people with impaired mobility, hearing or sight. The development of new cinema buildings has meant improvements with respect to physical access, with at least some screens in multiplexes having spaces for wheelchair users.

A programme is now underway to substantially increase both the number of cinemas equipped to show films with digital subtitles and audio description and the number of films that are available. For information on subtitled and audio-described films and where they are being shown, visit:
Ⓦ www.yourlocalcinema.com

If you are a registered blind person or receive Disability Living Allowance or Attendance Allowance, the **Cinema Exhibitors' Association (CEA)** offers a national card verifying entitlement to a free ticket for a person accompanying you to the cinema. There is a £5.50 administration charge and the card has to be renewed each year.

Application forms are available from participating cinemas or from www.ceacard.co.uk. The CEA card is administered and run by The Card Network, Network House, St Ives Way, Sandycroft CH5 2QS. Telephone 0845 123 1292; Textphone 0845 123 1296; email info@ceacard.co.uk

Activity holidays

Some people choose their holiday destination based on a particular leisure interest. This section includes a selection of organisations that provide outdoor activity, boating and skiing holidays as well as breaks for people who want to volunteer, take a course or follow a special interest while away.

Outdoor activity holidays

These centres cater for individuals or groups on organised programmes of outdoor and indoor activities including horse riding and rock climbing. Some also offer facilities for self-led groups.

Activenture Holidays

Hindleap Warren, Wych Cross, Forest Row, East Sussex RH18 5JS.
📞 01342 828215
✉️ activenture@hindleap.com
🌐 www.londonyouth.org
Run week-long activity holidays for young people with disabilities or special needs aged 8-18 during school holidays, and a weekend for over 18s, at Hindleap Warren Outdoor Centre. Owned by London Youth, the Centre has a 300-acre site in Ashdown Forest and offers 24-hour one-to-one care if required. Activities available with trained instructors include abseiling, canoeing, archery, and obstacle courses. 30 people are accommodated on each holiday with young and adult staff as companions. Nurse in attendance. Early booking essential.

Avon Tyrrell

Bransgore, Hampshire BH23 8EE.
📞 01425 672347
✉️ info@ukyouth.org
🌐 www.avontyrrell.org.uk
UK Youth activity centre on a 65-acre site in the New Forest for groups of all ages offering a wide range of activities with qualified instructors including climbing, canoeing, archery, zip wire, high and low rope courses and environmental studies. Accessible accommodation on either full board or self-catering basis.

Badaguish Centre

Aviemore, Inverness-shire PH22 1QU.
📞 01479 861285
✉️ info@badaguish.org
🌐 www.badaguish.org
Provide activity holidays with support predominately for people with learning disabilities. They offer a wide range of activities in an area that includes the Cairngorm Funicular Railway and Morlich Water Sports Centre. Respite care activity holidays with 24-hour care arranged for unaccompanied people with learning disabilities. For groups

there is also accommodation in fully accessible log cabins or under canvas as well as in new, fully accessible self-catering lodges.

Bendrigg Trust

Bendrigg Lodge, Old Hutton, Kendal, Cumbria LA8 0NR.

☎ 01539 722446
✉ office@bendrigg.org.uk
Ⓦ www.bendrigg.org.uk

Residential activity centre running courses for people of all ages and abilities and specialising in supporting people with learning disabilities. A wide range of outdoor and indoor activities available with qualified, experienced staff. Individual programmes are planned for each group. Open weeks are available for individuals and carers. Accommodation for up to 40 people in small dormitories. Lift and ramp to first floor. Adapted showers, washrooms and WCs.

Bowles

Eridge Green, Tunbridge Wells TN3 9LW.

☎ 01892 665665
✉ admin@bowles.ac
Ⓦ www.bowles.ac

Offer activity courses for groups of young people and adults including disabled people. Modern accommodation includes twin and single bedrooms with en-suite accommodation plus two twin bedrooms with en-suite shower rooms designed for wheelchair users.

There are also 96 rooms in dormitory accommodation available. Activities include skiing, rope courses, rock climbing, canoeing and archery. Some specialist equipment available.

Calvert Trust Exmoor

Wistlandpound, Kentisbury, Barnstaple, Devon EX31 4SJ.

☎ 01598 763221
✉ exmoor@calvert-trust.org.uk
Ⓦ www.calvert-trust.org.uk

Activity centre near the coast and Exmoor, designed for disabled people and their friends and families. All bedrooms have shower rooms accessible to wheelchair users. Indoor swimming pool, jacuzzi and steam room. Activities offered include climbing, bush craft, horse riding, sailing, canoeing, and archery. Self-catering units also available.

The Lake District Calvert Trust

Little Crosthwaite, Keswick, Cumbria CA12 4QD.

☎ 01768 772255
✉ enquiries@lakedistrict. calvert-trust.org.uk
Ⓦ www.calvert-trust.org.uk

Outdoor activity holidays and educational or personal development courses specifically designed around individual group requirements. The accommodation has recently been refurbished and is in a converted farmhouse with wheelchair access throughout. All bedrooms all have en-suite shower rooms. Facilities include

radar

Children First

A guide for everyone involved in the care and support of disabled children. It covers a wide range of topics including health, play, children's services, school and benefits.

Available from Radar's online shop
www.radar-shop.org.uk

sports hall, climbing wall, indoor pool, games room, TV lounge, library and brand-new this year; a state of the art hydrotherapy pool. Activities include rock climbing, abseiling, horse riding, water sports, fell walking, orienteering and archery. Specialist courses offered. Standard and adapted equipment available. Qualified staff. Self-catering accommodation also available.

Calvert Trust Kielder

Kielder Water, Hexham, Northumberland NE48 1BS.
☎ 01434 250232
✉ enquiries@calvert-kielder.com
🌐 www.calvert-trust.org.uk
Purpose-built holiday centre by Northumberland National Park for disabled people and their families and friends. Activities include water sports, climbing, abseiling, archery and zipwire with king swing and low ropes course. Instruction and equipment available. There is a hydrotherapy pool and recreation hall. All accommodation is fully accessible for wheelchair users with level entry showers throughout. Care packages available.

Clyne Farm Centre

Westport Avenue, Mayals, Swansea SA3 5AR.
☎ 01792 403333
✉ info@clynefarm.com
🌐 www.clynefarm.com
Accredited activity centre, three miles from central Swansea. Offers a range of activities both on-site and off

including horse riding, archery, quad biking, surfing, rock climbing, canoeing and an assault course. Special interest courses are also offered for groups and individuals. Entrance level. Dining room/lounge level. Ramp or one step to other rooms. Nine self-catering cottages sleeping four-16 people, up to 51 in total. 'The School Rooms' are recommended for wheelchair users being on the ground floor with specially adapted wet rooms.

Coldwell Activity Centre

Back Lane, Southfield, Burnley BB10 3RD.
☎ 01282 601819
✉ bookings@coldwell.org.uk
🌐 www.coldwell.org.uk
Group holiday accommodation in the Pennines by Coldwell Reservoir. Outdoor activity programme available including archery, canoeing and climbing. Reserved parking bay. Entrance ramp. Public rooms level. Unisex WC. Lift to first floor. Adapted shower room. Accommodation for up to 27 in 12 bedrooms. Minimum group size 16.

The Kepplewray Centre

Broughton-in-Furness, Cumbria LA20 6HE.
☎ 01229 716936
✉ web1@kepplewray.org.uk
🌐 www.kepplewray.org.uk
Fully accessible and inclusive indoor and outdoor activity centre in southern Lake District designed for groups of

disabled and non-disabled people. Accommodation for up to 45. Ramp to side door. Lift to upper floor. Variety of bedrooms, bathrooms and toilets fitted for a range of disabilities. Equipment includes Clos-o-Mat WC, adjustable height bed, shower chair and electric hoist. A wide variety of outside and indoor activities are available including environmental studies. Programmes offered for families, schools and organisations.

Loch Insh Watersports
Insh Hall, Kincraig, Inverness-shire PH21 1NU.
☎ 01540 651272
✉ office@lochinsh.com
🌐 www.lochinsh.com
Privately run watersport centre in Cairngorm National Park between Aviemore and Kingussie offering courses for families and groups. The jetty is accessible for wheelchair users from the car park and boathouse/restaurant. Archery and an adapted

catamaran are available for wheelchair users. Advance booking required.

Mersea Island Festival
East Mersea Youth Camp, Rewsalls Lane, East Mersea, Colchester CO5 8SX.
☎ 01206 383226
✉ info@merseyfestivals.org.uk
🌐 www.merseafestival.org.uk
Two activity breaks of five and three days are offered in August each year comprising sport, music and art. The programme is designed to be accessible to everyone and includes water-sports, climbing, archery, circus skills and workshops in music, dance, arts and crafts all with qualified instructors. The 70-acre site on the coast has camping accommodation and associated facilities for up to 350 people.

Plas Menai National Watersports Centre
Llanfairisgaer, Caernarfon, Gwynedd LL55 1UE.
☎ 01248 670964
✉ info@plasmenai.co.uk
🌐 www.plasmenai.co.uk
Centre owned by Sports Council for Wales offering watersports courses for groups including disabled people. Accommodation entrance level. 43 bedrooms in separate blocks with level entry and two fully adapted bathrooms with wheelchair accessible shower rooms available and designed for disabled people.

Riding for the Disabled Association

Lavinia Norfolk House, Avenue R, Stoneleigh Park, Warwickshire CV8 2LY.

☎ 0845 658 1082

✉ info@rda.org.uk

🌐 www.rda.org.uk

Has local riding and carriage driving groups for disabled people throughout the country. Organise group, county, regional and national holidays for its members.

Queen Elizabeth II Silver Jubilee Activities Centre

Manor Farm Country Park, Pylands Lane, Bursledon, Hampshire SO31 1BH.

☎ 023 8040 4844

✉ qe2centre@aol.com

🌐 www.qe2activitycentre.co.uk

Residential activity centre in Country Park by Hamble River near Southampton. Accommodation is in six self-catering cabins each for up to eight people. Adapted cooking facilities, showers and toilets are available for participants with disabilities. Activities offered include canoeing, orienteering and indoor sports. Facilities adapted for disabled people include a motor boat and a climbing wall.

Whitewave – Skye's Outdoor Centre

No. 19 Lincro, Kilmuir, Isle of Skye IV51 9YN.

☎ 01470 542414

✉ info@whitewave.co.uk

🌐 www.white-wave.co.uk

Family-run centre in north Skye offering activities including canoeing,

archery, Gaelic language courses and informal breaks in self-catering accommodation. Apply to Anne Martin and John White.

Woodlarks Camp Site Trust

Tilford Road, Lower Bourne, Farnham GU10 3RN.

☎ 01252 715238

✉ enquiries@woodlarks.org.uk

🌐 www.woodlarks.org.uk

A woodland site for tented camping with some indoor accommodation including toilets and washing facilities. Tents and beds provided. Totally accessible and equipped for wheelchair users. Heated swimming pool, aerial runway and barbeque sites. Available for group bookings, and for seven weeks are open to individuals as disabled participants and volunteer helpers.

Special interest centres and courses

The following centres and organisations offer residential courses on a variety of non-vocational subjects and areas of special interest from photography and literature to environmental studies and personal development.

Ammerdown Centre

Ammerdown Park, Radstock, Somerset BA3 56W.

☎ 01761 433709

✉ centre@ammerdown.org

🌐 www.ammerdown.org

Conference and retreat centre set within a country estate 20 minutes from both Bath and Wells offering a variety of holistic courses suitable for people with disabilities. Specialist break available for people with ME run in September. Entrance level access, public lecture rooms ground floor. Lift to first floor. One twin and two single bedrooms with bathrooms designed for disabled guests. Programme of events and further information is available on request.

Higham Hall

Bassenthwaite Lake, Cockermouth, Cumbria CA13 9SH.
☎ 01768 776276
✉ admin@highamhall.com
🌐 www.highamhall.com
Residential adult education college in northern Lake District offering a varied programme of short courses all year round. Main public areas and all ground floor rooms are accessible to disabled people and there is a stair lift on the main staircase. Induction loop in the lecture room and also a portable loop for other classes is available. Bungalow in the grounds adapted for wheelchair users and friends and family.

Holton Lee

East Holton, Poole, Dorset BH16 6JN.
☎ 01202 631063
✉ facilities@holtonlee.co.uk
🌐 www.holtonlee.co.uk
Offer a range of accessible, short-term, self-catering accommodation for individuals and groups of up to 22 people, set within 350 acres of diverse landscape. Ideally situated for the Isle of Purbeck and the Jurassic Coast World Heritage Site. In 2012, introduced Mobility Safaris with Countryside Mobility South West. Guides take groups of disabled people into the countryside and run courses on a variety of subjects including photography and habitat management. From August, four-week long learning breaks will be available covering mixed crafts, wildlife observation and gardening skills.

The Kingcombe Centre

Toller Porcorum, Dorchester, Dorset DT2 0EQ.
☎ 01300 320684
✉ office@kingcombecentre.org.uk
🌐 www.kingcombe.org
Study centre in converted farm buildings surrounded by a nature reserve. A variety of residential and day courses are organised throughout the year, many drawing on the natural history of the surrounding area. Small step to main building, ramp available. Main public rooms on ground floor, level or ramped. Unisex WC. Two bedrooms in annexe, single and twin, designed for disabled people. Roll-in shower room opposite, handrails, transfer space by WC and shower chair available. Accessible paths and boardwalks and all-terrain buggy available.

Knuston Hall Residential College

Irchester, Wellingborough,
Northamptonshire NN29 7EU.
☎ 01933 312104
✉ enquiries@knustonhall.org.uk
🌐 www.knustonhall.org.uk
Offers short residential courses on
literature, arts, crafts and music.
Reserved parking bays. Entrance level,
automatic doors. Main public rooms
have level access. Most teaching rooms
level and fitted with induction loop.
Ramp to six ground floor bedrooms
with en-suite bathrooms, one adapted
for people with disabilities. Stair lift
to first floor bedrooms. Individual
requirements should be checked when
enquiring about a course.

Sport Wales

Sophia Gardens, Cardiff CF11 9SW.
☎ 0845 0450904
✉ info@sportwales.org.uk
🌐 www.sportwales.org.uk
Sports centre in central Cardiff offering
residential breaks for people of all
abilities including specialist residential
courses for people with disabilities.
Entrance ramp and automatic doors
with lift to all floors. Two twin
bedrooms designed for guests with
disabilities including shower rooms with
sliding doors and space for side transfer
to WC. Waterproof sheets available.
Tactile signs and Braille plan of the
premises also available.

Holidays afloat

These organisations and projects run
holidays for both self-led and skippered
boating holidays ranging from breaks
on a canal barge to full ocean sailing.

Accessible Boating

31 Burns Avenue, Church Crookham,
Fleet GU52 6BN.
☎ 01252 622520
✉ bookings@accessibleboating.org.uk
🌐 www.accessibleboating.org.uk
Operate two boats specially designed
and equipped with facilities for
less-mobile passengers and their
companions. 'Madame Butterfly' is a
seven-berth cruising canal boat based
at Odiham on the Basingstoke Canal.
It is equipped with hydraulic lifts at the
prow and stern, power assisted steering
and hoists for the WC and shower as
well as over one bed. 'Dawn', a day
boat suitable for six wheelchair users is
also available.

The Bruce Trust

Hungerford, Berkshire RG17 9YY.

📞 01264 356451

✉ enquiries@brucetrust.org.uk

🌐 www.brucetrust.org.uk

Operate four specially designed boats, two 12 berth, one 10 berth and one six berth in the Kennet & Avon Canal. These are based at Great Bedwyn, for cruising between Reading and Devizes Locks from where return cruises to Bath are possible. Each boat is equipped with a hydraulic lift and specially designed toilet. Full training can be given to group leaders.

The Bruce Wake Charitable Trust

Oakam, Rutland LE15 0ET.

📞 08448 793349

✉ info@brucewaketrust.co.uk

🌐 www.brucewaketrust.co.uk

Operate two narrow boats; 'Isabella' & 'Liilia' designed for use by disabled people, based at Upton-on-Severn between Tewkesbury & Worcester. Both boats are designed to accommodate one wheelchair user and their family or friends with berths for six-seven people for holidays on the rivers and canals of the south Midlands. They have two hydraulic lifts, a hoist over one bed and a specially designed WC & shower. Also have the 'Charlotte III', a wide beamed boat available for use on the rivers Severn & Avon & on the Gloucester-Sharpness Canal.

The Canal Boat Project

Lock View, Burnt Mill Lane, Essex CM20 2QS.

📞 01279 424444

✉ admin@canalboat.org.uk

🌐 www.canalboat.org.uk

Have a small fleet of purpose built or specially adapted accessible boats for hire to disabled people and community groups on the rivers Lee and Stort. Two wide-beamed residential boats sleep 12 or eight people respectively and can only be hired by self steering parties. Two day boats are also offered with a skipper and crew; one accommodating 12 passengers with the possibility of having six wheelchair users aboard and one for up to 10 passengers that will only accommodate one wheelchair user. Each has a lift giving access to most parts of the boats and some have specialist control equipment to enable people with mobility problems to steer.

Docklands Canal Boat Trust

8 Lloyd Villas, Roman Road E6 3SW.

📞 07511 622747

✉ bookings@dcbt.org.uk

🌐 www.dcbt.org.uk

'MV Challenge' is a wide-beamed barge based on the Lee & Stort Canal on the Hertfordshire/Essex border. The barge sleeps 10 passengers or 12 people for a day-trip and can take up to five wheelchair users onboard. It has a lift between decks and other accessible features including a wet room for disabled people. A skipper is provided. Bookings are taken from April to

October with special Christmas outings available in December.

Jubilee Sailing Trust

12 Hazel Road, Woolston, Southampton SO19 7GA.

📞 02380 449108

✉ info@jst.org.uk

🌐 www.jst.org.uk

Offer adventure holidays as crew members of 'Lord Nelson' and 'Tenacious'; purpose built, square-rigged tall sailing ships. Voyages last between four and 10 days and run around the UK, off the Canary Islands and sometimes further afield. Anyone aged over 16 can sail and bursary funding is sometimes available to cover fees. People with disabilities, including wheelchair users, sail alongside an equal number of non-disabled people. Special equipment includes flat wide decks, audio compasses, lifts between decks and an adjustable seat at the helm.

The Lyneal Trust

Lyneal Trust, Shirehall, Abbey Foregate, Shrewsbury SY2 6ND.

📞 01743 252728

✉ pushkar.trivedi@shropshire.gov.uk

🌐 www.lynealtrust.org

Provide canal and canal side holidays on the Llangollen Canal in North Shropshire for people with disabilities and their families and friends from Lyneal Wharf. At the Wharf there is a games room, kitchen and showers and two accessible chalets and a bungalow that can accommodate up to 16

people. 'Shropshire Lass' is a purpose built, eight berth canal boat that can accommodate up to three wheelchair users and has a specialist WC and shower for people with disabilities. 'Shropshire Lad' is available for day trips and holidays for people staying in the chalets or bungalow. Both boats have a hydraulic lift and hydraulic steering which allows wheelchair users to take part in running the boat. All parts of the boats can be accessed by people in wheelchairs.

Peter Le Marchant Trust

Canalside Moorings, Beeches Road, Loughborough LE11 2NS.

📞 01509 265590

✉ lynnsmith@
peterlemarchanttrust.co.uk

🌐 www.peterlemarchanttrust.org.uk

Have three boats designed for people with disabilities and long term health conditions. 'Serenade' takes up to 10 people on holidays ranging from four days to a fortnight, 'Melody' is available for weekly hire by small groups and 'Symphony' takes up to 26 people on day trips. All boats have hydraulic

ReachOut Plus

We are an established and exciting charity working to create opportunities that change people's lives. We run two facilities of interest to disabled groups and individuals:

Canal boats and sailing: A fleet of three, 12-passenger canal boats, adapted to be accessible for people with disabilities and special needs, operates from our boat base in Nash Mills, Hemel Hempstead. The boats are ideal for all abilities, for learning outside the classroom and expedition-based learning (including overnight). The base also houses a 50-seater fully-accessible Education and Visitor Centre/Training Room and kitchen (available for hire). In summer 2012 we will welcome a new 35-passenger boat (17 overnight) and an 8-berth family holiday boat. Both boats have a special complex needs cabin and bed. Our *Enable Adventure and Development Programme*, for young people aged 11-22, includes sailing, powerboating and adventure and development opportunities.

Conference and residential facilities: The Chellington Centre is our youth residential and conference facility in a wonderfully refurbished 12th century church set in stunning North Bedfordshire countryside (next to Harrold Country Park and Lake). The fully-accessible centre sleeps 30 in bunks, has room for 10 in camp-beds or sleeping bag rolls, seats 80 and is a fantastic setting for people to experience as part of their learning.

The charity works with over 200 community groups a year, offering support and services to over 4000 people. Our community-based *Circles of Support* projects enable inclusion and engagement for disabled young people in Herts and Beds and we are seeking funding to extend this to Northants and Bucks. We offer our facilities to businesses for team-building and client events. To hire facilities, volunteer or make a donation, please contact us.

Director Ron Overton says: *"ReachOut Plus is all about creating opportunities that change people's lives. I have had many conversations with young people and people with disabilities who have told me how grateful they are for the opportunities afforded by our programmes – and how transforming they have been. The experience of the canal, the environment, the boat, the team-working and relationships, the fun, the exercise, the sense of achievement and individual affirmation, all provide a very real and lasting contribution to their personal development. Those experiences are hugely affirming and should not be underestimated. It really does change lives!"*

lifts, toilets and showers designed for wheelchair users.

Reach Out Plus

Suite 3, Citygate, 17 Victoria Street, Hertfordshire AL1 3JJ.

📞 0845 2160080

✉ info@reachoutplus.org

🌐 www.reachoutplus.org

Three 12-berth canal boats operate from their boathouse in Hemel Hempstead. All are fully accessible for people with disabilities and ideal for people of all abilities. From summer 2012, a new 35 passenger boat (17 overnight) and an eight-berth family holiday boat will be available. Both new boats include a special complex needs cabin and bed. The Boat Base also includes a 50 seater fully accessible Education and Visitor Centre.

Seagull Trust Cruises

Bantasksine Park, Falkirk FK1 5PT.

📞 01324 620768

🌐 www.seagulltrust.org.uk

Offer one six-berth boat that can accommodate a family with a wheelchair user for cruises on the Scottish lowland canals. Two toilets on board can be used by a disabled person, one of which can be combined with a shower. There are lifts at the fore and rear and a skipper can be provided. Day cruises for disabled people and their families and friends are also organised from Falkirk, Kirkintilloch and Ratho.

Yorkshire Waterways Museum

Dutch River Side, Goole DN14 5TB.

📞 01405 768730

✉ info@waterwaysmuseum.org.uk

🌐 www.waterwaysmuseum.org.uk

The 'Sobriety' is a converted, wheelchair accessible barge used for groups of up to 12 people for residential trips on the waterways of Yorkshire and Lincolnshire. A lift is provided between the cabin and deck level and a skipper can be made available. Week-long, weekend and day bookings can be taken.

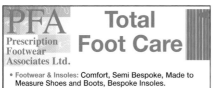

Snowsport holidays

If holidays on the water are not for you, you may fancy a holiday on the slopes. These organisations provide holidays that involve skiing activities specially adapted for disabled people.

Disability Snowsport UK

Glenmore Grounds, Aviemore, PH22 1QU.

☎ 01479 861272

✉ admin@disabilitysnowsport.org.uk

🌐 www.disabilitysnowsport.org.uk

Offer ski instruction by fully qualified instructors for disabled people at a purpose built adaptive ski school at Cairngorm. Similar services are based at the ski slopes around the country. In addition, activity weeks are held in Europe and USA.

Redpoint Holidays

Trinity Hall, Llangollen Road LL14 3SF.

☎ 0345 6801214

✉ sales@redpoint.co,uk

🌐 www.redpoint.co.uk

Mainstream winter sports company that also offer adaptive ski programmes for disabled people wanting a skiing holiday with their family or friends. They also offer a 'Buddy Course' for companions.

Working holidays

Whilst on holiday, you may wish to volunteer on a project and meet others who are interested in getting involved in similar activities or causes. The following organisations may be able to provide you with these opportunities:

British Trust for Conservation Volunteers

Sedum House, Mallard Way, Doncaster DN4 8DB.

☎ 01302 388883

✉ information@btcv.org.uk

🌐 www.btcv.org.uk

Run an extensive programme of conservation holidays all year round in some of the most beautiful landscapes across the UK. Many of the holidays are suitable for disabled people but please call before booking to explain your needs and check suitability. Full details of the holidays offered can be found on their website.

Toc H Projects

PO Box 15824, Birmingham B13 3JU.

☎ 0121 4433552

✉ info@toch.org.uk

🌐 www.toch-uk.org.uk

Projects of varying lengths are arranged throughout the year bringing together volunteers to work to help local communities.

Days out

What you do on your day out – from shopping to visiting stately homes or taking a walk in the forest – will depend on where you are and what you enjoy. Even a day trip can take some planning, so try and find out as much as you can before you head off. Here are some of the things to think about and ideas on where you could go.

Checking accessibility

While most modern tourist attractions should be able to cater for disabled visitors, it is advisable to check in advance if you have any specific requirements, if the attraction is large or for particular events.

Sites with a conservation aim, including historic buildings, nature reserves, forests, industrial heritage displays etc, can have limitations for disabled visitors. Several organisations have improved facilities for their disabled visitors. The following organisations have specialist publications and web pages providing information about their facilities.

Cadw: Welsh Historic Monuments
Plas Carew, Unit 5/7 Cefn Coed, Parck Nantgarw, Cardiff CF15 7QQ.
- ☏ 01443 336000
- ✉ cadw@wales.gsi.gov.uk
- ⓦ www.cadw.wales.gov.uk

www.disabledgo.info provides online access guides including detailed information gathered by personal inspection around the UK at a wide range of entertainment venues, places to visit, restaurants and shops.

English Heritage
Customer Services Department, Kemble Drive, PO Box 567, Swindon SN2 2YP.
- ☏ 0870 333 1181
  Textphone 0800 015 0516
- ✉ customers@english-heritage.org.uk
- ⓦ www.english-heritage.org.uk

Historic Scotland
Longmore House, Salisbury Place, Edinburgh EH9 1SH.
- ☏ 0131 668 8600
- ⓦ www.historic-scotland.gov.uk

The National Trust
PO Box 39, Warrington WA5 7WD.
- ☏ 0844 800 1895
  Textphone 0844 800 4410
- ✉ accessforall@nationaltrust.org.uk
- ⓦ www.nationaltrust.org.uk

National Trust for Scotland

Hermiston Quay, 5 Cultins Road EH11 4DF.
- ☎ 0844 493 2100
- ✉ information@nts.org.uk
- ⓦ www.nts.org.uk

Royal Society for the Protection of Birds

The Lodge, Potton Road, Sandy SG19 2DL.
- ☎ 01767 680551
- ⓦ www.rspb.org.uk

Sport

There are lots of local and national organisations providing and promoting sport opportunities and facilities for disabled people.

In some areas, local organisations have been formed to provide a range of sporting and other recreational activities for disabled people. These groups may use premises owned by the local council or other bodies but a number have their own purpose-built Centres.

Specialist organisations often have an important role in introducing people to sport and for those wishing to be involved in competitions. 'Taster' sessions, which give the opportunity to try a range of activities, are often arranged locally at local sports or leisure centres.

GENERAL INFORMATION

For information on facilities and sporting groups in your local area, contact the local authority Sports Development Officer. The following organisations may also be able to point you in the right direction.

English Federation of Disability Sport (EFDS)

Sport Park, Loughborough University, 3 Oakwood Drive, Loughborough LE11 3QF.
- ☎ 01509 227 760
- ✉ federation@efds.co.uk
- ⓦ www.efds.co.uk

EFDS is an umbrella group of disability sports organisations that works with policy makers and mainstream sports governing bodies to develop opportunities for disabled people to become more involved as competitors, recreational participants, administrators, officials and coaches. It seeks to create greater co-operation between disability sports organisations and works with the following national disability sports organisations that are recognised by Sport England: BALASA

(British Amputee & Les Autres Sports Association), British Blind Sport, CP Sport, Dwarf Athletics, Mencap Sport, Special Olympics, UK Deaf Sport and WheelPower – British Wheelchair Sport.

The British Paralympics Association (BPA)

60 Charlotte Street, London W1T 2NU.
- 020 7842 5789
- 020 7842 5777
- info@paralympics.org.uk
- www.paralympics.org.uk

Aside from being the representative organisation for elite paralympians, the BPA also provides, through its website, Parasport, which has been designed to inspire, educate, inform and signpost disabled people, and those interested in disability sport, to high quality opportunities. Parasport aims to help you find your personal best.

For other parts of the UK contact:

Disability Sport Northern Ireland,

Adelaide House, Falcon Road, Belfast BT12 6SJ.
- 028 9038 7062
- www.dsni.co.uk

Scottish Disability Sport

Caledonia House, South Gyle, Edinburgh EH12 9DQ.
- 0131 317 1130
- www.scottishdisabilitysport.com

Disability Sport Wales

Welsh Institute of Sport, Sophia Gardens, Cardiff CF11 9SW.
- 0845 846 0021
- www.disabilitysportwales.org

During 2012, Disability Rights UK are publishing 'Doing Sport Differently', a comprehensive guide to accessing sporting and leisure activities. Generously sponsored by VISA, the guide covers a wide range of sport and fitness activities from rambling to archery. It will be available for free download from the online shop on their website at www.disabilityrightsuk.org

SPECIFIC SPORTING ACTIVITIES

The following are just some of the organisations and projects concerned with helping disabled people to take part in specific sporting activities. More information on this can be found in this section under Activity Holidays.

British Disabled Angling Association (BDAA)

9 Yew Tree Road, Delves, Walsall WS5 4NQ.
- 01922 860912
- www.bdaa.co.uk

Represents disabled anglers across UK, including coarse, sea, specimen and game fishing. Services include: courses, group development, access audits of fishing areas, training people to coach disabled people and disability awareness training.

Inclusive Fitness Initiative (IFI)

Sport Park, Loughborough University, 3 Oakwood Drive, Loughgborough LE11 3QF.

📞 01509 227 750

📧 info@inclusivefitness.org

🌐 www.inclusivefitness.org

Launched by the English Federation for Disability Sport, IFI promotes the provision and management of integrated facilities for disabled people in general fitness centres. It accredits venues that provide accessible facilities, inclusive fitness equipment, appropriate staff straining and inclusive marketing.

> **www.activeplaces.com** is a database giving details of over 50,000 public and private sports facilities in England including activities available, charges, membership and accessibility for disabled people.

SPECTATOR FACILITIES

Facilities for disabled spectators have improved considerably following creation of new and enlarged stadia, greater awareness of the needs of disabled people and the impact of the Disability Discrimination Acts and other regulations.

But there are still limitations. Some arise from the nature of the feature provided, such as a commentary for visually impaired spectators at a football match or a raised viewing platform for wheelchair users at a

racecourse. Others result from lack of provision, particularly where spectator arrangements are made for a particular event. Contact venues in advance to find out about availability of accessible facilities.

Association of Wheelchair & Ambulant Disabled Supporters (AWADS)

c/o 2 Coopers Fold, Ribbleton, Preston PR2 6HW.

📞 01772 700788

🌐 www.awads.co.uk
www.awads.com

The website contains access information and member comments on league and many non-league football grounds in England and Scotland.

Event Mobility Charitable Trust

8 Bayliss Road, Kemerton, Tewkesbury GL20 7JH.

☎ 01386 725391

✉ eventmobility@hotmail.co.uk

🌐 www.eventmobility.org.uk

Some events can be problematic for disabled people to attend because they extend over a large area or the facilities for spectators are temporary. Event Mobility provides powered scooters and wheelchairs at a range of events including flower shows, agricultural and countryside shows, major golf championships and horse shows. Bookings need to be made in advance. A donation is requested (£18 for scooters and £10 for manual wheelchairs). Visit the website for a list of events that will provide the service or send a stamped addressed envelope to the address above.

Level Playing Field

The Meridian, 4 Copthall House, Station Square, Coventry, CV1 2FL.

☎ 0845 230 6237

✉ info@nads.org.uk

🌐 www.nads.org.uk
www.levelplayingfield.org.uk

Formerly The National Association of Disabled Supporters) Level Playing Field promotes good facilities for disabled spectators at sports grounds. They have links with Disabled Supporters Associations at many clubs and their website includes information on facilities for disabled fans at grounds around the country.

Other activities

Here are a few of the organisations devoted to encouraging the participation of disabled people. To find out what's available locally – ask local disability organisations, libraries, or look on the internet.

Disabled Photographers' Society

PO Box 85, Longfield, Kent DA3 9BA.

☎ 01454 317754

✉ secretary@disabled
photographers.co.uk

🌐 www.disabledphotographers.
co.uk

The Disabled Photographers' Society provides information on how you can adapt cameras and other photographic equipment and has access to engineers who can help. It arranges an annual exhibition of members' work and organises occasional photographic holidays and other events. The DPS has close ties with mainstream photographic bodies.

Motorsport Endeavour

123 Ealing Village, London W5 2EB.

☎ 020 8991 2358

✉ info@motorsportendeavour.com

🌐 www.motorsportendeavour.com

Motorsport Endeavour runs events involving disabled people in all forms of motorsport. A wide-ranging programme includes rallies, karting and visits to motorsport venues. The club is open to drivers as well as people wishing to take other roles including as navigators, marshals, timekeepers and spectators. It is also establishing links for disabled people who are seeking employment in the motorsport industry.

'Get Caravanning' is an introductory guide to caravans and motor caravans for leisure use published by Radar with the support of The Caravan Club. The guide is available from Disability Rights UK; Telephone 020 7250 3222 or visit the website www.radar-shop.org.uk.

Thrive

The Geoffrey Udall Centre, Beech Hill, Reading RG7 2AT.

T 0118 988 5688

E info@thrive.org.uk

W www.thrive.org.uk

Thrive's aim is to improve the lives of elderly and disabled people through gardening and horticulture. It runs demonstration gardens, supports a network of community and therapeutic gardening projects and runs an extensive programme of training courses, many about running community gardening projects. It runs the Blind Gardeners' Club and produces publications and factsheets offering practical advice on a wide variety of gardening topics. Their website www.carryongardening.co.uk provides information about equipment and techniques to make gardening easier. Launched in April 2011, www.accessiblegardens.org.uk has a directory of gardens with accessibility reviews written by people with disabilities. The site also contains information on accessibility, and articles about people, organisations, schools and groups involved with gardens.

The Wheelyboat Trust

North Lodge, Burton Park, Petworth GU28 0JT.

T 01798 342222

E info@wheelyboats.org

W www.wheelyboats.org

The Trust places specially designed Wheelyboats on lakes and other waters in all parts of the British Isles where they can be used for fishing, bird-watching or other activities. The boats have a bow door which lowers to form a boarding ramp and the open level deck provides access throughout. Contact the Director, Andy Beadsley at the above address or look on the website for a list of locations.

Further information

There are further ideas for days out in the Useful resources section of this Guide. You will also find details of a publication called *The Rough Guide to Accessible Britain*. This book contains over 170 ideas and recommendations for days out for disabled people with all suggestions having been reviewed by writers with disabilities.

Public toilets

Accessible toilets can be found in most shopping centres, theatres, theme parks, sports centres and next to public toilet facilities.

Finding accessible toilets

All public toilets in Britain should have an accessible toilet close by. Accessible toilets usually have a level or ramped entrance, a bigger floor space to accommodate a wheelchair or a carer, grab bars and a low-level sink. They may also have a red alarm string that you pull in an emergency.

You might find that many accessible public toilets in Britain are locked – this is to prevent them being vandalised or misused. If you need a key to use an accessible toilet then you can join the Radar National Key Scheme (see below).

TOILET PROVISION

Traditionally, public conveniences or toilets were provided by local authorities. In many areas, accessible features for disabled people have been included for many years, although you may still find inaccessible public conveniences still in use.

Changes in provision

In recent years, there has been an overall reduction in the number of traditional public conveniences,

including some unisex units for disabled people operated by local authorities. However, as a result of greater awareness and the impact of Building Regulations and anti-discrimination law, appropriately designed toilets have become more common in privately owned buildings used by the public such as large shops, restaurants and bars and also in public premises including parks and libraries.

There have also been significant changes in the ways that toilets in public places are provided and managed.

In many instances the cleaning and routine maintenance will have been contracted out. Pre-built, self-cleaning toilets (sometimes referred to as 'automatic' or 'superloos') have been installed in an increasing number of locations, and these generally are maintained by the supplier.

In some districts the responsibility for public conveniences has been handed over to other bodies such as Parish Councils or to private companies that are responsible for managing elements of town centre public spaces.

Community toilet schemes have been established in some areas to provide public access to toilets in privately owned places such as pubs and cafes.

Toilets inside the growing number of shopping centres and other semi-public areas are usually the responsibility of the owners or managers of the premises.

The **Just Can't Wait** card is for people who may need to get to a toilet quickly when a public one is not available. The idea is that the card is shown in a shop or other premises as a request to use a staff or other toilet. Although some high street outlets have signed up to accept it there is no guarantee that the request will be granted, or that those that do accept it will have a toilet available with particular features. The Card, for which a £5 donation is requested, and other information are available from Bladder & Bowel Foundation, SATRA Innovation Park, Rockingham Road, Kettering NN16 9JH. Phone 01536 533255, or visit www.bladderandbowelfoundation. org for more information.

Just Can't Wait!

The holder of this card has a medical condition and needs to use a toilet quickly.

Please help

NATIONAL KEY SCHEME FOR TOILETS FOR DISABLED PEOPLE

The National Key Scheme (NKS), sometimes referred to as the Radar key scheme, is widely used throughout the UK. It was introduced over 30 years ago because an increasing number of local authorities and other bodies were finding that they had to lock their toilets for disabled people to prevent them being vandalised, or misused.

How the Scheme works

If toilets have to be locked, providers are asked to fit the standard NKS lock and to make keys available to disabled people in their area. Whenever possible a key should be held somewhere nearby for use by disabled people who have not got one.

The scheme has now been adopted by over 400 local authorities and the NKS lock has also been fitted to over 9000 toilets provided by other organisations including transport undertakings, pub companies, visitor attractions, shops and community bodies.

The National Key Scheme guide

When the scheme was first introduced, Radar (now Disability Rights UK) agreed to keep and maintain a list of all toilets fitted with the NKS lock. This list is regularly updated and published annually in our National Key Scheme Guide. For news on the latest edition visit www.disabilityrightsuk.org.

This information is also available and continually updated as a Smartphone app, priced at £4.99 and available from the Applestore, Blackberry World and various e-stores for Android users.

You can order a key from Disability Rights UK by clicking on shop at their website at www.disabilityrightsuk.org or by calling 020 7250 3222.

You can also get a list of accessible toilets from the following website which was set up by a disabled person who was having problems finding accessible toilets:

www.needaloo.org

Changing Places toilets

Some disabled people need facilities that go beyond those found in a 'standard' toilet for disabled people.

Changing Places toilets have:
- an adjustable height adult changing table;
- a hoist with tracking, or a mobile one if necessary;
- space both sides of the WC for assistants.

There are around 375 Changing Places toilets around the country. Access may be limited depending on opening times for the premises they are situated in.

For further information about the *Changing Places* campaign or to find details of current and planned Changing Places toilets locations, visit www.changing-places.org

Useful resources

This section lists national tourist boards, voluntary and commercial organisations involved in holiday services and tourism for disabled people, leisure providers and equipment and vehicle hire companies. We've also included some specialist organisations offering holidays to destinations outside the UK, in case you're thinking about travelling further afield in the future.

Statutory bodies

Directgov
Ⓦ www.direct.gov.uk/disabledpeople
The government's consumer website giving information on public services with links to government departments and agencies and a wide range of other organisations. It includes information about 'package holidays', travel and transport.

Equality & Human Rights Commission
Ⓣ 08456 046610 Helpline England
08456 045510 Helpline Scotland
08456 048810 Helpline Wales
Ⓔ englandhelpline@
equalityhumanrights.com
scotlandhelpline@
equalityhumanrights.com
waleshelpline@equality
humanrights.com
Ⓦ www.equalityhumanrights.com
Provide advice and guidance on equality and discrimination issues including disability discrimination. Provide advice via their helplines to people who feel they may have experienced discrimination. They produce a series of factsheets available to download free of charge from their website.

Tourist boards

The organisations listed below are the key tourist boards in Great Britain and Ireland and include VisitBritain. VisitBritain are primarily sponsored by the Department of Culture, Media and Sport and are responsible for promoting all of the countries within Great Britain & Ireland to visitors from outside of Great Britain. Each country within Great Britain and Ireland also has its own national tourist board which are all listed below. These board's primary objectives are to provide information for all visitors on public transport, accommodation and tourist attractions within their countries and this will often cover giving information on accessibility.

VisitBritain
1 Palace Street, London SW1E 5HX.
Ⓣ 0207 5781000
Ⓦ www.visitbritain.com

VisitEngland

1 Palace Street, London, SW1E 5HX.

☎ 020 7578 1400

🌐 www.visitengland.com

National tourist board of England. Provide travel and tourism information for all visitors including those with disabilities. There is a huge amount of useful information available free of charge on the VisitEngland website. Most of the listings show the appropriate National Accessible Scheme symbols to indicate those establishments meeting the relevant criteria.

Visit Scotland

VisitScotland, Ocean Point One, 94 Ocean Drive, Edinburgh EH6 6JH.

☎ 0845 859 1006

✉ info@visitscotland.com

🌐 www.visitscotland.com

Scotland's national tourism organisation provides information on Scottish travel, vacations, tours, holidays and accommodation. To order a brochure call or email with details of your requirements. Information on accessible accommodation can be found at:

🌐 www.visitscotland.com/guide/
   where-to-stay/accessible-scotland

Visit Wales

☎ 08708 300 306 (Contact Centre)

✉ info@visitwales.co.uk

🌐 www.visitwales.co.uk

Welsh Assembly Government's tourism team within the Department of Heritage. First port of call for information on holidays and short breaks in Wales including information on accessible accommodation.

Discover Ireland

☎ 0800 313 4000

🌐 www.discoverireland.ie

Official Site of Failte Ireland (the Irish Tourist Board). Visit their website for information about accommodation, accessibility, attractions, activities and events in Ireland.

Northern Ireland Tourist Board

☎ 0289 0231221

🌐 www.discovernorthernireland.com

Official Tourist Board for Northern Ireland. Provide tips and guidance on accommodation, activities and things to do and see for all visitors including those with disabilities.

Channel Islands Tourist Board

🌐 www.visitchannelislands.com

Official Tourist Board for the Channel Islands where you can find information about Jersey, Guernsey, Alderny, Herm and Sark.

Isle of Man Department of Tourism & Leisure

Sea Terminal Buildings, Douglas IM1 2RG.

☎ 01624 686766

✉ tourism@gov.im

🌐 www.visitisleofman.com

The Isle of Man's official tourism organisation. They provide details of accommodation, events and attractions.

Accommodation groups

The hotel groups and other organisations listed below are not specialist providers of accommodation for disabled people but have some properties which may be suitable and include an indication of this in their directories and brochures.

Accor

☎ UK Reservations 0871-663-0624

Ⓦ www.accorhotels.com

Accor Hotels include Sofitel, Pullman, MGallery, Suite Novotel, Mercure, Adagio, All Seasons, Ibis, Etap hotel, Formule 1, hotelF1 and Orbis.

Best Western Hotels GB

Consort House, Amy Johnson Way, Clifton Moor, York YO30 4GP.

☎ Reservations 0845 773 7373

Ⓦ www.bestwestern.co.uk

A consortium of independently owned hotels in England, Scotland, Wales and the Channel Islands. Some member hotels have been inspected for accessibility

Campanile Hotels

Europa House, Church Street, Old Isleworth TW7 6DA.

Ⓔ contactclient@louvre-hotels.com

Ⓦ www.campanile.com

A chain of purpose-built hotels by main roads and in city centres. Parking is adjacent to the bedrooms and to the building housing reception, bar, restaurant and meeting room. All have rooms designed for disabled guests.

The Camping and Caravanning Club

Greenfields House, Westwood Way, Coventry CV4 8JH.

☎ 0845 130 7633 (also Textphone)

Ⓦ www.campingandcaravanningclub.co.uk

Operate sites throughout Great Britain, most of which are open to non-members. About 70 have unisex toilet and shower facilities designed for disabled people. This together with information on their sites and membership can be obtained from the above address.

Camping in the Forest

Bath Yard, Moira, Derbyshire DE12 6BD.

☎ 0845 130 8224 (campsites)
   0845 130 8223 (cabins)

Ⓔ contact@forestholidays.co.uk

Ⓦ www.campingintheforest.co.uk

The Forestry Commission has 20 caravan and camping sites, most of which have WCs and showers for wheelchair users, and also three self-catering log cabin sites in Cornwall, North Yorkshire and The Trossachs that each have six-person cabins designed for disabled people.

The Caravan Club

East Grinstead House, East Grinstead RH19 1UA.

☎ 01342 326944

Ⓦ www.caravanclub.co.uk

Has about 200 sites throughout UK. Over 140 have unisex toilet/shower rooms designed for wheelchair users and a further 24 have handrails in amenity blocks. 70 sites have been assessed under the National Accessible Scheme and received the M1 grading. Full details are given in their annual brochure, The Site Collection, which is available free on their website or by calling 0800 521 161.

Choice Hotels Europe

Premier House, 112 Station Road, Edgware HA8 7BJ.

- ☎ 0800 444444
- ✉ infouk@choicehotels.com
- Ⓦ www.choicehotelsuk.co.uk

A hotel group including Sleep Inn, Comfort, Quality and Clarion Hotels. Their directory indicates those with facilities for disabled guests.

The Circle

20 Church Road, Horspath, Oxford OX33 1RU.

- ☎ 0845 345 1965
- ✉ info@circlehotels.co.uk
- Ⓦ www.circlehotels.co.uk

A consortium of individual family run hotels, located throughout the British Isles, with a central reservations office. The Circle Hotel Directory indicates those whose managers say have access to bedrooms for disabled guests.

Days Inn

- ☎ 08000 280400
- Ⓦ www.daysinn.com

Accommodation, mainly at Welcome Break Service Areas on motorways and main routes, which have rooms for disabled guests.

Formule 1 Hotels

- Ⓦ www.hotelformule1.com

Budget hotels; each with two rooms for disabled guests with a double and bunk beds. One shared shower room has a roll-in shower, handrails and space for side transfer to the WC. Continental breakfast served. When reception is not open an electronic machine will sell rooms by credit card; an entry code is provided for pre-paid bookings.

Reservations may be made through the website or by contacting the hotel.

Haven Holidays

Reservations, 1 Park Lane, Hemel Hempstead HP2 4TU.

- ☎ 0870 242 2222
- Ⓦ www.havenholidays.com

Operate 34 holiday parks in Great Britain, mainly on the coast. Their brochure, available from travel agents or by calling the above telephone number, indicates that most of these have some units designed for use by disabled people. For detailed information contact a Special Needs Advisor on ☎ 0870 381 1111. Haven also have some parks with accessible units in France.

Helpful Holidays

Mill Street, Chagford, Devon TQ13 8AW.

- ☎ 01647 433593
- ✉ help@helpfulholidays.com
- Ⓦ www.helpfulholidays.com

Offer over 500 self-catering properties in Cornwall, Devon, Dorset and Somerset, all of which are regularly inspected. Several have been designed for wheelchair users. These are indicated in their brochure, and can be searched for on the website, as are others that may be suitable for people with mobility difficulties.

Hilton Hotels

Maple Court, Watford WD24 4QQ.

- ☎ 0870 551 5151
- Ⓦ www.hilton.co.uk

International hotel group with hotels in cities, at airports and in other locations throughout the country. Although mainly used for business travel during the week, special offers for leisure guests are available at weekends.

InterContinental Hotel Group

☎ 0800 405060

🌐 www.ichotelsgroup.co.uk

An international hotel group comprising the Express by Holiday Inn brand, middle range Holiday Inn hotels, high class Crowne Plaza hotels and luxury InterContinental hotels. They have a programme of improving their accessibility and services for disabled guests. Information on weekend breaks and other special offers is available by phoning Central Reservations and on their website.

Ibis Hotels

255 Hammersmith Road, London W6 8SJ.

☎ Reservations 0871 6630624

🌐 www.ibishotel.com

A group of two star hotels, part of the international Accor group, which have rooms designed for disabled guests.

Innkeeper's Lodge

☎ 0845 1551551

🌐 www.innkeeperslodge.com

A chain of lodge hotels attached to Mitchells & Butlers pubs and restaurants. The more recent properties have rooms for disabled guests and are indicated in their directory.

National Trust

Holiday Cottage Booking Office, PO Box 536, Melksham SN12 8SX.

☎ 0844 800 2072 (brochures)

✉ cottages.nationaltrust.org.uk

🌐 www.nationaltrustcottages.co.uk

Have holiday cottages with adaptations for disabled people in a number of parts of England, Wales and Northern Ireland. Further information on these and on other cottages with ground floor accommodation that may be suitable for people with restricted mobility can be obtained from the above address and website.

Novotel Hotels

255 Hammersmith Road, London W6 8SJ.

☎ 08716 630626

🌐 www.novotel.com

A group of three star hotels, part of the international Accor group, all with rooms designed for disabled guests.

Parkdean Holidays

2nd Floor, 1 Gosforth Park Way, Gosforth Business Park, Newcastle upon Tyne NE12 8ET.

☎ 0870 220 4646

✉ enquiries@parkdeanholidays.co.uk

🌐 www.parkdeanholidays.co.uk

Operate 20 holiday parks in South West England, East Anglia, Wales and Scotland. Most have some units that have been adapted for disabled guests.

Premier Cottages

☎ 0845 0739421

🌐 www.premiercottages.co.uk

An annual brochure of independently owned and managed holiday cottages in many parts of Great Britain. Bookings are made direct with the owners who can answer enquiries.

Premier Travel Inn

Houghton Hall Business Park, Porz Avenue, Dunstable LU5 5XE.

☎ 0870 242 8000

🌐 www.premiertravelinn.com

A group of over 470 lodge hotels around Great Britain mainly adjoining restaurants or pubs where meals are available, although some have integral restaurants. Almost all have rooms designed for disabled guests and the number of these is indicated in their directory. Bookings can be made online, or by telephone to the central reservations number or to the individual hotels which are listed on their website.

Recommended Cottage Holidays
Eastgate House, Eastgate, Pickering YO18 7DW.
☎ 01751 475547
Ⓦ www.recommended-cottages.co.uk
Company offering self-catering holiday cottages in many parts of Great Britain. Their brochure and website indicate those that have adaptations for wheelchair users and also those with some ground floor accommodation.

Travelodge
Ⓦ www.travelodge.co.uk
Located beside main roads and in city centres in over 300 locations. Most have rooms designed for disabled guests and guests with limited mobility. These can be specified when booking. A directory is available.

Venuemasters
The Workstation, Paternoster Row, Sheffield S1 2BX.
☎ 0114 249 3090
Ⓔ info@venuemasters.co.uk
Ⓦ www.venuemasters.com
Offer holiday accommodation at Universities and Colleges throughout Britain during vacations on self-catering, bed & breakfast and fully serviced terms.

Youth Hostels
Youth Hostels offer inexpensive accommodation with meals or self-catering. A small but growing number of hostels have some adaptations for disabled people. Other hostels vary considerably in the extent of their accessibility. Especially for groups it is recommended that an advance visit is made before booking. Some hostels can be block-booked by groups or offer special activity programmes. For information on membership, hostels and other matters contact the Associations at the addresses logical.

Youth Hostels Association (England & Wales)
Trevelyan House, Dimple Road, Matlock DE4 3YH.
☎ 0870 770 8868
Ⓦ www.yha.org.uk

Scottish Youth Hostels Association
7 Glebe Crescent, Stirling FK8 2JA.
☎ 0870 155 3255
Ⓦ www.syha.org.uk

Hostelling International Northern Ireland
22-32 Donegal Road, Belfast BT12 5JN.
☎ 028 9032 4733
Ⓦ www.hini.org.uk

Irish Youth Hostel Association
61 Mountjoy Street, Dublin 7.
☎ +353 (0)1 830 4555
Ⓦ www.irelandyha.org

Voluntary organisations

The following voluntary organisations are involved in various ways in holiday provision for disabled people. Other organisations with a more localised remit are listed in the regional sections.

Tourism for All

- ☎ 0845 124 9971
  Textphone 0845 124 9976
- ✉ info@tourismforall.org.uk
- 🌐 www.tourismforall.org.uk

Registered charity and the UK's central source of holiday and travel information and support for disabled and older people and carers. Provide information on accessible accommodation, visitor attractions and transport, both in the UK and at selected overseas destinations. Identify sources of funding for disabled people on low incomes. Reservations service for inspected accessible accommodation is also offered. Work with all sectors of the tourism industry to improve accessibility and carry out inspections under the National Accessible Scheme. They have developed the Open Britain brand, including website, magazine and Smartphone app and aim to become a one-stop shop on UK tourism and holidays for anyone needing accessibility information and assistance.

3H Fund

Unit 2B, Speldhurst Business Park, Langdon Road, Tunbridge Wells, Kent TN1 2RA.
- ☎ 01892 860207
- ✉ info@3hfund.org.uk
- 🌐 www.3hfund.org.uk

Organise subsidised group holidays for physically disabled people accompanied by volunteer carers, giving the disabled person a chance to have a unique and enjoyable experience, and providing a break from the routine of caring for the carer or family of that person.

Action Against Allergy

PO Box 278, Twickenham TW1 4QQ.
- ☎ 020 8892 2711
- ✉ AAA@actionagainstallergy.freeserve.co.uk
- 🌐 www.actionagainstallergy.co.uk

Publish a large number of information leaflets for people with allergies including the leaflet Holiday Accommodation – a useful list of places to stay for people with allergies, price £2.

Action for Blind People

14-16 Verney Road, London SE16 3DZ.
- ☎ 020 7635 4800
- ✉ helpline@rnib.org.uk
- 🌐 www.actionforblindpeople.org.uk
  www.visionhotels.co.uk

Action for Blind People operate four Vision Hotels for blind and partially sighted people in South Devon, West Sussex, Somerset and Windermere. Self-catering units also available at Teignmouth (South Devon) and Windermere. The hotels aim to be accessible for all and welcome visually impaired guests. Brochures are available in large print, braille and cassette format.

Arthritis Care

18 Stephenson Way, London NW1 2HD.
- ☎ 020 7380 6500
  Advice Line 0808 8004050
- ✉ info@arthiritiscare.org.uk
- 🌐 www.arthritiscare.org.uk

Campaign and provide a range of services and information for people with arthritis and their families. Free and confidential helpline offers specific advice on arthritis and holidays.

Asthma UK
Summit House, 70 Wilson Street, London EC2A 2DB.
- ☎ 020 7786 4900
  Advice Line 08457 010203
- ✉ info@asthma.org.uk
- ⓦ www.asthma.org.uk

Run Kick Asthma adventure holidays for children and young people with asthma and related conditions. Fun and adventure activities are combined with educational sessions on managing asthma. Holidays held at a variety of locations in the UK divided into 6-11 and 12-17 age groups. For more information contact the Kick Asthma information team.
- ☎ 0845 603 8143
- ✉ holidays@asthma.org.uk

BREAK
Davison House, 1 Montague Road, Sheringham NR26 8WN.
- ☎ 01263 822161
- ✉ office@break-charity.org
- ⓦ www.break-charity.org

Charity that supports children, adults and families with special care needs at a centre in Norfolk. Offer supported holidays, short breaks, respite care and day care support. Provide special care services for children and adults with learning or physical disabilities and their families. Services include holidays and respite care, children's homes, adult day care and residential assessments for families in crisis. Also operate a mentoring scheme where volunteers support young people who have recently left local authority care. Also

have two holiday chalets in Westward Ho!, Devon

British Kidney Patient Association
Bordon, Hants GU35 9JZ.
- ☎ 01420 541424
- ✉ info@britishkidney-pa.co.uk
- ⓦ www.britishkidney-pa.co.uk

Offer financial assistance to kidney patients for holidays and any requests should be made on their behalf by their renal social worker. Group holidays arranged for young kidney patients at three activity centres and arrangements can be made for adults at some Mediterranean resorts. For information contact the Holiday Secretary.

British Limbless Ex-Service Men's Association (BLESMA)
Frankland Moore House, 185/187 High Road, Chadwell Heath RM6 6NA.
- ☎ 020 8590 1124
- ✉ headquarters@blesma.org
- ⓦ www.blesma.org

Holiday accommodation available at BLESMA residential and nursing homes in Blackpool for limbless ex-service men and their wives and to widows of former members. Convalescent and holiday accommodation may also be available to other ex-service men.

British Lung Foundation
73-75 Goswell Road, London EC1V 7ER.
- ☎ 020 7688 5555
- ✉ adminassistant@blf-uk.org
- ⓦ www.lunguk.org

Among a range of free information sheets and booklets on lung diseases and related issues is *Going on Holiday with a Lung Condition*. Some information on services in other countries can also be given.

British Polio Fellowship

Unit A, Eagle Office Centre, The Runway, Ruislip HA4 6SE.

☎ 0800 0180586

✉ info@britishpolio.org.uk

🌐 www.britishpolio.org.uk

Run a self-catering bungalow equipped for wheelchair users at Burnham-on-Sea. Holiday information and grants available to their members.

Calvert Trust

🌐 www.calvert-trust.org.uk

Have three outdoor activity centres equipped for disabled people in the Lake District, Northumbria and Exmoor. At each there is also accessible self-catering for families and similar sized groups. For information on each centre please see the section in this Guide on Activity Holidays.

Contact a Family

209-211 City Road, London EC1V 1JN.

☎ 0808 808 3555

　　Textphone 0808 808 3556

✉ helpline@cafamily.org.uk

🌐 www.cafamily.org.uk

Among a range of publications offering information to families with disabled children is a free factsheet – *Holidays, Play and Leisure.*

Cystic Fibrosis Trust

11 London Road, Bromley BR1 1BY.

☎ 020 8464 7211

✉ enquiries@cftrust.org.uk

🌐 www.cftrust.org.uk

Can give information to people with cystic fibrosis and their families on holidays, travel and travel insurance.

Diabetes UK

Macleod House, 10 Parkway, London NW1 7AA.

☎ 020 7424 1000

✉ info@diabetes.org.uk

🌐 www.diabetes.org.uk

Offer advice to people with diabetes on travel planning and have a Travel Guide booklet (price £2). Also available are guides on around 60 countries. Activity holidays are arranged at a number of locations during the summer for children and young people with diabetes. A catalogue and information are available from Careline at the above address or

☎ 0845 120 2960

　　Textphone 020 7424 1031

　　(9am-5pm weekdays).

DIAL UK

☎ 01302 310123 (also Textphone)

✉ response@scope.org.uk

🌐 www.dialuk.info

National network of local disability advice centres run by and for disabled people. Provide independent advice on all aspects of disability, mainly by phone but also in person. DIAL merged with Scope in 2008 and in November 2011 the DIAL UK office in Doncaster closed. Some local DIAL groups are listed in the regional sections of this Guide.

Disabled Christians Fellowship/Through the Roof

PO Box 353, Epsom KT18 5WS.
- ☎ 01372 749955
- ✉ info@throughtheroof.org
- 🌐 www.throughtheroof.org

Organise holidays for disabled people of all ages both in the UK and overseas. Personal help may be available as required.

Disabled Holiday Information

PO Box 185, Oswestry, Shropshire SY10 1AF.
- ✉ info@disabledholidayinfo.org.uk
- 🌐 www.disabledholidayinfo.org.uk

Provide information on the accessibility of places to visit and some places to stay largely based on the direct experience of a wheelchair user. In addition to a regularly expanding website, they have printed information on facilities in and around Shropshire.

Disabled Ramblers

c/o 14 Belmont Park Road, Maidenhead SL6 6HT.
- 🌐 www.disabledramblers.co.uk

Organisation of disabled people promoting improved access in the countryside. Run an annual programme of one and two day supported rambles in a variety of settings mainly for users of mobility vehicles including wheelchairs, scooters and buggies. Advice on accommodation can be given to participants if required.

Disaway Trust

55 Tolworth Park Road, Surbiton, Surrey KT6 7RJ.
- ☎ 020 8390 2576
- ✉ lynnesimpkins@hotmail.com
- 🌐 www.disaway.co.uk

Organise group holidays for physically disabled people, putting holiday packages together including visiting the venues to ensure suitability and accessibility throughout the holiday. Volunteer helpers are paired with disabled holidaymakers to provide assistance during the holiday.

Epilepsy Society

Chalfont Centre for Epilepsy, Chalfont St Peter, Bucks SL9 0RJ.
- ☎ 01494 601400
  Advice line 01494 601400
- ✉ enquiries@epilepsy.org.uk
- 🌐 www.epilepsysociety.org.uk

Provide respite and residential care and medical services including assessments for people living with epilepsy.

Fieldfare Trust

69 Crossgate, Cupar, Fife KY15 5AS.
- ☎ 01334 657708
- ✉ info@fieldfare.org.uk
- 🌐 www.fieldfare.org.uk

Work with people with disabilities and countryside managers to improve access to the countryside for everyone. Run projects which can enable people to take action locally, provide information on accessible places to visit and run events.

Handicapped Aid Trust

Northchapel House, North Street, Horsham, RH12 1RD.
- ☎ 0800 028 0647
- ✉ secretary@handicappedaidtrust.org.uk
- 🌐 www.handicappedaidtrust.org.uk

Give grants towards the cost of helpers to assist disabled people on holiday, and towards the cost of holidays and helpers to give carers a break.

Holidays for All

☎ 08451 249973

🌐 www.holidaysforall.org

Group of UK disability charities and specialist tour companies. Work together to promote quality, accessible holiday breaks providing improved choice and flexibility for holidaymakers. Offer leisure activities and accommodation throughout the UK and abroad for people with sensory and physical impairments, their friends and families.

Holidays for Disabled People

Holidaymaker Liaison Team, PO Box 164, Totton, Southampton SO10 9WZ.

✉ disholspw@aol.com

🌐 www.holidaysfordisabled.com

Organise an annual group holiday for people with physical disabilities at a holiday centre in the UK. Assistance provided by volunteers as required with medical and nursing cover. Participants can take their own companions.

Holidays with Help

4 Pebblecombe, Adelaide Road, Surbiton, Surrey KT4 6LL.

☎ 020 8390 9752

✉ hwhholidays@btinternet.com

🌐 www.holidayswithhelp.org.uk

Run group holidays for disabled people at holiday centres in England. Activities and outings arranged. Applications accepted from groups, families and individuals. Experienced helpers and medical and nursing personnel are available. Apply to Rosemary McIntyre at the above address.

Incontact

SATRA Innovation Park, Rockingham Road, Kettering NN16 9JH.

☎ 01536 533255

✉ info@bladderandbowelfoundation.org

🌐 www.incontact.org

Provide advice and information for people with bowel and bladder control problems, including guidance on taking a holiday.

Livability Holidays

50 Scrutton Street, London EC2A 4XQ.

☎ 0845 658 4478

✉ holidays@livability.org.uk

🌐 www.livability.org.uk

Offer a range of holiday accommodation including hotels at Minehead and Llandudno and self-catering units, houses and flats around England and Wales including units at holiday parks and self-contained houses and flats equipped for disabled holidaymakers.

MENCAP

Advice & Information Service, 4 Swan Courtyard, Coventry Road, Birmingham B26 1BU.

☎ 0121 707 7877

✉ help@mencap.org.uk

🌐 www.askmencap.info

Local Gateway Clubs offer a range of leisure activities for people with learning disabilities. Also administer the AdCare Holiday Fund which gives grants to enable people with learning disabilities to go on holiday.

Mind

15-19 Broadway, London E15 4BQ.
- 020 8519 2122
- contact@mind.org.uk
- www.mind.org.uk

The leading mental health charity in England and Wales. Have an information sheet, updated every couple of years, on holidays (available from the website above).

Multiple Sclerosis Society

MS National Centre, 372 Edgware Road, London NW2 6ND.
- 020 8438 0700
  Advice Line 0808 800 8000
- www.mssociety.org.uk

Publish information on holidays suitable for people with multiple sclerosis including an online respite directory. Own several respite care homes and hotels.

The National Autistic Society

393 City Road, London EC1V 1NG.
- 020 7833 2299
- nas@nas.org.uk
- www.autism.org.uk

Issue Holiday Help: a guide giving information on places that may be appropriate for children and adults with autism and Asperger syndrome.

National Blind Children's Society

Bradbury House, Market Street, Highbridge, Somerset TA9 3BW.
- 01278 764764
- enquiries@nbcs.org.uk
- www.nbcs.org.uk

Provide and organise activity holidays for children with a visual impairment and family weekends among other services. They have a specially adapted mobile home at Burnham-on-Sea.

National Deaf Children's Society

37a Great Charles Street, Birmingham B3 3JY.
- 0121 234 9820 (also Textphone)
- events@ndcs.org.uk
- www.ndcs.org.uk

Among the services and events organised for deaf children and their families, arrange a series of residential and day adventure and activity events. Volunteer interpreters and lip speakers provide communication support.

National Kidney Federation

6 Stanley Street, Worksop S81 7HX.
- Helpline 0845 601 0209
- nkf@kidney.org.uk
- www.kidney.org.uk

The holiday pages on the website give general advice for kidney patients travelling away from home and contact details for dialysis units in the UK that are particularly geared up for people on holiday.

Papillon Holidays

1 Exeter Drive, Ashton-under-Lyne OL6 8BZ.
- 0774 959 8423
- papillonholidays@aol.com
- www.papillonholidays.co.uk

Offer a range of holidays with support in Britain particularly for people with learning and physical disabilities. The programme, which runs through the year, includes a variety of activity and themed breaks as well as less structured seaside holidays.

Parkinson's Disease Society of the UK

215 Vauxhall Bridge Road, London SW1V 1EJ.
- 020 7931 8080/0808 800 0303
  Textphone 020 7963 9380

📧 hello@parkinsons.org.uk
🌐 www.parkinsons.org.uk
Advice and information on Parkinson's Disease and travel is available through the Helpline. Publish an information sheet on International Travel & Parkinson's.

Phab England, Summit House
50 Wandle Road, Croydon CR0 1DF.
☎ 020 8667 9443
📧 info@phab.org.uk
🌐 www.phab.org.uk
Their Phab Kids Integrated Living Experience offer one week breaks at activity centres for disabled young people aged 9-18. Details on these and information on the network of Phab clubs throughout the country are available from the above address.

PINNT
PO Box 3126, Christchurch BH23 2XS.
☎ 01202 481625
📧 info@pinnt.com
🌐 www.pinnt.com
A self-help organisation for people requiring intravenous, naso-gastric and other artificial nutrition therapy. Produce holiday guidelines giving information on planning a holiday, transporting and obtaining equipment and supplies and other matters.

The Ramblers
2nd Floor, Camelford House, 87-90 Victoria Embankment SE1 7TW.
☎ 0207 3398500
📧 ramblers@ramblers.org.uk
🌐 www.ramblers.org.uk
Britain's only walking charity, working to safeguard footpaths, countryside and other places and to encourage more people to take up walking. Many local groups and are a good source of local information and some cater for people with disabilities or mobility impairments. You can find your local group by visiting their website.

Rethink
5th Floor, Royal London House, 22-25 Finsbury Square, London EC2A 1DX.
☎ 0845 456 0455
📧 info@rethink.org
🌐 www.rethink.org
Provide services and advice to people affected by severe mental illness including information on holidays and respite care. A factsheet on respite care is available on their website.

The Royal Blind Society
☎ 01827 722574
📧 Peterhards@royalblindsociety.org
🌐 www.royalsociety.org.uk
Charity who offer self-catering holidays at 37 UK seaside holiday parks for people with a visual impairment.

Royal British Legion
48 Pall Mall, London SW1Y 5JY.
☎ 0845 772 5725
🌐 www.britishlegion.org.uk
Has four Poppy Break Centres for service and ex-service people, their dependants and carers recovering from an illness or bereavement. Centres are in Bridlington, Portrush, Southport and Weston-super-Mare. Personal and nursing care is not provided.

Royal National Institute of the Blind

Leisure Services, 105 Judd Street, London WC1H 9NE.

- ☎ 0303 1239999
- ✉ helpline@rnib.org.uk
- 🌐 www.rnib.org.uk

Provide holiday and leisure information for people with sight loss and run vacation schemes together with Action for Blind People for blind and partially sighted children. They also work with the leisure industry to improve access to leisure.

Royal Yachting Association (RYA) - Sailability

RYA House, Ensign Way, Hamble, Southampton SO31 4YA.

- ☎ 0845 345 0403
  Textphone 023 8060 4248
- ✉ sailability@rya.org.uk
- 🌐 www.rya.org.uk/sailability

An initiative of the RYA with the aim of promoting and co-ordinating participation by disabled people in the sailing community. It provides information to the public on where they can sail and supports sailing centres and clubs in improving opportunities open to people with disabilities.

Scope

Scope Response, PO Box 833, Milton Keynes MK12 5NY.

- ☎ 0808 800 3333
- ✉ response@scope.org.uk
- 🌐 www.scope.org.uk

National disability organisation with a focus on people with cerebral palsy. For more information contact Scope Response, 9am-7pm weekdays and 10am-2pm Saturdays.

Scout Holiday Homes Trust

Gilwell Park, Bury Road, Chingford, London E4 7QW.

- ☎ 020 8433 7290
- ✉ scout.holiday.homes@scouts.org.uk
- 🌐 www.holidayhomestrust.org

Offer low cost self-catering holidays in six-berth chalets and caravans at a number of holiday parks. Any family with a disabled member welcomed - not only those in Scouting. The season is generally from Easter-October and bookings are taken from the previous October.

Scripture Union Holidays

207-209 Queensway, Bletchley, Milton Keynes MK2 2EB.

- ✉ holidays@scriptureunion.org.uk
- 🌐 www.scriptureunion.org.uk

Organise holidays for young people. One holiday each year caters for disabled youngsters alongside non-disabled children aged 15-19 and another for 13-19 year-olds with learning difficulties. Applications via the Holidays Administrator.

Sense

101 Pentonville Road, London, N1 9LG.

- ☎ 0845 127 0060
  Textphone 0845 127 0062
- ✉ holidays@sense.org.uk
- 🌐 www.sense.org.uk

Organise over 25 holidays each year for 120 deafblind children and adults. Each holiday has one or more paid leader supported by a team of volunteers to ensure that it is centred on individual needs and choices of holidaymakers. Sense holidays enable participants to have fun in a supportive environment, gain new experiences and meet new people. For further information contact the Holidays Co-ordinator.

Spinal Injuries Association

SIA House, 2 Trueman Place, Oldbrook, Milton Keynes MK6 2HH.

T 0845 678 6633

E sia@spinal.co.uk

W www.spinal.co.uk

Website includes information on holiday opportunities taken from information provided by members and articles and advertisements placed in the Association's magazine.

Vitalise

212 Business Design Centre, 52 Upper Street N1 0QH.

T 0303 3030147

E info@vitalise.org.uk

W www.vitalise.org.uk

Provide breaks for disabled people and carers in five accessible centres in Southampton, Bodmin, Chigwell, Nottingham and Southport. Each centre offers a programme of short breaks with care on-call and personal support. Over 500 activities are offered throughout the year with over 35 special interest weeks, including special Alzheimer's and MS Society weeks. Also run holidays for visually impaired people accompanied by sighted guides, and offer independent holidays, without care support, at selected accessible hotels in Germany and Spain. Holidays for disabled groups can be arranged.

Commercial organisations

The following companies and organisations offer holidays or other tourist services specifically geared to meet the needs of disabled people.

Access at Last Ltd

18 Hazel Grove, Tarleton, Preston PR4 6XL.

T 01772 814555

W www.accessatlast.com

Travel company formed by a wheelchair user. Website details accessible hotels, adapted vehicles, equipment and holiday packages, and users can post comments. All of these inspected hotels have at least one room with a wheel-in shower.

Accessible Travel & Leisure

Avionics House, Naas Lane, Quedgeley, Gloucester GL2 2SN.

T 01452 729739

E info@accessibletravel.co.uk

W www.accessibletravel.co.uk

Offer a wide range of holidays and related services for disabled people including Mediterranean holidays, cruises and tours in South Africa and Egypt. Accessible villas, apartments and hotels are offered together with accessible transfers or car hire, local representatives and insurance.

ATS Travel Ltd

1 Tank Lane, Purfleet, Essex RM19 1TA.

E aatstravel@aol.com

W www.assistedholidays.com

Tour operator arranging holidays for disabled people and their families in Britain and abroad. Accessible accommodation is used and transport, trips and holiday insurance can be arranged. A variety of hotel, self-catering, and touring holidays are offered throughout the country.

Can Be Done Ltd
11 Woodcock Hill, Harrow HA3 0XP.
T 020 8907 2400
E holidays@canbedone.co.uk
W www.canbedone.co.uk

Tour Operator founded by a wheelchair user, offering holidays for people with access or mobility problems. Their brochures include a wide range of destinations in Europe (including Britain and Ireland), Asia, Australia, Africa and America but tailor made holidays can be arranged anywhere.

Chalfont Line
Chalfont House, 4 Providence Road, West Drayton UB7 8HJ.
T 01895 459540
E info@chalfont-line.co.uk
W www.chalfont-line.co.uk

Long-established adapted coach hire company with a programme of leisurely paced holidays for wheelchair users and others with impaired mobility mainly to destinations in Britain and Europe. Their own wheelchair accessible coaches are used for these. Also run worldwide cruise holidays. A door-to-door service can be provided at an extra cost. Assistance with planning can be given to groups hiring coaches for their own programmes.

Diana's Supported Holidays
18 Parish Close, St Peters, Broadstairs, Kent CT10 2UU.
T 0844 800 9373
E enquiries@dsh.org.uk
W www.dianassupportedholidays.com

A range of holidays are offered with support for people with learning disabilities at seaside resorts and countryside areas in Britain and a number of destinations abroad. Groups are of at least six with a qualified leader and support staff, with one-to-one support if required although a lower ratio is normally provided. In addition to the programmed holidays, other destinations can be arranged for groups.

Mosaic Community Care Ltd
Unit 1 Chiswick Court, Chiswick Grove, Preston New Road, Blackpool FY3 9TW.
T 01772 325350
E info@mosaiccommunitycare.co.uk
W www.mosaiccommunitycare.co.uk

Specialise in the provision of supported luxury holidays and respite breaks for disabled people who require support and care with daily living tasks. Their programme includes cruises and destinations in Florida and UK.

William Forrester
1 Belvedere Close, off Manor Road, Guildford GU2 9NP.
T 01483 575401

A wheelchair user who is a registered Blue Badge tour guide. Can help plan an itinerary in London or throughout the country, give lectures and assist visiting study groups. A telephone advice service is offered for wheelchair users visiting the country.

Matching Houses
W www.matchinghouses.com

A website for disabled people who wish to house-swap for their holidays based on the principle that if an exchange can be arranged between people with similar access needs they should both be able to travel with greater confidence within this country or further afield. They have over 600 members worldwide.

Countryside information

Areas of Outstanding Natural Beauty (AONB)

Ⓦ www.aonb.org.uk

The website has details and links to all AONB across the UK. Many have information about accessibility and have published easy access walks.

Keep Britain Tidy (Green Flag)

Ⓦ www.keepbritaintidy.org/greenflag

The Green Flag Award® Scheme recognises and rewards the best green spaces in the country. For 2011/2012, a record number of awards were made with 1200 parks and green spaces currently flying a Green Flag or Green Flag Community Award. These areas generally have good disabled access and facilities

National Parks

Ⓦ www.nationalparks.gov.uk

There are 15 parks that are members of the National Parks scheme. They are areas of protected mountains, meadows, moorlands, woods and wetlands and each one has an organisation that looks after the landscape and wildlife and helps people enjoy and learn about the area. Each park has its own website which can be reached through the website above and publish details of accessibility and facilties.

National Trails

Ⓦ www.nationaltrail.co.uk

Long distance routes for walking, cycling and horse riding through the finest landscapes in England and Wales. Most National Trails have their own website which can be reached through the central address above and some have information on sections of trails suitable for wheelchair users and buggies

The Wildlife Trusts

Ⓦ www.wildlifetrusts.org

The largest UK voluntary organisation dedicated to protecting wildlife and wild places. There are 47 local Trusts across the UK, the Isle of Man and Alderney. Many local trusts publish accessibility information and you can find your local trust through their main website above.

Shopping

The following organisations, shopping areas and shopping centres offer specially adapted facilities and support to disabled people so that you can enjoy getting out and around the shops.

National Federation of Shopmobilty

PO Box 6641, Christchurch, BH23 9DQ.

Ⓣ 0844 4141850

Ⓔ info@shopmobility.org

Ⓦ www.shopmobilityuk.org

Provide wheelchairs and scooters for use in around 300 shopping centres and other shopping areas throughout UK. Services can provide a great deal of support and independence when you are shopping. Some schemes provide children's wheelchairs, escorts or special services for people visiting their area. The locations of regional branches and the services offered change all the time so although you will find some details in our regional listings, you must call the number above or visit the online directory on their website to double check the costs and what is available in your local area.

Capital Shopping Centres Group PLC

📞 020 7887 4220

✉ feedback@capshop.co.uk

Own some of the biggest shopping centres in the country including five of the UK's top six – The Trafford Centre, Manchester; Lakeside, Thurrock; Metrocentre, Gateshead; Braehead, Glasgow and The Mall at Cribbs Causeway, Bristol plus nine 'in-town centres' including Cardiff, Manchester, Newcastle, Norwich and Nottingham. They have made efforts to make their shopping experience fully accessible for disabled shoppers.

The Glades, Bromley, Kent

🌐 www.theglades.uk.com

Shopping centre that is completely step-free. There are lifts to the second floor and disabled toilets on the ground level. Good selection of popular stores and leads out on to the High Street, where you will find more accessible shops. Surrounded by a number of car parks with free disabled parking and wheelchair/scooter hire.

The Whitgift Centre & Centrale Centres, Croydon, Surrey

🌐 www.thewhitgiftcroydon.co.uk

Shopping centres in Croydon divided by the High Street. Both contain large department stores, as well as independent and high street shops. There are lifts and disabled toilets in the malls and in some of the shops. Both the shopping centres have car parks with disabled bays close to the entrances. The Whitgift Centre car park offers wheelchair hire on 0208 688 7336.

Romford, Essex

If you are looking for somewhere to shop but want to avoid the London crowds, Romford offers the Brewery and the Liberty joint shopping centre. The Brewery has a wide range of shops, bars and accessible restaurants and also has 85 disabled pay and display car parking spaces. There is a 16 screen VUE cinema with spaces for wheelchairs and a 24 lane bowling alley. For children, there is Kidspace, Europe's largest play area. The Liberty has over 100 shops, with a mixture of mainstream, and specialist stores. It leads out on to the High Street and Market Place where more shops and banks lie. The shopping streets are step-free with lifts to go upstairs so is accessible for all. The shops are very spacious and the restaurants have disabled toilets.

St David's Dewisant, Cardiff

🌐 www.stdavidscardiff.com

Brand new shopping centre in the heart of Cardiff city centre. Home to designer shops, big high street names and a large restaurant quarter housing a variety of restaurants. The centre offers car parking spaces for disabled visitors and there is level access entry to most entrances. A lift gives you access to all floors and accessible toilets and one Changing Places room is also available.

Trafford Centre, Manchester

Ⓦ www.traffordcentre.co.uk

Large indoor shopping and leisure facility situated five miles from the centre of Manchester and the largest shopping centre in the UK by actual size. Every toilet block in the centre contains an accessible toilet which can be opened by a National Key Scheme (Radar) key that can be collected from a member of the centre's staff. Further facilities for disabled visitors include an assisted changing facility with a Clos o Mat WC and an electric hoist. There are 260 designated parking spaces for disabled visitors situated near various entrances to the centre and there are ramps, or dropped kerbs at every entrance and a talking lift to all floors.

Westfield, London

Ⓦ http://uk.westfield.com/london

Shopping centres based in Stratford, East London and Shepherds Bush in the West with 300 designer and high street shops, a variety of restaurants and a large VUE cinema. The centres are step-free with disabled toilets, wheelchair-friendly malls and lifts. Over 5% of the parking bays are dedicated to disabled parking and customers can book a free wheelchair or motorised scooter. Parking is free Monday – Friday for Blue Badge holders.

Theme parks & attractions

This section includes details of some of the UK's most popular theme parks and attractions. Most major theme parks and attractions have concessions for disabled children and adults. Ask in advance what evidence you will need to bring with you to get a concession. It is normally a Disability Living Allowance (DLA) or Attendance Allowance (AA) award letter but it's worth confirming this before you go to avoid any disappointments or difficulties. Parks may allow a limited number of friends, carers or support workers to go on rides with you or into the park at a discount.

Alton Towers

Alton Towers Resort, Alton, Staffordshire, ST10 4DB.

☏ 0871 222 3330

Ⓦ www.altontowers.com

Charge full entry fee for disabled visitors but offer concessions for up to three helpers. A Guide for Visitors with Disabilities can be downloaded from their website.

Chessington World of Adventures

Chessington World of Adventures Resort, Leatherhead Road, Chessington, Surrey KT9 2NE.

☏ 01372 731582

Ⓦ www.chessington.com

Offer discounted rates for disabled guests and up to two carers. They publish a guide for guests with disabilities available at www.chessington.com/plan-your-trip/disabled-guide.aspx

Drayton Manor Park and Zoo
Drayton Manor Park, Tamworth B78 3TW.
- 📞 01827 252 400
- 🌐 www.draytonmanor.co.uk

Offer discounts for disabled people and your carer on the day.

The Eden Project
Bodelva, Cornwall PL24 2SG.
- 📞 01726 811911
- 🌐 www.edenproject.com

Offers one free entry for a carer when accompanied by the disabled person.

Hatton Country World
Hatton Farm Village, Dark Lane, Hatton, Warwick, Warwickshire CV35 8XA.
- 📞 01926 843 411
- ✉️ hatton@hattonworld.com
- 🌐 www.hattonworld.com/farmvillage/contact

Offer discounted rates for a disabled person and free entry for their carer.

Howletts Wild Animal Park
Bekesbourne, Nr Canterbury, Kent CT4 5EL
- 📞 0844 842 4647
- 🌐 www.aspinallfoundation.org/howletts

Offer discounted rates for disabled children.

Legoland Windsor
Winkfield Road, Windsor, Berkshire, SL4 4AY.
- 📞 01753 626182
  Textphone 18001 0871 2222 001
- ✉️ customer.services@legoland.co.uk
- 🌐 www.legoland.co.uk

Offer free entry for the carer who is looking after a disabled child for the day, documentary evidence will be required.

Offer free admission for registered personal assistants with documented proof of disability. Publish a guide for disabled guests, available at:
- 🌐 www.legoland.co.uk/Plan/Guests-With-Disabilities

Lightwater Valley
Lightwater Valley Attractions Ltd, North Stainley, Ripon, North Yorkshire HG4 3HT.
- 📞 0871 720 0011
- 🌐 www.lightwatervalley.co.uk

Offer discounted rates for a disabled person and up to two helpers on proof of disability.

Madame Tussauds
London: Marylebone Road, London NW1 5LR.
- 📞 0871 894 3000
- 🌐 www.madametussauds.com

Blackpool: 89 Promenade, Blackpool FY1 5AA.
- 📞 0871 282 9200
- 🌐 www.madametussauds.com/Blackpool

Museum that contains wax models of famous people including the Royal Family, world leaders and sports and music stars, welcomes disabled visitors and one helper, without charge. You will need to provide documentary proof of disability e.g. blue/orange badge or similar.

Oakwood Theme Park
Canaston Bridge, Narberth, Pembrokeshire SA67 8DE.
- 📞 01834 891373 (General enquiries)
- 📞 01834 891376 (24-hour info line)
- ✉️ info@oakwoodthemepark.co.uk
- 🌐 www.oakwoodthemepark.co.uk

Theme Park in Pembrokeshire that offers

discounts for disabled visitors and easy entry on to rides. Offer concessions for the disabled person and a carer at their discretion.

Thorpe Park

Thorpe Park, Staines Road, Chertsey, Surrey KT16 8PN.
📞 0871 663 1673 (9am to 5pm)
🌐 www.thorpepark.com
Theme park in Surrey that offer concessions for disabled children and their carer.

Warwick Arts Centre

Warwick Arts Centre, University of Warwick, Coventry CV4 7AL.
📞 024 7652 4524 (Box office)
✉ arts.centre@warwick.ac.uk
🌐 www.warwickartscentre.co.uk
Allow disabled visitors to bring a companion or carer with them free of charge subject to availability.

Vehicle hire

Adapted Vehicle Hire

Head office: Unit 508 Stone Close, West Drayton, Middlesex UB7 8JU
📞 0845 2571670
✉ info@adaptedvehiclehire.com
🌐 www.adaptedvehiclehire.com
Rent out adapted cars and wheelchair accessible vehicles and have launched a 'Car and driver' service. They have branches around the UK and offer **a delivery & collection service.**

Atlas Vehicle Conversions

3 Aysgarth, Road, Waterlooville, Hampshire PO7 7UG.
📞 023 9226 5600
🌐 www.avcltd.co.uk
In addition to selling adapted cars, Atlas have a number of wheelchair accessible vehicles for hire including the Renault Kangoo, which can carry one passenger in a wheelchair and a minibus with removable seats that can carry up to two. Daily, weekly and monthly terms are available with special rates for weekends. Drivers must be over 25.

Autobility

Tower Garage, Main Road, Abernethy, Perth PH2 9JN.
📞 0800 2989290
🌐 www.autobility.co.uk
Have wheelchair accessible vehicles for hire on weekend, weekly and monthly rates. From their base in central Scotland they can arrange delivery throughout Britain or to airports and railway stations for an additional charge.

Brotherwood Automobility

Lambert House, Pillar Box Lane, Beer Hackett, Sherborne, Dorset DT9 6QP.

T 0844 8227939

E sales@brotherwood.com

W www.brotherwood.com

Convert cars for wheelchair users and have a range of cars available for long or short-term hire from their premises in North Dorset.

Caldew Coaches

6 Caldew Drive, Dalston, Carlisle CA5 7NS.

T 01228 711690

E caldewcoachesltd@aol.com

W www.caldewcoaches.co.uk

Company with a range of accessible coaches for hire. These are available for holidays and day trips for groups of eight and above.

John Flanagan Coach Travel

2 Reddish Hall Cottages, Broad Lane, Grappenhall, Warrington WA4 3HS.

E admin@flanagancoaches.org.uk

W www.flanaganscoaches.org.uk

Have coaches equipped with lifts that can carry passengers in wheelchairs that are available for hire by groups for day and longer trips. Holidays can be arranged in UK, Ireland and Holland for groups.

Motorvation Hull & East Riding

31a Northfield Close, West End, South Cave, Brough HU15 2EW.

T 01430 422809

E mikliz.ten@virgin.net

Have three vehicles adapted to carry a passenger in a wheelchair and three others. Mainly used in East Yorkshire. Available with a voluntary driver on a daily basis. A donation towards running costs based on mileage used is requested.

Nirvana Motorhomes

Court Farm, Pilgrims Road, Upper Halling, Rochester, Kent ME2 1HR.

T 0800 328 1475

E info@nirvanarv.com

W www.nirvanarv.com

Hire out a motor home that is purpose-designed to be accessible for a wheelchair user and companions. It is equipped with a lift at the wide entrance, lower level kitchen fitments and a shower room with sliding walls to increase the size. Clamps are available to enable a passenger in a wheelchair to sit alongside the driver or both front seats can swivel to aid transfer. This can be used both in Britain and continental Europe. Similar models are available for sale.

Pyehire

Ovangle Road, Morcambe LA3 3PF.

T 01524 598641

E pye.hire@pye-motors.co.uk

W www.pyemotors.co.uk

Have a range of self-drive accessible vehicles that can carry between one and four passengers in wheelchairs and two to eight other people. These are available on daily or weekly hire.

Thorntrees Garage

Wigan Road, Leyland, Lancashire PR25 5SB.

T 01772 622688

E julie@thorntreesgarage.co.uk

W www.thorntreesgarage.co.uk

Cars and vans that can carry passengers in wheelchairs are available for hire at daily, weekly and monthly rates. Thorntrees

Garage is near the M6, M61 and M65 or customers can be picked up from Preston mainline rail station.

Wheelchair Accessible Vehicles

Unit H4, Morton Park, Darlington DL1 4PH.

- 📞 01325 389900
- ✉️ hire@wheelchairaccessiblevehicles.co.uk
- 🌐 www.wheelchairaccessible vehicles.co.uk

This company has a range of self-drive adapted vans that can carry wheelchair users for hire. Delivery or collection from Darlington Station can be arranged at additional cost.

Wheelchair Travel

1 Johnston Green, Guildford GU2 9XS.

- 📞 01483 233640
- ✉️ trevor@wheelchair-travel.co.uk
- 🌐 www.wheelchairtravel.co.uk

A self-drive rental company with wheelchair accessible cars and minibuses available for any period of domestic and continental use by both UK and non-UK licence holders. Minibuses have lifts, wheelchair securing points and seatbelts. Fiat Doblo cars can carry one wheelchair only, driver and two passengers. Cars with hand controls also available. Vehicles can be delivered to home, hotel or airport. Also offered is a wheelchair taxi service, using luxury adapted minibuses.

Equipment hire

This section includes bodies that operate nationally or at least over a large part of the country. Some organisations that hire wheelchairs and other equipment to people living in or visiting their area are included in the regional sections of this guide. A full list can be obtained from:

British Healthcare Trades Association

Suite 4.06 New Loom House, Back Church Lane, London E1 1LU.

- 📞 020 7702 2141
- ✉️ bhta@bhta.com
- 🌐 www.bhta.net

Regulating body with over 400 professional members who sell equipment such as scooters, wheelchairs, bath lifts and stair lifts. If a company is listed with them or on their website, it means they have passed a special code of practice and therefore met high quality standards.

Ability2Travel

3 Mill Road, Kettering NN16 0RY.

- 📞 01536 501298
- ✉️ enquiry@ability2travel.co.uk
- 🌐 www.ability2travel.co.uk

Offer the services of travel companions / personal assistants to people with disabilities travelling in Britain or abroad. Assistance with making travel plans and arrangements can also be provided.

British Red Cross

44 Moorfields. London EC2Y 9AL.

- 📞 0870 170 7000
- ✉️ information@redcross.org.uk
- 🌐 www.redcross.org.uk

Most branches can help people with disabilities in some or all of the following ways – referring people to other holiday facilities, providing voluntary assistance to disabled holiday-makers, and providing short-term loan of equipment such as wheelchairs. Enquiries should be made to the area office, addresses in local telephone directories or on their website above.

Direct Mobility Hire Ltd

Warren House, 201A Bury Street, Edmonton, London N9 9JE.

T 0800 0929322

E info@directmobility.co.uk

W www.directmobility.co.uk

Hire and sell a wide range of mobility, bath, toilet and bed equipment. Pressure relief and incontinence products also available. Next day delivery in area around London.

St John Ambulance

National Headquarters, 27 St Johns Lane, London EC1M 4BU.

T 0870 010 4950

W www.sja.org.uk

For road ambulance services, escorts, nursing and other care services in England, Wales and Northern Ireland apply to the County Headquarters listed in the telephone directory or on the website.

Theraposture Ltd

Kingdom Avenue, Northacre Industry Park, Westbury BA13 4WE.

T 0800 834654

E info@theraposture.co.uk

W www.theraposture.co.uk

Offer a sale and rental scheme for adjustable beds for short-term use (two weeks minimum).

Publications & websites

AA Disabled Travellers' Guide

W www.theaa.com

Bi-annual publication available for free download from their website that gives information on facilities for disabled people at motorway service areas, toll bridges and tunnels. An overseas section gives information on the Channel Tunnel, car ferries, French motorways and some hotels in Europe.

Accessible Countryside for Everyone (ACE)

W www.accessiblecountryside.org.uk

This site promotes accessibility to the countryside of England and Wales. Highlights walks suitable for wheelchair users of varying difficulties. The listed sites are selected for the physical access aspect however a number also have facilities for those with sight or hearing impairments. Site also lists accessible taxis, pubs and restaurants and links to specialist sites for accessible camping.

Access at Last

W www.accessatlast.com

This website provides information on accessible holiday accommodation as well as suggestions for specialist equipment. The website is run by a disabled person and advertises only accommodation with at least one room with a level access shower. It includes detailed information and customer reviews

Accessible Accommodation

W www.accessibleaccommodation.com

This website helps you to find accessible accommodation in England, Ireland,

Scotland, Wales and Northern Ireland. They aim to provide relevant information to those who need accessible accommodation when they travel, whether families with children, older people or those with reduced mobility and whether wheelchairs are required or not. Properties are not inspected and are classified by the property owner. Requests for further information or to make a booking are made directly to the properties.

Caravanable

Ⓦ www.caravanable.co.uk

This website has been created by the mother of a wheelchair user. It lists caravan sites in the UK which have an adapted toilet, shower and basin with level or ramped access that are suitable for a disabled person.

Deaftravel

Ⓦ www.deaftravel.co.uk

This website has been launched for deaf people travelling independently abroad. As well as advice, information and local contacts, it includes travel stories both in written and signed video clip forms.

Direct Enquiries

Ⓦ www.directenquiries.com

This website holds the nationwide access register which gives information on the accessibility of a wide range of business premises around the country. It can be searched geographically, by type of business and by the nature of the access required. It also contains the list of toilets fitted with the National Key Scheme lock.

Disabled Holiday Directory

Ⓦ www.disabledholidaydirectory.co.uk

Online resource offering a large selection of holidays in the UK from country and coastal cottages to hotels, caravan sites and log cabins. Virtually all accommodation listed is wheelchair accessible with widened doorways. Some properties have disabled equipment such as hoists and electric beds and facilities such as lowered kitchen and bathroom units and accessible wet rooms.

Disabled Holiday Information

P.O. Box 186, Oswestry, Shropshire SY10 1AF.

Ⓔ info@disabledholidayinfo.org.uk

Ⓦ www.disabledholidayinfo.org.uk

A website designed to give travellers with disabilities (whether they are wheelchair users or have other mobility issues) appropriate information on accessible holiday accommodation, attractions and activities in order to help them choose suitable accessible holidays. Properties bearing their logo on the site have been visited and assessed by their researchers for accessibility. Other properties are self-assessed.

Disability Now

Ⓣ 0845 120 7001

Ⓔ dnsubs@servicehelpline.co.uk

Ⓦ www.disabilitynow.org.uk

Monthly magazine for disabled people. It includes regular features on holidays in Britain and abroad written by disabled people. Also includes holiday advertisements. Available on subscription, in print, on CD/cassette or via email for £18 per 12 editions. For a sample copy contact Disability Now Subscriptions. The website also contains information on accessible holidays and accommodation rated by disabled people.

Disability Rights UK

12 City Forum, 250 City Road, London
EC1V 8AF.

Ⓣ 020 7250 3222

Ⓔ reception@disabilityrightsuk.org

Ⓦ www.disabilityrightsuk.org

Disability Rights UK produce and stock
a wide range of publications on matters
affecting the lives of disabled people. Visit
the website for a full list of all Disability
Rights UK publications or to order online.
The following may be particularly relevant
to holiday-makers:

- *If Only I'd Known That A Year Ago*
  (2012)
- *National Key Scheme Guide* (2012)
- *Doing Transport Differently* (free to
  download, 2011)
- *Get Mobile: a guide to buying a scooter or
  power chair* (2007)
- *Get Motoring: a guide to buying a car*
  (2007)

Disabled Go

Ⓦ www.disabledgo.info

The website gives access details on premises
including shops, leisure facilities, catering
establishments, etc in an increasing number
of towns and cities.

Disabled Holiday Directory

Ⓦ www.disabledholidaydirectory.co.uk

Website giving detailed information on
accessible holiday accommodation in the
UK, Ireland and worldwide. The site also
gives a useful list of questions that disabled
people may wish to ask accommodation
owners before making a booking.

English Heritage: Access Guide

Ⓣ 0870 3331181
  Textphone 08000150516

Ⓔ customers@english-heritage.org.uk

Ⓦ www.english-heritage.org.uk/
  accessguide

An annual booklet giving information
on accessibility and facilities for disabled
people at around 100 historic buildings
and sites owned by English Heritage. The
booklet is available in alternative formats
and can be picked up from any staffed
property, from English Heritage Customer
Services Department, PO Box 569,
Swindon SN2 2YP or downloaded for free
from their website.

Farm Stay

Ⓣ 024 7669 6909

Ⓔ info@farmstayuk.co.uk

Ⓦ www.farmstay.co.uk

The official guide listing holiday
accommodation of all kinds on farms
throughout the UK. Some information on
accessibility is included. It can be obtained
from Farm Stay (UK) Ltd, National
Agricultural Centre, Stoneleigh Park,
Warwickshire CV8 2LG.

Go Gluten-free, Wheat-free

Ⓦ www.go-gluten-free-wheat-free.co.uk

An independent website giving
information on accommodation and travel
services in Britain and abroad suitable for
coeliacs and others needing a gluten-free
diet.

Good Beer Guide

Ⓣ 01727 867201

Ⓦ www.camra.org.uk/books

An annual publication with information
on 4500 pubs throughout the UK

recommended by members of the Campaign for Real Ale. Those that are said to have easy access for wheelchair users to bars and toilets are indicated. Available, price £12.99 (2012), from bookshops or from CAMRA, 230 Hatfield Road, St Albans AL1 4LW. A mobile phone based version of the guide is also now available for Smartphones.

The National Trust Access Guide

PO Box 39, Warrington WA5 7WD

T 0870 458 4000

Textphone 0870 240 3207

E accessforall@nationaltrust.org.uk

W www.nationaltrust.org.uk

An annual book giving information on the accessibility and services for disabled visitors at National Trust properties throughout England, Wales and Northern Ireland. A free copy can be requested by post or email to the addresses above and is available in audio and Braille formats.

Open Britain 2011

W www.openbritain.net/openbritain

Book containing a great amount of accessibility information supported by all national tourism authorities and Regional Development Agencies. Provides a comprehensive directory of accessible UK accommodation and travel.

Rough Guide to Accessible Britain

W www.accessibleguide.co.uk

Produced in association with Motability, this book is packed with ideas for days out for disabled visitors. Includes details of things to do across Britain, from the arts to gondola trips on the Nevis Mountain range, with colour photos. All sites have been reviewed by writers with disabilities.

An updated online guide will be available to buy in 2012. Visit the website for details.

Royal Society for the Protection of Birds

The Lodge, Sandy SG19 2DL.

T 01767 680551

E enquiries@rspb.org.uk

W www.rspb.org.uk

Welcomes disabled visitors to many of its nature reserves. Information on accessibility and facilities for disabled people is given on their website and in their monthly Bird Watching magazine.

Walks With Wheelchairs

W www.walkswithwheelchairs.com

Online database of walks in the countryside of the UK that have been tried and tested by wheelchair users.

The Yellow Book

The National Gardens Scheme, Hatchlands Park, East Clandon, Surrey GU4 7RT.

T 01483 211535

E webmaster@ngs.org.uk

W www.ngs.org.uk

The National Gardens Scheme's annual Guide to thousands of gardens, open for visiting by the public. Many are indicated in the Guide and on the website as being accessible to wheelchair users. Available from bookshops, by post or online from the addresses above. Price £9.99 (2012).

International holidays

This section includes details of companies and organisations that offer specialist holidays to destinations outside of the UK. Although this Guide is intended to cover Great Britain & Ireland, the following details may be of use to you if you decide to travel further afield in the future.

Access Travel Ltd

6 The Hillock, Astley, Manchester M29 7GW.

T 01942 888844

E office@access-travel.co.uk

W www.access-travel.co.uk

Offer a programme of holiday packages designed for disabled people in destinations around the Mediterranean, the Canaries and Florida. Holiday homes in France are also offered. A variety of self-catering and hotel accommodation options are available. ATOL protected.

Enable Holidays Ltd

39 Station Street, Walsall, West Midlands WS2 9JT.

T 0871 222 4939

W www.enableholidays.com

Offer overseas package holidays at selected resorts in the Mediterranean, Canaries and Florida at hotels chosen as being accessible. Powered wheelchairs and other equipment can be pre-booked, and adapted vehicles arranged for transfers and outings in many locations. All properties personally checked for accessibility.

Traveleyes

PO Box 511, Leeds LS5 3JT.

T 0870 922 0221

W www.traveleyes.co.uk

Travel company organising small group holidays for visually impaired and sighted people, with the latter acting as guides in exchange for a discounted price. Holidays have included walking trips in southern Spain and the Atlas mountains, visits to Tuscany, Sorrento, Greek Islands and Cuba with more destinations planned. Groups are kept to around 16 and the air holidays are ATOL protected.

Wings on Wheels

8 Cornfields, Church Lane, Tydd St Giles, Wisbech PE13 5LX.

T 01945 871111

E info@wingsonwheels.co.uk

W www.wingsonwheels.co.uk

Offer a programme of small escorted group holidays for disabled and non-disabled people throughout the year to overseas destinations and also tailored holidays for individuals and organisations in Britain, Europe and worldwide.

"

The National Accessible Scheme is great – giving you the confidence to book somewhere which suits your specific needs.

"

England

> Exceptional accessible tourism venues are recognised and awarded through the VisitEngland Awards for Excellence.

Visit England

England is a country of impressive diversity and variety. From the rolling hills of the Cotswolds and bustling city life of Manchester, to the charms of sleepy Cornish villages and the dramatic coastal splendour of the North East.

Importantly, England's tourism businesses are making it a top priority to ensure that their facilities and services are more accessible to their visitors. That means that holidays in England, with its plethora of exciting attractions and rich variety of accommodation, are becoming easier for everyone.

So whether The Great North Museum (Newcastle-upon-Tyne) takes your fancy, the National Theatre (London), Imperial War Museum North (Manchester), Windsor Castle (Berkshire) or the National Space Centre (Leicestershire), you are sure of a warm welcome.

Accessible England

VisitEngland runs a scheme to highlight those accommodation businesses which have improved their accessibility. The National Accessible Scheme (NAS) is great if you have a visual, hearing or mobility impairment giving you the confidence to book somewhere which suits your specific needs. A trained assessor has checked it out before you have checked in.

One new addition to the NAS is the University of Leeds, which provides accommodation to guests during the summer vacation. Storm Jameson Court has recently been awarded 'Access Exceptional' status, recognising its excellence in providing for mobility, hearing and visually impaired guests. It has 23 new fully accessible rooms, and provides an ideal base to explore the buzzing city of Leeds or the surrounding countryside.

So remember – next time you book your accommodation in England – look out for the NAS logos. You can find information about NAS and the logos in the advice and guidance part of this Guide.

Award-winning venues

Exceptional accessible tourism venues are recognised and awarded through the VisitEngland Awards for Excellence. The awards are the highest accolade in English tourism. The 'Access for All Award' is given to those who show a strong commitment to access resulting in excellent facilities.

Hoe Grange Holidays (2011 Gold winner) is a group of beautiful Four Star Gold self-catering cabins on the edge of Peak District National Park whose owners are dedicated to making their accommodation not only accessible but also horse friendly!

The Deep in Hull (2011 Gold winner) has gone above and beyond the call of duty offering 'Quiet Days' when lighting and sound levels are adjusted, BSL-signed presentations are available and there are multi-sensory and interactive experiences. Similarly, Cadbury World (2011 Silver winner) has made extra efforts to ensure a warm welcome to all of their visitors, no matter what their needs.

Information is key

All VisitEngland star rated accommodation and quality assured attractions are now required to provide information on their facilities and services to help you 'know before you go'. This information is presented as an Access Statement, which is simply a document that tells you lots of useful details about the premises and its surroundings.

Typical information may include, for example, the frequency of buses, useful telephone numbers, the number of steps to the front door and the availability of subtitles on televisions. The RSPB is working hard to produce improved Access Statements for all its nature reserves.

So, when you are next researching which accommodation to stay at and attractions to visit, ask to see their Access Statements.

The national tourist board website has a dedicated information section for people with physical or sensory needs. To make your travels around England easier and more enjoyable for you, we've put together some practical information and links to other useful websites, which we hope you'll find useful.

Find out more at
www.visitengland.com/accessforall

About London

London is one of the world's most important tourist destinations as well as hosting more British visitors than any other city or area. Whether your trip is for pleasure or business, for a particular event or general sightseeing, London will have something for you.

Many of London's major sights are well known – Buckingham Palace, Trafalgar Square, Marble Arch, Piccadilly Circus, Westminster Abbey, St Paul's Cathedral, Tower Bridge and the Tower of London. The Olympic Stadium and other aspects of the Olympic Park in Stratford will doubtless be added to the list of London's iconic sites.

London is the home of many internationally important museums and art collections including the British Museum, the National Gallery and the National Portrait Gallery both off Trafalgar Square. The national British Art collection is in Tate Britain near Westminster. The Victoria & Albert, the Natural History and the Science Museums are clustered in South Kensington. Other accessible attractions include the London Transport Museum in Covent Garden, the Imperial War Museum in Kennington and Somerset House between the river and the Strand.

A string of attractions now exist along the riverfront. The most dramatic are the London Eye opposite Westminster and the Tate Modern at Bankside with its international collection of 20th Century art. Nearby Southwark Cathedral has a recently opened visitor centre as does The Globe, a reconstructed Elizabethan theatre. Families may enjoy a visit to the London Aquarium in the old County Hall while adults can explore the history and taste of wine at Vinopolis near London Bridge.

Central London has more open spaces, large and small, than many comparable cities and these are home to attractions such as the Serpentine Gallery in Hyde Park and London Zoo in Regents Park. In the outer areas there are large open areas at Hampstead Heath to the north, Epping Forest in the east and Richmond Park in West London. Also to the west, the London Wetlands Centre is at Barnes across the river from Hammersmith and Kew Gardens is a designated World Heritage Site.

There is much to see outside the centre of London too. The accessible Docklands Light Railway serves the centre of Greenwich with its many historic buildings. An access leaflet covering the National Maritime Museum, the Queen's House and the Royal Observatory is available. Greenwich and the Thames Barrier can be visited by river.

English Heritage premises include the home of Charles Darwin at Down House in the extreme south east of Greater London and Eltham Palace with its restored 1930's interior.

Shopping opportunities include famous retail streets, stores and markets in both central London and major suburban centres. For live entertainment, London offers an enormous variety of theatre and concerts, many in venues with recently improved access. Visitors to London may well encounter an event, be it pageantry like the Changing of the Guards or a State Visit, celebrations such as the Lord Mayor's Show or the Chinese New Year, a colourful demonstration or a major exhibition or sports fixture.

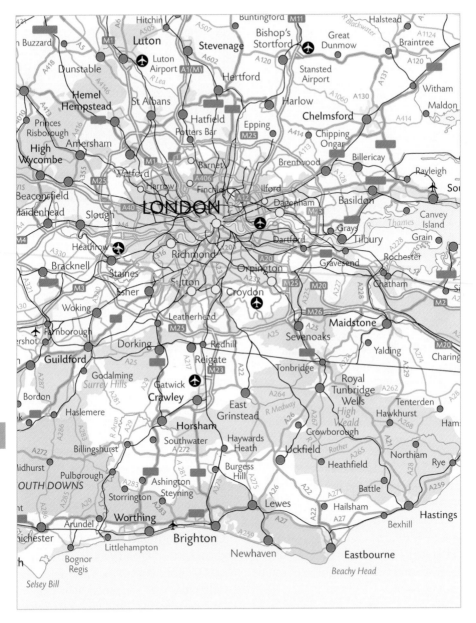

0   10   20 Km

0   10   Miles

Resources

Tourism

Visit London

6th Floor, 2 More London Riverside,
London SE1 2RR.

☎ 020 7234 5800

Ⓦ www.visitlondon.com

Organisation representing the tourist
industry in London. Some information
for disabled people is included on their
website.

Artsline

21 Pine Court, Wood Lodge Gardens,
Bromley BR1 2WA.

Ⓔ ceo@artsline.org.uk

Ⓦ www.artsline.org.uk

Free online-based advice service for
disabled people on arts and entertainment
venues in London. Full details are provided
on access and provision for disabled people
at London theatres, cinemas and other
venues. Access guides are available in print,
on tape and on the website.

Transport

Transport for London

☎ 0843 222 1234 (Information)
Textphone 020 7918 3015

Ⓦ www.tfl.gov.uk

Historically the public transport networks in
London were not designed for wheelchair
users and other people with mobility
problems. Although considerable barriers
still exist, a range of developments have
made it easier for disabled people to use
at least parts of London's public transport
system.

London Buses

All bus routes regulated by Transport for
London use buses that have low-level floors
with improved circulation, space for a
wheelchair user and entrance ramps. Along
some routes work has been carried out
to adjust the kerbs at bus stops. However,
accessibility to wheelchair users may be
limited due to the bus being unable to draw
up close to the pavement at bus stops.

London Underground

On the Underground all the stations on the
Jubilee Line Extension from Westminster
to Stratford have lifts between street
and platform levels with only a small gap
between platform and train. There are a
number of other stations with step-free
access to platforms either at the outer parts
of the network or where there has been
substantial work carried out. Transport
for London has a long-term programme
to create a network of 100 accessible
Underground stations and carry out other
improvements. A map showing which
stations are accessible for wheelchair users
is available.

Docklands Light Railway

☎ 084 3222 1234

Runs from near Tower Hill and Bank
to Stratford, Beckton, the Isle of Dogs,
Greenwich, Lewisham and London
City Airport with an extension under
construction to Woolwich. There are
lifts or ramps to all station platforms and
passengers in wheelchairs can be carried.

Tramlink

☎ 084 3222 1234

A network running through Croydon to Beckenham and Wimbledon in South London. Designed to be accessible for disabled passengers.

Journey Planner

🌐 journeyplanner.tfl.gov.uk

Transport for London's internet travel planner. It can be searched for routes using accessible vehicles and step-free stations and interchanges.

The Congestion Charge

🌐 www.tfl.gov.uk/roadusers/
   congestioncharging

Blue Badge holders can apply for 100% discount from the Congestion Charge in central London for an initial registration fee of £10. Therefore for disabled visitors to London it would be worth registering for the discount if they are going to be using a car in central London for more than 2 weekdays. The Registration Pack can be obtained by calling 0845 900 1234, Textphone 020 7649 9123. Vehicles exempt from Vehicle Excise Duty are automatically exempt from the charge.

Taxis

All licensed public hire taxis (Black Cabs) in London have space for a passenger in a manual wheelchair and carry or are equipped with a ramp.

Information & advice

DIAL

DIAL offers free, impartial and confidential information and advice by telephone to disabled people, their relatives and professionals. Local branches of DIAL are constantly changing but at the time of writing, the following groups were members of DIAL UK and may be able to help visitors in their areas. Please call before travelling to check whether the service and organisation is still available.

Disability Action Barnet
☎ 020 8446 6935

Bexley Association of Disabled People
☎ 01322 350988

Mind in Croydon
☎ 020 8763 2037

Greenwich Association of Disabled People
☎ 020 8305 2221
   Textphone 020 8858 9307

Choice in Hackney
☎ 020 7613 3206
   Textphone 020 7613 3208

DIAL Havering
☎ 01708 730226
   Textphone 01708 751844

Disability Network Hounslow
☎ 020 8758 2048
   Textphone 020 8758 2065

Kingston CIL
☎ 020 8540 9603

Lambeth DAS
☎ 020 7738 5656
   Textphone 020 7978 8765

Richmond A&ID
☎ 020 8831 6070
   Textphone 020 8831 6078

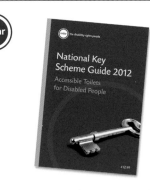

DAN Tower Hamlets
- 020 8980 2200

DIAL Waltham Forest
- 020 8539 8884
  Textphone 020 8539 8077

Wandsworth DAS
- 020 8333 6949

Bromley Association of People with Disabilities

Lewis House, 30 Beckenham Road, Beckenham BR3 4LS.
- 020 8663 3345
- respite@bath-disability.org

Organise a range of respite holidays for disabled people living in Bromley.

The Original Tour

Jews Row, Wandsworth, London SW18 1TB.
- 020 8877 1722
- info@theoriginaltour.com
- www.theoriginaltour.com

Largest provider of bus tours around central London with recorded and live commentaries in English and some other languages and the ability to get on and off at places of interest. Their most recent vehicles, introduced from 2005, have a ramp at the entrance and spaces on the lower deck for wheelchair users.

Healthcare and Transport Services

44 Weir Road, Wimbledon, London SW19 8UG.
- 084 5372 0999
- www.hatsgroup.com

Have a variety of vehicles for hire including wheelchair accessible vans and minibuses and drivers with a wide experience of disability. Available for outings and airport/station transfers.

Equipment hire

SHOPMOBILITY

The National Federation of Shopmobility UK (NFSUK), PO Box 6641, Christchurch, BH23 9DQ.
- 0844 41 41 850
- info@shopmobilityuk.org
- www.shopmobilityuk.org

Hires manual and powered wheelchairs and scooters. Have a range of branches around the UK. You can find the nearest Shopmobility Schemes to you on their on-line Directory. Access is obtained by clicking on the 'Shopmobility Directory' button on the top of the row to the left of their website and using the search criteria. You will need to contact a specific Shopmobility Scheme in order to make equipment bookings or find out detailed information. General and contact information is contained in their Directory.

City Mobility

267 Southwark Park Road, London SE16 3TP.
- 020 7394 0591
- www.citymobility.co.uk

Manual and electric wheelchairs and scooters are available to rent on daily, weekly or monthly rates.

Direct Mobility Hire Ltd

Warren House, 201A Bury Street, Edmonton N9 9JE.
- 0800 0929322
- info@directmobility.co.uk
- www.directmobility.co.uk

Hire and sell a wide range of mobility, bath, toilet and bed equipment. Pressure relief and incontinence products also available. Next day delivery in London and surrounding areas.

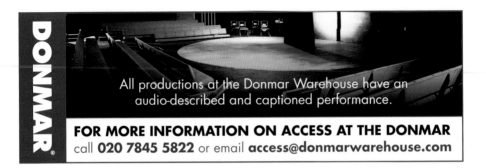

Keep Able

615-69 Watford Way, Apex Corner, London
NW7 3JN

📞 020 8201 0810

📧 apex@keepable.co.uk

Wheelchairs may be hired through
the above store where a wide range of
equipment is also available.

Opt4Mobility

9/11 The Causeway, Teddington TW11
0HA.

📞 020 8943 8890

📧 info@opt4mobility.com

🌐 www.opt4mobility.com

As well as selling a wide range of mobility
and daily living equipment, also offer a hire
service for transit and manual wheelchairs.

Publications

Access to London

🌐 www.accessinlondon.org

4th edition published in 2003. Prepared
by Pauline Hephaisto's Survey Projects
teams of disabled and able-bodied people.
Gives information on getting around the
London area, accommodation, attractions,
entertainment, sports venues, shopping,
places to eat and pubs. Price £9.99.
Available from the publishers, Access
Project, 39 Bradley Gardens, London W13
8HE.

Access London Theatre

📞 020 7557 6700

📧 enquiries@solttma.co.uk

Quarterly brochure listing audio-
described, sign-interpreted and captioned
performances in London theatres. The
Access Guide to London's Theatres,
published 2004, gives details on access and
facilities at 58 theatres including those in
the West End. These are available in print,
tape, Braille or large print from:
The Society of London Theatre, 32 Rose
Street, London WC2E 9ET.
Or can be downloaded together with
listings of assisted performances from:

🌐 www.officiallondontheatre.co.uk/
access

Access for Disabled People in the City of London

📞 020 7332 1995 (Typetalk available)

📧 access@cityoflondon.gov.uk

Regularly revised booklet listing parking
bays for blue badge holders, accessible
toilets and places of interest in The City
and information on Congestion Charging.
Also available in alternative formats, it can
be obtained from the Access Office, City
of London, PO Box 270, Guildhall, London
EC2P 2EJ. Also available on:

🌐 www.cityoflondon.gov.uk

Accommodation

KENSINGTON
Copthorne Tara
Scarsdale Place, London W8 5SR.
- 📞 020 7937 7211
- 📧 reservations.tara@
  milleniumhotels.co.uk
- 🌐 www.milleniumhotels.co.uk

Hotel off Kensington High Street in West London.

NAS ASSESSED ACCOMMODATION

BROMLEY
Best Western Bromley Court Hotel
Hotel
- 📞 0208 4618 600
- 📧 patrickwall@bromleycourthotel.co.uk
- 🌐 www.bw-bromleycourthotel.co.uk

CENTRAL LONDON
YHA London Central
Four star hostel
- 📞 0870 7708 868
- 📧 neilbaldwin@yha.org.uk
- 🌐 www.yha.org.uk

HOLBORN
SACO London
Four star serviced apartments
- 📞 0845 1220 405
- 📧 janejones@sacoapartments.co.uk
- 🌐 www.sacoapartments.co.uk

PROVIDENCE WHARF
Radisson Edwardian Providence Wharf
Four star hotel
- 📞 0208 7577 900
- 📧 vanderwm@radisson.com
- 🌐 www.radissonedwardian.com

SOUTH KENSINGTON
Meininger Hotel London Hyde Park
Four star hostel
- 📞 +44 020 7590 6907
- 📧 hlqg@meininger-hotels.com
- 🌐 www.meininger-hotels.com

THAMESIDE
YHA London
Two star hostel
- 📞 0870 7708 868
- 📧 neilbaldwin@yha.org.uk
- 🌐 www.yha.org.uk

WESTMINSTER
Tune Hotels.com
Accredited budget hotel
- 📞 0207 244 4100
- 📧 j.stenson@queensway.com

About South East England

Although sometimes over-shadowed by London, the counties of Kent, Surrey and East and West Sussex have their own special features and many attractions for holiday makers and day visitors.

Resorts large and small are found around the coast. Brighton with its distinctive Royal Pavilion and a thriving arts and entertainment scene can claim to be Britain's first seaside resort. Eastbourne has a long level seafront but is close to the South Downs, England's newest National Park, and the cliffs of Beachy Head. Other resorts include Hastings, Worthing, Littlehampton, Bognor Regis and Margate, home to the new Turner Contemporary Gallery.

Historically, the area has always been important. The Romans landed here and among the many reminders of their civilisation is Fishbourne Palace near Chichester. At the famous historic site of the Battle of Hastings, at Battle north of Hastings, English Heritage have opened a new visitor centre, although access difficulties remain for the battlefield itself.

Since 1066, the military emphasis on the area has been to repel invasions.

Examples of this include Dover Castle, the Military Aviation Museum at the Battle of Britain airfield at Tangmere in West Sussex and a cluster of attractions in north Kent including the Chatham Historic Dockyard. Also at Chatham, Dickens World is a new family attraction bringing to life the work of the region's leading literary figure.

At Canterbury, disabled people can get to most parts of the great Cathedral. There are also historic Cathedrals in Chichester and Rochester and a more modern one at Guildford. Historic secular buildings include the beautiful Leeds Castle near Maidstone, the imposing 17th century Petworth House in West Sussex owned by the National Trust and the modernist De La Ware Pavilion at Bexhill.

Before the Industrial Revolution the forested Weald was a major centre for iron manufacture. A variety of old industrial and transport buildings are on display at the Amberley Museum north of Arundel. The several heritage railways in the area include the Bluebell Railway, which has a coach for wheelchair users. More modern industries are represented at Mercedes-Benz World and the Brooklands Museum of motor racing and aviation at Weybridge and at The Body Shop Tour in Littlehampton.

Animal attractions in the area include the WWT Wetlands Centre at Arundel, Wildwood north of Canterbury,

Birdworld near Farnham and the South of England Rare Breeds Centre near Ashford, which is run by people with learning disabilities. Noted gardens include Painshill Landscape Garden near Cobham. Other outdoor attractions include the award-wining Seven Sisters Country Park in East Sussex and Capstone Farm Country Park near Gillingham. Thorpe Park in north west Surrey is a destination for family outings. There is also the possibility of a shopping trip to Bluewater near Dartford or a day trip to France by ferry from Dover or through the Channel Tunnel.

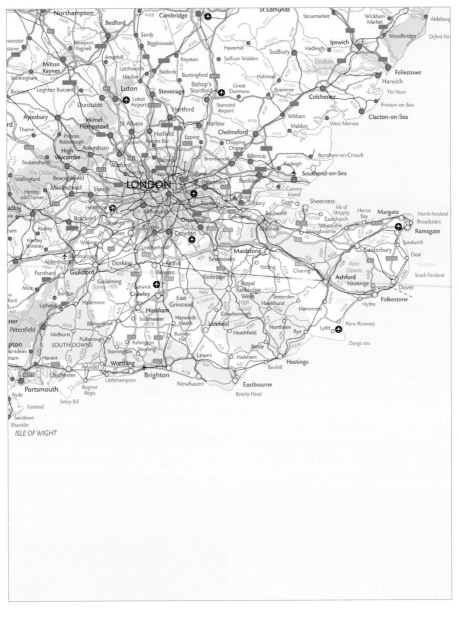

Resources

Tourism

Tourism South East
40 Chamberlayne Road, Eastleigh
Hampshire SO50 5JH.
- ☎ 023 8062 5400
- ⓦ www.visitsoutheastengland.com
Issue a number of publications on
accommodation and attractions in the
region.

Information & advice

East Sussex Disability Association
1 Faraday Close, Eastbourne BN22 9BH.
- ☎ 01323 514500
- ⓔ info@esda.org.uk
- ⓦ www.esda.org.uk
Provide a wide variety of services including
advice on equipment, welfare rights and an
information service.

Kent Association for Disabled People
The Chequers Centre Management Suite,
Pads Hill, Maidstone ME15 6AT.
- ☎ 01622 756444
Organise three one-week holidays for
disabled people at hotels on the south
coast. Voluntary helpers provide some care
but no medical or night care is available.

Voluntary Association for Surrey Disabled
10 Havenbury Estate, Station Road, Dorking
RH4 1ES.
- ☎ 01306 741500
- ⓔ info@vasd.org.uk
- ⓦ www.vasd.org.uk
Two adapted vehicles and manual
wheelchairs can be hired by individuals
and organisations in Surrey. Self catering
properties are available in Bognor Regis and
Bracklesham Bay.

West Sussex Association for Disabled People
9a South Pallant, Chichester PO19 1SU.
- ☎ 01903 264665
- ⓔ iaa@ilawestsussex.org
- ⓦ www.wsad.org.uk
Offer second-hand disability equipment,
information and advice services, a voice for
disability social groups and access groups
and discussion forums.

DIAL
DIAL offer free, impartial and confidential
information and advice by telephone
to disabled people, their relatives and
professionals. Local branches of DIAL
are constantly changing but at the time
of writing, the following groups were
members of DIAL UK and may be able to
help visitors in their areas. Please call before
travelling to check whether the service and
organisation is still available:

Brighton & Hove DAC
- ☎ 01273 203016 (also Textphone)

DIAL Kent
- ☎ 01227 771155
  Textphone 01227 771645

DIS Kent (Folkestone)
- ☎ 01303 226464 (also Textphone)

DIAL N W Kent
- ☎ 01474 537666 (also Textphone)

DIS Sussex
- ☎ 01273 585575

Equipment hire

SHOPMOBILITY

The National Federation of Shopmobility UK (NFSUK), PO Box 6641, Christchurch BH23 9DQ.

- **T** 0844 41 41 850
- **E** info@shopmobilityuk.org
- **W** www.shopmobilityuk.org

Hire manual and powered wheelchairs and scooters. Have a range of branches around the UK. You can find the nearest Shopmobility schemes to you on their on-line Directory. Access is obtained by clicking on the 'Shopmobility Directory' button on the top of the row to the left of their website and using the search criteria. You will need to contact a specific Shopmobility Scheme in order to make equipment bookings or find out detailed information. General and contact information is contained in their Directory.

Southern Mobility Centres

Mobility House, Cavendish Avenue, Eastbourne BN22 8EN.

- **T** 01323 645067
- **W** www.southernmobility.com

Manual wheelchairs and a range of hoists are available to hire at weekly and monthly rates.

Weald Mobility Care Centre

149 Tideswell Road, Eastbourne.

- **T** 01323 721223
- **W** www.wealdmobility.co.uk

Scooters and manual wheelchairs are available for hire for two days and over. Free local delivery and collection.

Publications

Access to places in and around Eastbourne

- **T** 0871 663 0031
- **W** www.visiteastbourne.com

Published annually, this booklet provides information on accessible places in and around Eastbourne and includes a wheelchair route map. The wheelchair route map can also be downloaded from the website. The booklet is available free of charge from Eastbourne Tourist Information Centre, Cornfield Road, Eastbourne, East Sussex BN21 4QA.

Accessible Worthing – an access guide

- **T** 01903 221066
- **W** www.visitworthing.co.uk

Available from Worthing Tourist Information Centre, Chapel Road, Worthing, West Sussex BN11 1HL.

Walks for All in Kent & Medway

- **W** www.kent.gov.uk/explorekent

Gives detailed information for disabled people on 16 country routes in the area. These can be downloaded free from the website.

Maidstone: a Disabled Person's Guide to the Town Centre

- **T** 01622 602169
- **E** tourism@maidstone.gov.uk

A map showing the location of dropped kerbs, reserved parking bays and toilets for disabled people. Available from Maidstone Visitor Information Centre, Maidstone Museum & Bentlif Art Gallery, St Faith's Street, Maidstone, Kent ME14 1LH.

Guildford Cathedral

From its commanding hilltop position, Guildford Cathedral is an imposing landmark. Inside there is tranquility, peace, simple beauty, light and space. Regular events and art exhibitions are held in the Cathedral. Facilities include a gift shop and modern restuarant, a large car and coach park with free parking, and full facilities for disabled visitors.

Opening times
Cathedral
Daily throughout the year 8:30 – 18:30

Restaurant and shop
9:00 – 16:30 most days

Admission
Free

T 01483 547860
E reception@guildford-cathedral.org
W www.guildford-cathedral.org
Stag Hill, Guildford, Surrey GU2 7UP

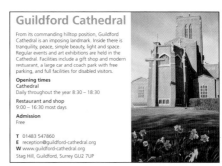

Hawthorn Farm Cottages
Ware, Near Sandwich, Kent.
Four self-catering cottages in a peaceful, rural setting. Single storey. Sleep 4-5. One suitable for wheelchair use. Ample parking. Pets welcome by arrangement.

Linen/towels and children's play equipment provided.

Tel: 01304 813560
Email: hawthornfarmcottages@dsl.pipex.com
www.hawthornfarmcottages.co.uk

Langney Shopping Centre

64 Kingfisher Drive
Eastbourne
East Sussex BN23 7RT

Telephone: 01323 761 730
Fax: 01323 761 477
www.langneyshopping.co.uk

The Wild Side of ARUNDEL WWT

Visit a Vole • Glide with a Guide on a Boat Safari • Spot a Species • Pond Dip & discover a wondrous world of Wetlands!

Wide accesible pathways.
Boat safari accepts wheelchairs without motors.

Arundel Wetland Centre
Mill Road, Arundel BN18 9PB
www.wwt.org.uk/arundel

the runnymede-on-thames
Windsor Road, Egham, Surrey TW20 0AG

4 star hotel in Egham, Surrey.
On the banks of the River Thames near Windsor, just minutes from Heathrow Airport. Our handy location makes us the ideal venue for meetings, weddings and short weekend hotel breaks. Family friendly, with gorgeous riverside dining and an award-winning spa there is so much to do here.

Tel: +44 (0)1784 220 960
www.runnymedehotel.com

Accommodation

BOGNOR REGIS, West Sussex

Invicta Warren

Elmer Sands, Middleton, Near Bognor
Regis, West Sussex.
Contact: Voluntary Association for Surrey
Disabled, 10 Havenbury Estate, Station
Road, Dorking RH4 1ES.
- 01306 741500
- www.vasd.org.uk
Self-catering bungalow designed for
wheelchair users.

Farrell House

27 Nelson Road, Bognor Regis, West Sussex
PO21 2RY.
- 08456 584478
- info@livability.org.uk
- www.livability.org.uk
Self-catering chalet-bungalow adapted and
equipped for disabled people.

Russell Hotel

King's Parade, Bognor Regis PO21 2QP.
- 01243 871300
- russell.hotel@
  actionforblindpeople.org.uk.
Hotel near the seafront and park designed
for blind and partially sighted people and
their companions.

BRACKLESHAM BAY, West Sussex

Tamarisk

Farm Road, Bracklesham Bay, West Sussex.
Contact: Livability (see voluntary
organisations in Useful resources)
- 020 7452 2087
- info@livability.org.uk
- www.livability.org.uk
Self-catering bungalow near the beach
adapted and equipped for disabled people.

VASD Holiday Chalet

Sussex Beach Holiday Village, Earnley,
Bracklesham Bay, West Sussex.
Contact: Voluntary Association for Surrey
Disabled, 10 Havenbury Estate, Station
Road, Dorking RH4 1ES.
- 01306 741500
- info@vasd.org.uk
- www.vasd.org.uk
Chalet designed for wheelchair users on a
holiday park by the beach is Sussex.

EAST PRESTON, West Sussex

Bradbury Hotel

Station Road, East Preston BN16 3AL.
- 01903 770339
- www.royalblindsociety.org.uk
Small hotel for visually impaired people and
their companions near the West Sussex
coast.

FARNHAM, Surrey

High Wray

73 Lodge Hill Road, Farnham GU10 3RB.
Contact: Mrs Alexine Crawford
- 01252 715589
- crawford@highwray73.co.uk
- www.highwray73.co.uk
'Rose' is a purpose-built, self-catering flat
for disabled people a mile from town.

FELPHAM, West Sussex

Beach Lodge

Strand Way, Felpham, Near Bognor Regis,
PO22 7LH.
Contact: Livability (see voluntary
organisations in Useful resources)
- 020 7452 2087
- info@livability.org.uk
- www.livability.org.uk
Detached house facing the sea – east of
Bognor.

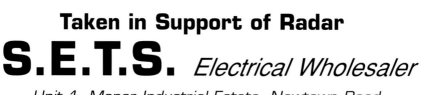

HERNE BAY, Kent

Strode Park Foundation

Strode Park House, Herne CT6 7NE.

T 01227 373292

E info@strodepark.org.uk

W www.strodepark.org.uk

Two self-catering holiday bungalows designed for disabled people and their companions.

HORLEY, Surrey

Brambles MS Respite Care Centre

Suffolk Close, Massetts Road, Horley RH6 7DU.

T 01293 771644

W www.brambles.org.uk

Purpose-built centre for respite care for people with multiple sclerosis.

NAS ASSESSED ACCOMMODATION

BIDDENDEN, Kent

Heron Cottage

Four star guest accommodation

T 01580 291358

E susantwort@hotmail.com

W www.heroncottage.info

BRIGHTON, Sussex

Myhotel Brighton

Four star metro hotel

T 01273 900 365

E benferrer@myhotels.com

W www.myhotels.com

CHICHESTER, Sussex

George Bell House

Five star guest house

T 01243 813 581

E gmenterprises@
chichestercathedral.org.uk

W www.chichestercathedral.org.uk

Eastmere House

Four star bed & breakfast

T +44 01243 544204

E bernardlane@hotmail.com

eastmere.com

Chichester Park Hotel

Three star hotel

T 01243 817 400

E dean@chichesterparkhotel.com

W www.chichesterparkhotel.com

Bishop Otter Campus - University Of Chichester

Two and Three star campus

T 0124 3812 120

E k.atkins@chi.ac.uk

CHIDDINGSTONE, Kent

Hay Barn & Straw Barn

Four star self-catering

T 01892 510117

E holiday@
gardenofenglandcottages.co.uk

W gardenofenglandcottages.co.uk

EASTBOURNE, Sussex

Hydro Hotel

Three star hotel

T +44 01323 720643

E ian.turnbull@hydrohotel.com

W www.hydrohotel.com

Best Western York House Hotel

Three star hotel

T 0170 3255 301

E goran.krgo@yorkhousehotel.co.uk

W www.yorkhousehotel.co.uk

EASTRY, Kent
The Old Dairy
Four star self-catering
- +44 01843 841656
- info@montgomery-cottages.co.uk
- www.montgomery-cottages.co.uk

FARNHAM, Surrey
High Wray
Two star self-catering
- +44 01252 715589
- alexine@highwray73.co.uk

FOLKESTONE, Kent
Shuttlesfield Barn
Four star self-catering
- 0130 3862 729
- geoffs.hirst@btinternet.com
- www.shuttlesfieldbarn.co.uk

HASTINGS, Sussex
Seaspray
Four star guest accommodation
- 01424 436583
- jo@seaspraybb.co.uk
- www.seaspraybb.co.uk

HEADCORN, Kent
Honywood At Curtis Farm
Three star self-catering
- 0162 2890 393
- curtis.farm@btopenworld.com
- www.curtis-farm-kent.co.uk

LISS, Sussex
The Jolly Drover
Four star inn
- 01730 893137
- thejollydrover@googlemail.com
- www.thejollydrover.co.uk

MAIDSTONE, Kent
Village Maidstone
Accredited hotel
- 0162 2672 200
- nicola.meredith@village-hotels.com

PEACEHAVEN, Sussex
Little Haven
Four star self-catering
- 0127 3587 365
- juliette.payne@yahoo.co.uk

PLUMPTON GREEN, Sussex
Heath Farm
Four star self-catering
- +44 01273 890712
- hanbury@heath-farm.com
- www.heath-farm.com

ROYAL TUNBRIDGE WELLS, Kent
Alconbury Guest House
Five star bed & breakfast
- 0189 2511 279
- camilla.robinson@live.co.uk
- www.alconburyguesthouse.com

STANWELL, Surrey
The Stanwell
Three star hotel
- 0178 4262 389
- gm@thestanwell.com

TENTERDEN, Kent
Little Silver Country Hotel
Three star hotel
- +44 01233 850321
- enquiries@little-silver.co.uk

TUNBRIDGE WELLS, Kent

The Brew House Hotel

Four star hotel

📞 01892 520 587

📧 info@brewhousehotel.com

🌐 www.brewhousehotel.com

WADHURST, Sussex

Bardown Farm

Five star self-catering

📞 01580 200452

📧 info@bardownfarm.co.uk

WEST MARDEN, Sussex

West Marsden Farm

Four and Five star self-catering

📞 0239 2631 382

📧 carole.edney@btinternet.com

🌐 www.barleycottage.co.uk

About the South of England

This is a large and varied region stretching from Buckinghamshire and Oxfordshire, through Berkshire and Hampshire to eastern Dorset and the Isle of Wight. It includes much of the Chiltern and Cotswold hills and the Thames Valley as well as the New Forest and stretches of attractive coastline.

There are many opportunities for seaside holidays. The largest resort is Bournemouth where there are entertainments and attractions for both young and old. Other resorts include Poole and Southsea, while Ryde, Sandown and Shanklin are on the Isle of Wight.

At Portsmouth, many attractions in the Historic Dockyard depict the military and naval heritage of the city including the Royal Naval Museum, the Mary Rose display and HMS Victory. An access trail has been laid out around the site and a panoramic view can be obtained from the Spinnaker Tower. The D-Day Museum and Overlord Embroidery are elsewhere in the city. There are other military museums in the region in Aldershot and Winchester.

There is also a full range of urban amenities in Reading and Southampton where part of the harbour has been redeveloped as Ocean City with waterfront restaurants, bars and shops. In Oxford, guided walks are open to disabled people around the historic university buildings. Other historic towns in the region include the cathedral city of Winchester, the Royal Borough of Windsor dominated by the castle, the old port of Poole and market towns such as Banbury and Aylesbury. Riverside towns along the Thames include Marlow,

Maidenhead and Henley, home of the River & Rowing Museum.

Two areas have their own specific characteristics - the New Forest National Park, and the Isle of Wight. A good starting point to learn more about the natural and human history of the former is the New Forest Museum and Visitor Centre at Lyndhurst. The Isle of Wight has been a tourist destination since the middle of the 19th century when Queen Victoria made her home at Osborne House near Cowes. This is now run by English Heritage and is partly accessible to disabled visitors. The many other attractions on the Island include the Isle of Wight Steam Railway, Needles Park overlooking Alum Bay and just watching the boats in the Solent.

Historic houses that can be visited elsewhere in the region include the National Trust's Basildon Park near Reading and Blenheim Palace at Woodstock in Oxfordshire. Beaulieu Abbey in the New Forest houses a large collection of veteran and classic cars. Outdoor attractions include the restored Greenham Common near Newbury, Marwell Zoo and Old Winchester Hill National Nature Reserve both in Hampshire and the Cotswold Wild Life Park at Burford. Most children, and many adults, will enjoy Legoland outside Windsor.

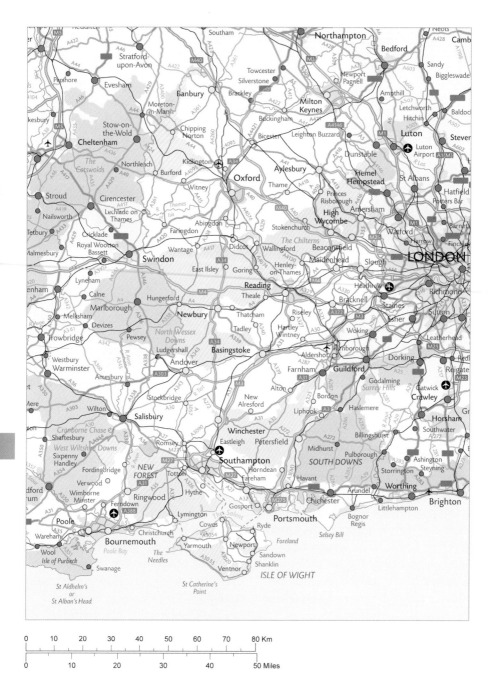

0   10   20   30   40   50   60   70   80 Km

0   10   20   30   40   50 Miles

Resources

Tourism

Tourism South East

40 Chamberlayne Road, Eastleigh
Hampshire SO50 5JH.
📞 023 8062 5505
🌐 www.visitsoutheastengland.com
Issue a number of publications and online
information on accommodation and
attractions in the region.

Transport

Hovertravel Ltd

Quay Road, Ryde, Isle of Wight PO33 2HB.
📞 01983 811000
🌐 www.hovertravel.co.uk
Operate a fast crossing for foot passengers
by hovercraft between Southsea
(Portsmouth) and Ryde on the Isle of
Wight. They have a lift and space for two
standard-sized wheelchairs on Solent
Express and one wheelchair on Island
Express and Freedom 90 crossings. For
accessibility information visit:
🌐 www.hovertravel.co.uk/
    accessibility-information.php

Red Funnel Ferries

12 Bugle Street, Southampton SO14 2JY.
📞 0870 444 8898
✉ post@redfunnel.co.uk
🌐 www.redfunnel.co.uk
Operate car ferries and hi-speed passenger
services between Southampton and Cowes
on the Isle of Wight. Ferries have lifts and
there are toilets for disabled passengers on
board and at terminals.

Wightlink Isle of Wight Ferries

PO Box 59, Portsmouth PO1 2XB.
📞 087 1376 1000
🌐 www.wightlink.co.uk
Operate car ferries on the Portsmouth-
Fishbourne and Lymington-Yarmouth
routes and FastCat catamaran services for
foot passengers only between Portsmouth
and Ryde. The vessels on the Portsmouth-
Fishbourne service are equipped with
lifts and toilets for disabled passengers.
Wheelchairs are available at all terminals. A
Wightlink Disabled Persons Card is available
giving discounted fares.
For assistance call:
📞 023 9281 2011

Several schemes may reduce the cost of
ferry travel for patients and their carers
attending hospital appointments on the
mainland. For more information:
🌐 www.redfunnel.co.uk/
    ferry-travel/healthcare-travel-scheme/
🌐 www.iwight.com

Information & advice

The Ark and Dis:Course

The Ark Studio, Ravenswood Village, Nine
Mile Ride, Crwothorne, Berkshire RG45
6BQ.
📞 013 4475 5528
✉ info@discourse.org.uk
🌐 www.theark.org.uk
A charity that enhances the lives of people
with disabilities through access to the arts
and new media. It also houses Dis:Course,
which provides information, advice and
support for people with disabilities.

British Red Cross Berkshire Branch
Community Services, 90 Eastern Avenue,
Reading RG1 5FS.
- 📞 0118 929 0500
- 🌐 www.redcross.org.uk

Provide some information on holidays for disabled and elderly people and may be able to provide transport for groups and individuals.

Green Island Holiday Trust
- 📞 01202 842880
- ✉️ webmaster@
  greenislandholidaytrust.com
- 🌐 www.greenislandholidaytrust.com

Organise holidays for disabled people with volunteer helpers at Holton Lee on the shore of Poole Harbour. Activities include birdwatching, painting, boat trips and barbecues. Priority will be given to people living in Dorset and Hampshire.

DIAL
Offer free, impartial and confidential information and advice by telephone to disabled people, their relatives and professionals. Local branches of DIAL are constantly changing but at the time of writing, the following groups were members of DIAL UK and may be able to help visitors in their areas. Please call before travelling to check whether the service and organisation is still available:

DIAL Isle of Wight
- 📞 01983 522823
  Textphone 01983 525424

Milton Keynes CIL
- 📞 01908 231344
  Textphone 01908 231505

New Forest DIS
- 📞 01425 628750
  Textphone 01425 610062

Dialability Oxford
- 📞 01865 763600
  Textphone 01865 203636

Sorrell DIAL, Portsmouth
- 📞 023 9282 4853

Disability Wessex, Bournemouth
- 📞 01202 589999

Equipment Hire

SHOPMOBILITY
The National Federation of Shopmobility UK (NFSUK), PO Box 6641, Christchurch BH23 9DQ.
- 📞 0844 41 41 850
- ✉️ info@shopmobilityuk.org
- 🌐 www.shopmobilityuk.org

Hire manual and powered wheelchairs and scooters. Have a range of branches around the UK. You can find the nearest Shopmobility schemes to you on their on-line Directory. Access is obtained by clicking on the 'Shopmobility Directory' button on the top of the row to the left of their website and using the search criteria. You will need to contact a specific Shopmobility Scheme in order to make equipment bookings or find out detailed information. General and contact information is contained in their Directory.

All Handling (Movability) Ltd
Branch Office, 133 High Street, Aldershot, Hants GU11 1TT.
- 📞 01252 319130
- ✉️ info@movability.com
- 🌐 www.movability.com

Hire manual and powered wheelchairs and scooters at weekly rates.

British Red Cross, Isle of Wight Branch

Red Cross House, Hunnycross way, Newport, Isle of Wight PO30 5ZD.

☏ 01983 537821

Can lend wheelchairs, walking and bathing equipment for holidaymakers. Advance booking required.

Buckingham Engineering Company

Old Leighton Farm, Mursley Road, Stewkley, Leighton Buzzard LU7 0ES.

☏ 01296 720800

Company hiring a range of manual, lightweight and powered wheelchairs and scooters for hire on weekly or monthly terms from their centres near Milton Keynes, Buckingham and Luton. A repair service is also offered.

Dunbar Dean Electric Transport Ltd

31 St Catherine's Road, Southbourne, Bournemouth BH6 4AE.

☏ 01202 426135

Electric and manual wheelchairs and scooters are available for hire. Delivery can be arranged.

Island Mobility

32 Dodnor Lane, Newport, Isle of Wight PO30 5XA.

☏ 01983 530000

🌐 www.islandmobility.co.uk

Manual wheelchairs, walkers and mobile hoists for hire on daily or weekly terms. Powered scooters available for experienced users on a weekly basis. A range of other equipment is stocked. Collection and delivery service offered throughout the Isle of Wight.

Publications

Bournemouth: Accessibility Guide

☏ 0845 051 1700

✉ accessibility@bournemouth.gov.uk

🌐 www.bournemouth.co.uk

Regularly updated guide giving information on accommodation, attractions, places to eat & drink and entertainment. Available free of charge from Bournemouth Tourism, Westover Road, Bournemouth BH1 2BU.

Accessible Portsmouth – A Guide for Visitors with Disabilities

☏ 023 92 82 6722

🌐 www.visitportsmouth.co.uk

Access guide produced by the City Council working with disabled people. The guide is available in print, audio, Braille and large print formats from ECCS, Portsmouth City Council, Civic Offices, Guildhall Square, Portsmouth PO1 2AD.

Winchester: Visitor Trail by Wheelchair

☏ 01962 840500

✉ tourism@winchester.gov.uk

🌐 www.visitwinchester.co.uk

A leaflet for visitors to the city prepared by Winchester Shopmobility and Winchester City Council. Available from the Tourist Information Centre, Guildhall, High Street, Winchester SO23 9GH.

Online resources

www.visitthames.co.uk

This website, managed by the Environment Agency, gives information on activities, attractions and places to stay along the Thames from its source in the Cotswolds to Teddington.

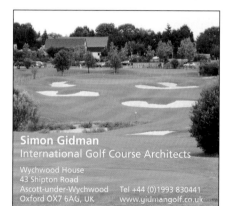

Accommodation

ABINGDON, Oxfordshire
Kingfisher Barn
Rye Farm, Abingdon, Oxfordshire OX14
3NN.
📞 01235 537538
📧 info@kingfisherbarn.com
🌐 www.kingfisherbarn.com
Bed & breakfast in barn conversion close to
town centre.

AYLESBURY, Buckinghamshire
Olympic Lodge
Guttmann Road, Stoke Mandeville,
Aylesbury, Buckinghamshire HP21 9PP.
📞 01296 484848
📧 stoke.mandeville@harperfitness.co.uk
🌐 www.stokemandevillestadium.co.uk
Accommodation in Stoke Mandeville
Stadium complex owned by British
Wheelchair Sports Foundation on the
outskirts of Aylesbury.

CHRISTCHURCH, Dorset
Number 31, Christchurch, Dorset
c/o 40 Walcott Avenue, Dorset BH23 2NG.
📞 01202 481597
📧 info@31aha.co.uk
🌐 www.31aha.co.uk
Self-catering bungalow originally adapted
for wheelchair using owner, a mile from
centre of coastal town.
Contact: Liz Cox

ISLE OF WIGHT
Brambles Chine Bungalow
194 Brambles Chine, Monks Lane,
Freshwater, Isle of Wight PO40 9SQ.
Contact: Mrs S Griffiths, Chalet Secretary,
Isle of Wight ASBAH, 3 Western Road,
Shanklin, PO37 7NF.
📞 01983 863658
🌐 www.iwasbah.co.uk
Chalet on holiday park at the west of Island.

LYMINGTON, Hampshire
Bench Cottage & Little Bench
Pennington, Near Lymington SO41 8HH.
📞 01590 673141
📧 enquiries@ourbench.co.uk
🌐 www.ourbench.co.uk
Cottages designed for wheelchair users in
grounds of owners' home near New Forest.
Contact: Mrs Mary Lewis, Our Bench,
Lodge Road, Pennington, Lymington SO41
8HH.

NEW MILTON, Hampshire
Scout Holiday Homes Trust Caravans
New Milton, Hampshire
Contact: Scout Holiday Homes Trust. See
resources section.
📞 020 8433 7290
Adapted units in New Milton, south west
Hampshire.

Smugglers View Chalets
New Milton, Hampshire.
Chalets adapted for wheelchair users.
Contact: Livability
📞 020 7452 2087
📧 info@livability.org.uk
🌐 www.livability.org.uk

POOLE, Dorset
Holton Lee
East Holton, Poole BH16 6JN.
📞 01202 631063
📧 admin@holtonlee.co.uk
🌐 www.holtonlee.co.uk
Purpose-built centre for disabled people
and carers in countryside overlooking Poole
Harbour.

Orton Rigg Hotel
53 Cliff Drive, Canford Cliffs, Poole BH13 7JF.
🌐 www.ortonrigghotel.co.uk
Hotel adapted for disabled guests in secluded setting.

Scout Holiday Homes Trust Caravan
Rockley Park, Hamworthy Poole BH15 4LZ.
Contact: Scout Holiday Homes Trust.
📞 020 8433 7290
✉ info.centre@scout.org.uk
🌐 www.scoutbase.org.uk
Adapted unit for on holiday park overlooking Poole Harbour.

SOUTHAMPTON, Hampshire
Vitalise Netley Waterside House
Abbey Hill, Netley Abbey, Southampton SO31 5FA.
📞 023 8045 3686
🌐 www.vitalise.org.uk
Centre by Southampton Water purpose-built for breaks for people with disabilities.
Contact: Vitalise
📞 0845 345 1970

NAS ASSESSED ACCOMMODATION

ABINGDON, Oxfordshire
Abbey Guest House
Four star guest house
📞 01235 537020
✉ info@abbeyguest.com
🌐 www.abbeyguest.com

BORTHWOOD, Isle of Wight
Borthwood Cottages
Four star self-catering
📞 01983 403967
✉ anne@borthwoodcottages.co.uk
🌐 www.borthwoodcottages.co.uk

BRIGHSTONE, Isle of Wight
Yafford Mill Barn
Five star self-catering
📞 0192 9481 555
✉ enq@islandcottageholidays.com
🌐 www.islandcottageholidays.com

COGGES, Oxfordshire
Swallows Nest
Four star self-catering
📞 01993 704919
✉ jan@strainge.fsnet.co.uk

GURNARD, Isle of Wight
The Blue House
Five star self-catering
✉ tim@houseblue.eu
🌐 www.houseblue.eu

LECKHAMPSTEAD, Buckinghamshire
Weatherhead Farm
Four star farmhouse
📞 +44 01280 860502
✉ weatherheadfarm@aol.com
🌐 www. weatherheadfarm.co.uk

MAIDENHEAD, Berkshire
Holiday Inn Maidenhead
Hotel
📞 0870 400 9053
✉ simon.hall@ihg.com
🌐 www.holidayinn.co.uk

MARLOW, Buckinghamshire
Granny Anne's
Four star bed & breakfast
📞 01628 473086
✉ enquiries@grannyannes.com
🌐 www.marlowbedbreakfast.co.uk

MILTON KEYNES, Buckinghamshire
South Lodge
Five star bed & breakfast
- ☎ 01908 582946
- ✉ info@culturevultures.co.uk

NEWCHURCH, NEAR SANDOWN, Isle of Wight
Mulberry Rest
Five star self-catering
- ☎ 0198 3400 096
- ✉ donnadempsey@me.com

OXFORD, Oxfordshire
YHA Oxford
Four star hostel
- ☎ 0870 7708 868
- ✉ neilbaldwin@yha.org.uk
- 🌐 www.yha.org.uk

RYDE, Isle of Wight
Doranes
Four star self-catering
- ☎ 0189 5233 557
- ✉ vyvyanrichards@yahoo.co.uk

SANDOWN, Isle of Wight
Fort Holiday Park
Three star holiday park
- ☎ 01983 402858
- ✉ bookings@fortholidaypark.co.uk
- 🌐 www.fortholidaypark.co.uk

Sandown Bay Holiday Park
No 6 & No 113
Three star self-catering
- ☎ 01983 810294
- ✉ holidays@maherross.com

SHANKLIN, Isle of Wight
The Marine Villa
Five star self-catering
- ☎ 0168 9606 060
- ✉ mowe@totalise.co.uk

Sunny Bay Apartments
Four star self-catering
- ☎ 01983 861 555
- ✉ rda7376401@aol.com

STOKE MANDEVILLE, Buckinghamshire
Olympic Lodge
Three star guest accommodation
- ☎ 0129 6484 848
- ✉ stoke.mandeville@harpersfitness.co.uk
- 🌐 www.olympic-lodge.co.uk

SWAY, Hampshire
The Nurse's Cottage Restaurant with Rooms
Four star guest accommodation
- ☎ 0159 068 3402
- ✉ nurses.cottage@lineone.net

About the West Country

This region comprises Somerset, Wiltshire, Gloucestershire, much of Dorset and the area around Bristol. It includes the rolling chalk uplands of the Salisbury Plain in the east, part of the Exmoor National Park in the west, the Mendip Hills, the Forest of Dean, much of the Cotswolds, the Somerset Levels and two distinctive coastlines.

Many of the most important signs of prehistoric Britain can be found in the area. Stonehenge in Wiltshire is world famous. Perhaps of equal significance are the stone rings of Avebury and there are several examples of ancient figures cut into chalk hillsides, such as the Cerne Abbas Giant in Dorset. Much of the Dorset and East Devon 'Jurassic coast' has been declared a World Heritage Site because the many fossils found in the area were vital in the development of knowledge of early life on Earth.

The region's leading city is Bristol. As well as a history that equals any other major town, there are a range of modern museums, theatrical and music performances, shops and a thriving nightlife. The docks in the heart of the city now contain many attractions including the SS Great Britain, the M Shed displaying the history of the city and its people and @ Bristol with its interactive displays of science and wildlife.

The city of Bath has attracted visitors since the Romans bathed in its thermal springs, a practice that today's visitors can replicate. Its status as a World Heritage Site comes from the later tourist development at the end of the 18th Century when it was the smartest resort in the country. The hilly nature of the town means that there are restrictions for some disabled people, but a number of attractions are accessible, including the Assembly Rooms and medieval Abbey, and the massed Georgian architecture which can all be appreciated by disabled visitors.

Other towns to visit include Salisbury with its famed Cathedral and Close. Wells boasts a magnificent Cathedral and the oldest continuously populated street in Europe. Gloucester Cathedral made famous in the Harry Potter films and the city's docks that now house a waterways museum are also worth a visit. Also in Gloucestershire, Cheltenham has developed as a Georgian spa town. Dorchester, the historic county town of Dorset, was Thomas Hardy's

Casterbridge. In part of the old railway works at Swindon is Steam a museum that depicts the history of the Great Western Railway and its workers.

On the Bristol Channel coast the largest resort is Weston-Super-Mare with a long, level seafront and a wide range of entertainment. Other resorts on this coast include Minehead on the edge of Exmoor and Burnham-on-Sea. The Dorset coast includes Weymouth on a sheltered bay behind Portland Bill and picturesque Lyme Regis.

Other attractions in the area with facilities for disabled visitors include the Tank Museum at Bovington in Dorset and Longleat House and Safari Park in Wiltshire. The West Somerset Railway has coaches adapted to carry wheelchair users between Minehead and the outskirts of Taunton.

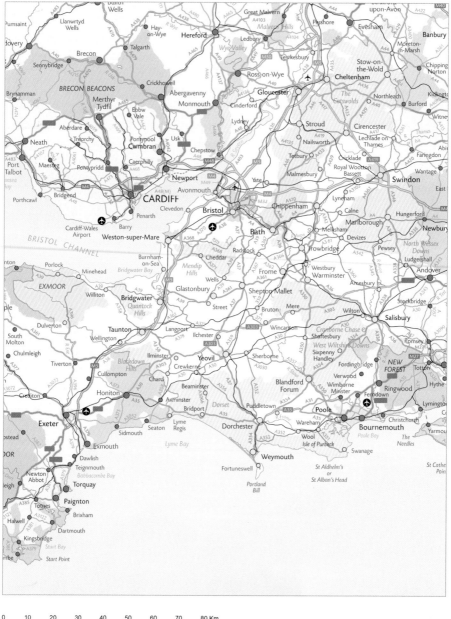

Resources

Tourism

South West Tourism

Woodwater Park, Exeter EX2 5WT.

- ☏ 0870 442 0880
- ✉ post@swtourism.co.uk
- 🌐 www.visitsouthwest.co.uk

General tourist information is given on their website. Specific information for disabled people is provided at:

- 🌐 www.accessiblesouthwest.co.uk

Information & advice

Dorset Association for the Disabled

Unit 18a, Enterprise Park, Piddlehinton, Dorchester DT2 7UA.

- ☏ 01305 849122
- ✉ dad.hq@tesco.net

Provide holidays for Association members and can respond to enquiries.

DIAL

Offer free, impartial and confidential information and advice by telephone to disabled people, their relatives and professionals. Local branches of DIAL are constantly changing but at the time of writing, the following groups were members of DIAL UK and may be able to help visitors in their areas. Please call before travelling to check whether the service and organisation is still available:

DIAS Bristol

- ☏ 0117 983 2828 (also Textphone)

Nailsea Disability Initiative

- ☏ 01275 812183

NORDIS Gillingham

- ☏ 01747 821010

Dial Weston-Super-Mare

- ☏ 01934 419426 (also Textphone)

Disability Wessex

- ☏ 01202 589999

Wiltshire & Bath ILC

- ☏ 01380 871007
  Textphone 01380 871747

Equipment hire

SHOPMOBILITY

The National Federation of Shopmobility UK (NFSUK), PO Box 6641, Christchurch BH23 9DQ.

- ☏ 0844 41 41 850
- ✉ info@shopmobilityuk.org
- 🌐 www.shopmobilityuk.org

Hire manual and powered wheelchairs and scooters. Have a range of branches around the UK. You can find the nearest Shopmobility schemes to you on their on-line Directory. Access is obtained by clicking on the 'Shopmobility Directory' button on the top of the row to the left of their website and using the search criteria. You will need to contact a specific Shopmobility Scheme in order to make equipment bookings or find out detailed information. General and contact information is contained in their Directory.

Purbeck Mobility Limited

Mobility Centre, St Johns Hill, Wareham BH20 4NB.

- ☏ 01929 552623
- ✉ info@purbeckmobility.com

Provide wheelchairs and scooters to visitors to the Purbeck area on daily and weekly rates.

Weston Mobility Centre

215 Milton Road, Weston-super-Mare BS22
8EG.

☎ 01934 642071

✉ miltonmobility@gmail.com

🌐 www.westonmobilitycentre.co.uk

In addition to hiring wheelchairs, they
supply a wide range of other disability
equipment, including spare parts.

Publications

South Somerset: a Guide for People with
Disabilities

☎ 01935 462462

✉ tourism@southsomerset.gov.uk

Published by the South Somerset District
Council. A booklet giving information
for disabled people on attractions,
accommodation, car parking, public
toilets and organisations. Available from
information centres in the area or from
Tourism Unit, South Somerset District
Council, Brympton Way, Yeovil BA20 2HT.

West Dorset for Visitors with Special
Needs

✉ tourism@westdorset-dc.gov.uk

🌐 www.westdorset.com

A free booklet published by West Dorset
District Council. It gives information on
visiting the towns of Dorchester, Bridport,
Sherborne, Beaminster and Lyme Regis.
Available from Tourist Information
Centres in the area or from West Dorset
District Council, Community Enabling
Division, Stratton House, High West Street,
Dorchester DT1 1UZ.

Online resources

www.accessiblesouthwest.co.uk

A website giving information on accessible
accommodation and attractions in the
region that also includes sections on
equipment hire, services and public toilets
for disabled people.

www.visitforestofdean.co.uk

Contains 'Facilities and Information for
those with disabilities visiting the Forest of
Dean', with information regularly updated
by Forest of Dean Council's Tourism &
Marketing Services.

www.visitsomerset.co.uk

☎ 01934 750833

✉ somersetvisitorcentre@
somerset.gov.uk

The website of Somerset Tourism includes
information for disabled visitors to the
county including accommodation that
has been inspected for accessibility and
attractions that are said to have facilities
for disabled visitors, a county wide list of
unisex public toilets and organisations that
can provide further information. General
advice on the area is also available from the
Somerset Visitor Centre.

Accommodation

BATH, Somerset

Carfax Hotel

13-15 Great Pulteney Street, Bath BA2 4BS.

☎ 01225 462089

✉ reservations@carfaxhotel.co.uk

🌐 www.carfaxhotel.co.uk

Townhouse hotel in city centre of Bath.

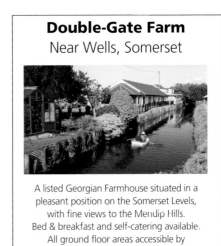

BLANDFORD FORUM, Dorset
The Ellwood Centre
Wooland, Blandford Forum DT11 0ES.
- 01258 818196
- admin@ellwoodcottages.co.uk
- www.theellwoodcentre.co.uk
Single storey self-catering cottages designed for disabled people in the countryside between Blandford and Shaftesbury.

BURNHAM-ON-SEA, Somerset
BPF Bungalow
Contact: British Polio Fellowship, Eagle Office Centre, The Runway, Ruislip HA4 6SE.
- 0800 018 0586
  01903 529057
- holidays@britishpolio.org.uk
- www.britishpolio.org.uk
Purpose-built bungalow on the seafront in Burnham-on-Sea.

Scout Holiday Homes Trust Caravan
Burnham-on-Sea Holiday Village, Burnham-on-Sea TA8 1LA.
Contact: Scout Holiday Homes Trust (see voluntary organisations in Useful resources)
- 020 8433 7290
Adapted units on holiday park near the town centre.

MINEHEAD, Somerset
Promenade Hotel
Esplanade, Minehead TA24 5QS.
- 01643 702572
- promenadehotel@livability.org.uk
- www.livability.org.uk
Hotel owned by Livability specially adapted for disabled guests.

SALISBURY, Wiltshire
Websters
11 Hartington Road, Salisbury SP2 7LG.
- 01722 339779
- www.websters-bed-breakfast.com
Bed & breakfast house in the city of Salisbury.

WESTON-SUPER-MARE, Somerset
The Lauriston Hotel
6-12 Knightsbridge Road, Weston-super-Mare BS23 2AN.
- 01934 620758
- lauriston.hotel@
  actionforblindpeople.org.uk
Hotel in own grounds near the seafront for blind and partially sighted people and their companions.

WEYMOUTH, Dorset
Anchor House
3 Holland Road, Weymouth, Dorset.
Contact: Livability.
- 08456 584478
- info@livability.org.uk
- www.livability.org.uk
Victorian house owned by Livability, adapted for wheelchair users.

Wimborne & Ferndown Lions Club Caravans
Littlesea Holiday Park, Near Weymouth.
Contact: Frank Fortey, 23 Egdon Drive, Wimborne BH21 1TY.
- 01202 886022
- www.lions.org.uk/wimborne-ferndown
Caravan designed for disabled people. Sited on Haven holiday park by Chesil Beach.

NAS ASSESSED ACCOMMODATION

AWRE NEAR NEWNHAM ON SEVERN, Gloucestershire
Priory Cottages
Four star self-catering
- 01594 516260

BATH, Somerset
Carfax Hotel
Two star townhouse
- 0122 546 2089
- sylvia.back@carfaxhotel.co.uk

SACO Bath
Four star Ssrviced apartments
- 0845 1220 405
- janejones@sacoapartments.co.uk
- www.sacoapartments.co.uk

BEAMINSTER, Dorset
Stable Cottage
Four star self-catering
- +44 01308 862305
- meerhay@aol.com

BOOKHAM, ALTON PANCRAS, Dorset
Bookham Court
Four and Five star self-catering
- 01300 345511
- andy.foot1@btinternet.com

BOURNEMOUTH, Dorset
BOD
Four star self-catering
- 01202 423046
- admin@afash.co.uk
- www.afash.co.uk

BRISTOL
Malago Bed and Breakfast
Three star guest accommodation
- 0117 9394 692
- info@themalago.com

BURTON BRADSTOCK, Dorset
Norburton Hall
Four and Five star self-catering
- 0130 8897 007
- info@norburtonhall.com
- www.norburtonhall.com

CHARD, Somerset
Tamarack Lodge
Four star self-catering
- +44 01823 601270
- matthew.sparks@tamaracklodge.co.uk

CHEDDAR, Somerset
YHA Cheddar
Three star hostel
- 0870 7708 868
- neilbaldwin@yha.org.uk
- www.yha.org.uk

CHICKERELL, Dorset
Tidmoor Self Catering Cottages
Four star self-catering
- 0130 578 7867
- sarah@tidmoorstables.co.uk
- tidmoorstales.co.uk

The Lugger Inn
Three star Inn
- 0130 5766 611
- ralph@theluggerinn.co.uk
- www.theluggerinn.co.uk

CORFE CASTLE, Dorset
Mortons House Hotel
Three star hotel
- 01929 480988
- bev@mortonshouse.co.uk
- www.mortonshouse.co.uk

CROSCOMBE, WELLS, Somerset
St Marys Lodge
Four star self-catering
- 01749 342157
- st.maryslodge@talktalk.net
- www.st-marys-lodge.co.uk

DORCHESTER, Dorset
Aquila Heights
Four star guest accommodation
- 01305 267145
- enquiries@aquilaheights.co.uk
- www.aquilaheights.co.uk

EXFORD, Somerset
Westermill Farm
Three star self-catering
- +44 01643 831238
- holidays@westermill-exmoor.co.uk

FAULKLAND, Somerset
Lime Kiln Farm Cottages
Five star self-catering
- 0122 5830 830
- limekilnfarm@live.co.uk

FERNDOWN, Dorset
Birchcroft
Four star self-catering
- holidayinndorset@btinternet.com

GLOUCESTER, Gloucestershire
Deerhurst Cottages
Four star self-catering
- 01684 275845
- enquiries@deerhurstcottages.co.uk
- www.deerhustcottages.co.uk

GODNEY, Somerset
Double-Gate Farm
Four star farmhouse
- 01458 832217
- doublegatefarm@aol.com
- www.doublegatefarm.com

GORWELL, Dorset
Gorwell Farm Cottages
Four star self-catering
- 01305 871401
- mary@gorwellfarm.co.uk

HIGH LITTLETON, Somerset
Greyfield Farm Cottages
Four and Five star self-catering
- 0176 1471 132
- june@greyfieldfarm.com
- www.greyfieldfarm.com

HORSINGTON, Somerset
Half Moon Inn
Three star Inn
- +44 01963 370140
- halfmoon@horsington.co.uk
- www.horsington.co.uk

HUNTWORTH, Somerset
Lakeview Holiday Cottages
Four star self-catering
- 0127 866 1584
- jayne@snotaroholdings.co.uk
- www.lakeviewholidaycottages.co.uk

LANGTON HERRING / RODDEN, Dorset

Character Farm Cottages

Four star self-catering

- 01305 871347
- jane@characterfarmcottages.co.uk
- www.characterfarmcottages.co.uk

LITTLEDEAN, Gloucestershire

Orchard Barn & Meadow Byre

Five star self-catering

- 01594 827311
- geoff@searanckes.com
- www.forestbarnholidays.co.uk

LONG BREDY, Dorset

Stables Cottage

Four star self-catering

- 0130 5789 000
- shane@dream-cottages.co.uk
- www.dream-cottages.co.uk

LYDNEY, GLOUCESTERSHIRE, Gloucestershire

The Lodge

Four star self-catering

- 01594 843745
- allaston-lodge@hotmail.co.uk

LYTCHETT MINSTER, Dorset

South Lytchett Manor Caravan & Camping Park

Five star holiday, touring and camping park

- 01202 622 577
- info@southlytchettmanor.co.uk
- www.southlytchettmanor.co.uk

MALMESBURY, Wiltshire

Best Western Mayfield House Hotel

Three star hotel

- 0166 657 409
- reception@mayfieldhousehotel.co.uk
- www.mayfieldhousehotel.co.uk

MINEHEAD, Somerset

Woodcombe Lodges

Four star self-catering

- +44 01643 702789
- nicola@woodcombelodge.co.uk

NEWENT, Gloucestershire

Leadon View Barn

Four star self-catering

- 0153 1660 362
- alan@muchmarcle.f9.co.uk

NR LYDNEY, Gloucestershire

2 Danby Cottages

Four star self-catering

- 0117 9422301
- glawes@talktalk.net

PARKEND, Gloucestershire

The Fountain Inn & Lodge

Three star Inn

- 01594 562189
- thefountaininn@aol.com

POOLE, Dorset

Gateway and Woodland Cottages

Three star self-catering

- 0120 2631 063
- facilities@holtonlee.co.uk
- www.holtonlee.co.uk

The New Beehive Hotel

Three star Small hotel

- 0120 270 1531
- info@thenewbeehive.co.uk
- www.thenewbeehive.co.uk

RADSTOCK, Somerset

The Garden House

Five star self-catering

- 0176 124 1080
- jclayton@janeclayton.co.uk
- www.lilycombe.co.uk

SOUTH BARROW, Somerset

The Stables

Four star self-catering

- 0196 3440 421
- a-nixon@btconnect.com

STATHE, Somerset

Walkers Farm Cottages

Four star self-catering

- 01823 698229
- info@walkersfarmcottages.co.uk

STAWELL, Somerset

Buzzard Heights B & B

Four star guest accommodation

- 0127 8722 743
- teresa@buzzardheights.co.uk
- www.buzzardheights.co.uk

STOKE ABBOTT, Dorset

Lewesdon Farm Holidays

Four star self-catering

- 01308 868270
- lewesdonfarmcottages@tiscali.co.uk

TAUNTON, Somerset

Holly Farm Cottages

Four star self-catering

- 0182 349 0828
- robhembrow@btinternet.com

TINCLETON, Dorset

Tincleton Lodge and Rose Cottage

Five star self-catering

- 01305 848391
- enquiries@dorsetholidaycottages.net
- www.dorsetholidaycottages.net

TYTHERINGTON, Somerset

The Lighthouse

Four star guest accommodation

- 01373 453585
- kay@lighthouse-uk.com
- www.lighthouse-uk.com

UPWEY, Dorset

Millspring

Four star self-catering

- 0130 5789 000
- shane@dream-cottages.co.uk
- www.dream-cottages.co.uk

WEST MILTON, Dorset

Lancombes House

Four star self-catering

- 01308 485375
- info@lancombes-house.co.uk
- www.lancombes-house.co.uk

WESTON SUPER MARE, Somerset

Spreyton House

Four star bed & breakfast

- 0193 4416 887
- info@spreytonguesthouse.com

The Royal Hotel

Three star hotel

- 0193 4423 100
- jonathan@royalhotelweston.com
- www.royalhotelweston.com

WEYMOUTH, Dorset

Jubilee View Apartment

Three star self-catering

- jendeagle@aol.com
- www.jubileeview.webeden.co.uk

WINFORD, Somerset

Winford Manor Hotel

Three star hotel

- 0127 5472 292
- traceybeck@winfordmanor.co.uk
- www.winfordmanor.co.uk

WINSLEY, Wiltshire

Church Farm Country Cottages

Four star self-catering

- 01225 722246
- stay@churchfarmcottages.com
- www.churchfarmcottages.com

WOOLLAND, Dorset

Ellwood Cottages

Four star self-catering

- 01258 818 196
- admin@ellwoodcottages.co.uk
- www.ellwoodcottages.co.uk

About Devon & Cornwall

The two counties of England's south west peninsula have long been a major holiday destination and offer a wide range of attractions for visitors.

Nowhere is far from the sea and there are a series of resorts around the coast. The Torbay towns of Torquay and Paignton are known as the English Riviera because of their mild climate and high-class entertainment. Parts of the coast are hilly, although east Devon resorts such as Exmouth and Sidmouth are fairly level as is Penzance in the far west. At other resorts such as Ilfracombe, St Ives, Newquay or Falmouth a car may be needed away from the seafront itself.

Much of the coastal scenery is dramatic. Among the places where this can be experienced are at the cliff-top National Trust car park at Wheel Coates near St Agnes, with its view over the North Cornwall cliffs and old tin mines, and Lands End. Marine life can be experienced at the National Seal Sanctuary near Helston and the National Marine Aquarium at Plymouth.

Inland, the countryside can also be wild, particularly in the National Parks of Dartmoor and Exmoor and areas such as Bodmin Moor in Cornwall. However, there are plenty of opportunities to experience the countryside and its activities at attractions such as Mount Edgcumbe Country Park overlooking Plymouth Sound, or the Crealy Farm Adventure Park in east Devon. At the Eden Project, outside St Austell, a dramatic global garden has been developed in a disused china clay pit.

Longer established planting can be enjoyed at the Royal Horticultural Society's Rosemoor Garden at Torrington.

Historic buildings in the area include Okehampton Castle in Devon owned by English Heritage, Buckfast Abbey and a number of National Trust properties such as Saltram House and Killerton House & Garden both near Exeter.

In Plymouth, the region's largest city, the National Marine Aquarium is a major attraction and the Plymouth Dome, on the Hoe, uses multi-media displays to show the civic and maritime history of the area. Exeter, county town of Devon, still has many old buildings especially in the area around the Cathedral. Truro is the location of the Royal Cornwall Museum. Other attractive towns include Barnstaple and Bideford in north Devon.

For family outings there is Flambards Theme Park near Helston or a trip on the Seaton Tramway in East Devon, both having facilities for disabled visitors. Finally, this is a region with distinctive food, be it genuine Cornish Pasties, fresh caught fish or the widely available cream teas.

Resources

Tourism

South West Tourism

Woodwater Park, Exeter EX2 5WT.

- 013 9222 9168
- info@swtourism.org.uk
- www.visitsouthwest.co.uk

The official tourist board for the South West. General tourist information is provided on their website. See also www.accessiblesouthwest.co.uk which provides more specific information for disabled people.

Transport

Richard Willson Accessible Transport Services

49 Carne View Road, Probus, Truro TR2 4HZ.

- 01726 883460
- Richard.willson@btconnect.com
- www.carehomemoves.co.uk

A well-established transport provider offering ambulance and accessible minibus services for wheelchair users, with or without their companions. Escorts and care attendants can be supplied. Journeys to and from the region are undertaken and guided tours can be arranged. Information on a range of disability matters can be given.

Information and Advice

DIAL

Offer free, impartial and confidential information and advice by telephone to disabled people, their relatives and professionals. Local branches of DIAL are constantly changing but at the time of writing, the following groups were members of DIAL UK and may be able to help visitors in their areas. Please call before travelling to check whether the service and organisation is still available.

DIAC Plymouth

- 01752 201065
  Textphone 01752 201766

Cornwall Disabled Association

1 Riverside House, Heron Way, Newham, Truro TR1 2XN.

- 01872 273518
- 01872 273518
- info@cornwalldisabled.co.uk
- www.cornwalldisabled.co.uk

Provide holidays, in conjunction with Social Services, for disabled residents of Cornwall and has adapted caravans at Par Sands and Rejerrah that are also available to people from outside the county. The Association also has 20 and 48 seat accessible coaches for group hire and runs monthly outings.

Equipment Hire

SHOPMOBILITY

The National Federation of Shopmobility UK (NFSUK), PO Box 6641, Christchurch, BH23 9DQ.

- 0844 41 41 850
- info@shopmobilityuk.org
- www.shopmobilityuk.org

Hire manual and powered wheelchairs and scooters. Have a range of branches around the UK. You can find the nearest Shopmobility schemes to you on their on-line Directory. Access is obtained by clicking on the 'Shopmobility Directory' button on the top of the row to the left of their website and using the search criteria. You

Bocaddon Holiday Cottages

Three cottages, specially designed to accommodate the needs of the less able-bodied.

Accessible throughout, fitted with large bathrooms with level flooring, roll-in shower seats and plenty of hand rails.

Bocaddon Farm, Lanreath,
Looe, Cornwall PL13 2PG.
Contact: Mrs Alison Maiklem
Tel: 01503 220192
Email: holidays@bocaddon.com
www.bocaddon.com

**is committed
to being accessible
to all**

www.torbay.gov.uk/disability

Brean Park Farm

Luxury holiday accommodation in
South East Cornwall

Converted barn, fully equipped and able to accommodate up to eight people plus a cot, with two double and two twin bedrooms. An ideal choice for those who want both quality and luxury in a rural idyll.

Email enquiries@breanparkfarm.co.uk
Telephone 01208 87218
www.breanparkfarm.co.uk

Devon's Hotel of The Year 2010/11

M5 exit 29, A30 to Honiton, 15mins
Open Daily, including Mondays
For Coffee, Lunch, Afternoon Tea & Dinner

"In Top 3 Best Foodie Hotels
in South West England"
*as voted by readers of
FOOD Magazine 2012*

Combe House Devon
HOTEL, RESTAURANT & GARDENS
Gittisham, Nr Honiton,
EXETER, Devon EX14 3AD
Tel: 01404 540 400
www.combehousedevon.com

will need to contact a specific Shopmobility Scheme in order to make equipment bookings or find out detailed information. General and contact information is contained in their Directory.

Braunton Mobility

3 Cross Tree Centre, Braunton, Devon EX33 1AA.
- 01271 814577
- www.mobilityinbraunton.co.uk

Manual wheelchairs and scooters are available for hire as well as a wide range of equipment for sale.

Exeter Community Transport Association

8-10 Paris Street, Exeter EX1 1GA.
- 01392 494001
- exetercta@aol.com
- www.exetercta.co.uk

In association with Exeter Shopmobility there is a long term loan service for both residents and visitors for use anywhere. They have manual wheelchairs at £2.50 a day and two portable scooters at £5 per day.

HSC Mobility

Mobility House, Unit 16 Marsh Lane Industrial Park, Hayle, Cornwall, TR27 5JR.
- 01736 755927
- info@hsc-mobility.co.uk
- www.hsc-mobility.co.uk

Wheelchairs, scooters, hoists, adjustable beds and other equipment are available for hire.

Pluss

The Pluss Organisation, 22 Marsh Green Rd, Marsh Barton, Exeter, EX2 8LB
- 01271 347934
- www.pluss.org.uk

Have manual and electric wheelchairs, scooters and some other equipment available for hire.

Tremorvah Industries

Unit 8, Threemilestone Industrial Estate, Truro, Cornwall TR4 9LD.
- 01872 324340
  Textphone 01872 324364
- enquiries.tremorvah@cornwall.gov.uk
- www.tremorvah.co.uk

Hire and sell manual and powered wheelchairs, scooters, commodes, hoists and a range of other equipment. Deliveries can be made throughout Cornwall.

Publications

Easy-Going Dartmoor
- 01822 890414
- www.dartmoor-npa.gov.uk

A guide giving information on walks, driving routes, viewpoints and access information to Dartmoor towns and villages suitable for disabled people. Produced by Dartmoor National Park Authority, The High Moorland Visitor Centre, Old Duchy Hotel, Princetown, Yelverton PL20 6QF. Also available to download from the website.

The English Riviera: Access for All

Regularly updated leaflet for Torquay, Paignton and Brixham. Available free at Tourist Information Centres in each town or from English Riviera Tourist Board, The Tourist Centre, Vaughan Parade, Torquay TQ2 5JG.
- 01803 211211 or 084 4474 2233
- holiday@englishriviera.co.uk
- www.englishriviera.co.uk

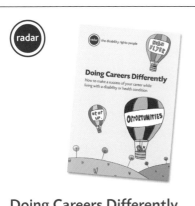

Online resources

www.accessiblesouthwest.co.uk

A website providing information on accessible accommodation, attractions, places of interest, places to eat, public toilets, and beaches in the region. There is also information on disability groups and organisations that can assist the disabled traveller whilst staying away from home, as well as local suppliers of accessibility equipment to hire.

www.dartmoor.co.uk

Dartmoor's official tourism website contains information about places to stay, things to do and routes to further information. Information about accommodation grading can be found at:

- www.dartmoor.co.uk/where-to-stay/grading

Dartmoor iPhone app

Updated regularly, the app provides a comprehensive and interactive guide to Dartmoor National Park and surrounding towns. Information on where to stay, what to do, eating out and what's on. Maps show you where you are in relation to nearby hotels, activities, attractions, shops and events. Search and refine results for prices, opening times, directions and descriptions. The app can be downloaded at:

- www.dartmoor.co.uk/plan-your-visit/dartmoor-iphone-app

Accommodation

BARNSTAPLE, Devon

Calvert Trust Exmoor

Wistlandpound, Kentisbury, Barnstaple EX31 4SJ.

- 01598 763221 (also Textphone)
- exmoor@calvert-trust.org.uk

Self-catering units attached to Activity Centre for disabled people with their families and friends.

BEAWORTHY, Devon

Blagdon Farm Country Holidays

Ashwater, Beaworthy EX21 5DF.

- 01409 211509
- info@blagdon-farm.co.uk
- www.blagdon-farm.co.uk

Self-catering cottages designed to be useable by disabled people, in the countryside 1½ miles from the village in West Devon.

BODMIN, Cornwall

Churchtown Lodges

Churchtown, Lanlivery, Bodmin PL30 5BT.
Apply: Vitalise Bookings Office

- 0845 345 1970

Vitalise chalets designed for disabled people at their Adventure Centre.

Penrose Burden Cottages

St Breward, near Bodmin PL30 4LZ.
Apply: Mrs Hall

- 01208 850277
- www.penroseburden.co.uk

Cottages designed for disabled people in Cornwall.

COLYTON, Devon

Smallicombe Farm

Northleigh, Colyton EX24 6BU.

T 01404 831310

E stay@smallicombe.com

W www.smallicombe.com

Converted barns designed for disabled people in Devon.

EXMOUTH, Devon

Scout Holiday Homes Trust Caravans

Apply: Scout Holiday Home Trust (see voluntary organisations in useful resources)

T 020 8433 7290

Adjacent adapted units in Exmouth, Devon.

IVYBRIDGE, Devon

Hannah's Holiday Lets

Dame Hannah Rogers School, Ivybridge PL21 9HQ.

T 01752 898100

E jane@dhrs.co.uk

Bungalows designed for wheelchair users in Ivybridge, Devon.

PAIGNTON, Devon

Scout Holiday Homes Trust Caravan

Hoburne Torbay, Grange Road, Goodrington, Paignton TQ4 7JP.

Apply: Scout Holiday Home Trust (see voluntary organisations in useful resources)

T 020 8433 7290

Adapted units with views over Torbay.

PAR, Cornwall

CDA Caravan

Par Beach Sands Holiday Park, Par Beach.

Apply: Cornwall Disabled Association

T 01872 273518

Purpose-built caravan on coastal holiday park near the Eden Project.

REJERRAH, Cornwall

CDA Caravan

Monkey Tree Holiday Park, Scotland Road, Rejerrah TR8 5QR

Apply: Cornwall Disabled Association.

T 01872 273518

Purpose-built caravan site in central Cornwall a few miles from the north coast.

ST AUSTELL, Cornwall

Scout Holiday Homes Trust Caravans

Pentewan Sands Holiday Park, St Austell PL26 6BT.

Apply: Scout Holiday Home Trust (see voluntary organisations in useful resources)

T 020 8433 7290

Adjacent adapted units on coastal site.

TEIGNMOUTH, Devon

Cliffden

Dawlish Road, Teignmouth TQ14 8TE.

T 01626 770052

E cliffden@visionhotels.co.uk

W www.visionhotels.co.uk

Hotel in large grounds near seafront and town centre for visually impaired people and their companions.

TORQUAY, Devon

Park House

1 Park Road, St Marychurch, Babbacombe, Torquay.

Apply: Livability

T 08456 584478

E info@livability.org.uk

W www.livability.org.uk

Self-catering ground floor flat in Torquay, fully adapted for wheelchair users.

TRURO, Cornwall

Trenona Farm
Trenona Farm, Ruan High Lanes, Truro, Cornwall TR2 5JS.
📞 01872 501339
📧 info@trenonafarmholidays.co.uk
🌐 www.trenonafarmholidays.co.uk
Contact – Pam Carbis
Enjoy a warm welcome on Trenona's working farm on the Roseland Peninsula. Set in an 'Area of Outstanding Natural Beauty', they offer four star accessible holiday cottages and three star en-suite bed and breakfast accommodation in a Victorian farmhouse. Children and pets welcome.

WESTWARD HO! Devon

BREAK Chalets
Golden Bay Holiday Village, Westward Ho!, near Bideford.
Apply: BREAK, 1 Montague Road, Sheringham NR26 8WN.
📞 01263 822161
📧 office@break-charity.org
🌐 www.break-charity.org
Chalets on holiday park overlooking Bideford Bay.

WOOLACOMBE, Devon

Lions Bungalow
Golden Coast Holiday Village, Woolacombe.
Apply: Mr Taylor, Ilfracombe & District Lions Club, Danesbury, King Street, Combe Martin EX34 0AD.

📞 01271 883677
Purpose-built bungalow for wheelchair users and their families.

NAS ASSESSED ACCOMMODATION

AXMINSTER, Devon

Goodlands
Five star self-catering
📞 0129 7320 36
📧 info@hedgehogcorner.co.uk
🌐 www.hedgehogcorner.co.uk

BODMIN, Cornwall

Lanhydrock Hotel and Golf Club
Three star hotel
📞 01208 262570
📧 manager@lanhydrockhotel.com
🌐 www.lanhydrockhotel.com

BOSCASTLE, Cornwall

Reddivallen Farmhouse
Five star guest accommodation
📞 01840 250854
📧 liz@redboscastle.com
🌐 www.redboscastle.com

The Old Coach House
Four star guest accommodation
📞 0184 025 0398
📧 info@old-coach.co.uk
🌐 www.old-coach.co.uk

BRAUNTON, Devon

Phoenix Retreat
Four star self-catering
📞 0127 1816 577
📧 phoenixcare@tdlmail.co.uk
🌐 www.phoenixholidayretreat.co.uk

BUCKLAND BREWER, Devon
West Hele
Three and Four star self-catering
- 01237 451044
- lorna.hicks@virgin.net
- www.westhele.co.uk

BUDLEIGH SALTERTON, Devon
Badgers Den
Four star self-catering
- 0139 544 3282
- mandydickinson3@btinternet.com
- www.holidaycottagedevon.com

CHAPEL AMBLE, Cornwall
The Olde House
Three and Four star self-catering
- 01208 813 219
- info@theoldehouse.co.uk
- www.theoldehouse.co.uk

COLYTON, Devon
Smallicombe Farm
Four star self-catering
- +44 01404 831310
- maggie_todd@yahoo.com
- www.smallicombe.com

CROWS-AN-WRAY, Cornwall
Tredinney Farm Holiday Cottage
Three and Four star self-catering
- 01736 810352
- rosemary.warren@btopenworld.com
- www.tredinneyfarm.co.uk

DAVIDSTOW, Cornwall
Pendragon Country House
Five star guest accommodation
- 01840 261131
- enquiries@
  pendragoncountryhouse.com
- www.pendragoncountryhouse.com

EXETER, Devon
Hue's Piece
Four star self-catering
- +44 01392 466720
- annahamlyn@paynes-farm.co.uk

GOLANT, Cornwall
South Torfrey Farm
Four and Five star self-catering
- 01726 833126
- stf7@onetel.com
- www.southtorfreyfarm.com

Penquite Farm
Five star self-catering
- 0172 6833 319
- ruth@penquitefarm.co.uk
- www.penquitefarm.co.uk

GOLBERDON, NEAR CALLINGTON, Cornwall
Berrio Mill
Four star self-catering
- 01579 363252
- ivan@berriomill.co.uk
- www.berriomill.co.uk

GUNNISLAKE, Cornwall
Todsworthy Farm Holidays
Four star self-catering
- 01822 834744
- jon@todsworthyfarmholidays.co.uk
- www.todsworthyfarmholidays.co.uk

HARLYN BAY, Cornwall
Yellow Sands Cottages
Three and Four star self-catering
- +44 01637 881548
- yellowsands@btinternet.com

HAYLE, Cornwall
Rowan Barn
Four star farmhouse
- 0173 685 1223
- info@rowanbarn.co.uk

HIGH BICKINGTON, N.DEVON, Devon
Country Ways
Three and Four star self-catering
- 01769 5605305
- kate@country-ways.net
- www.country-ways.net

HOLCOMBE ROGUS, Devon
Whipcott Water Cottages
Four star self-catering
- +44 01823 672339
- bookings@oldlimekiln.freeserve.co.uk

ILFRACOMBE, Devon
Mullacott Farm
Four star guest accommodation
- 0127 1866 877
- relax@mullacottfarm.co.uk
- www.mullacottfarm.co.uk

KILKHAMPTON, Cornwall
Forda Lodges & Cottages
Four and Five star self-catering
- 0128 832 1413
- info@forda.co.uk
- www.forda.co.uk

LANREATH, LOOE, Cornwall
Bocaddon Holiday Cottages
Four star self-catering
- 0150 3220 192
- holidays@bocaddon.com

LIZARD, Cornwall
YHA Lizard Point
Four star hostel
- 0870 7708 868
- neilbaldwin@yha.org.uk
- www.yha.org.uk

LOOE, Cornwall
Lesquite
Bed & breakfast and self-catering apartments
- +44 01503 220315
- stay@lesquite.co.uk
- www.lesquite.co.uk

LOSTWITHIEL, Cornwall
Brean Park
Five star self-catering
- 01208 872184
- breanpark@btconnect.com
- www.breanpark.co.uk

Hartswell Farm
Four star self-catering
- 0120 8873 419
- hartswheal@connexions.co.uk
- www.connexions/hartswheal.co.uk

MORETONHAMPSTEAD, Devon
Budleigh Farm
Three star self-catering
- 01647 440835
- judith@budleighfarm.co.uk

MORVAL, Cornwall
Tudor Lodges
Four star self-catering
- 01579 320 344
- mollytudor@aol.com
- www.tudorlodges.co.uk

MOUNT HAWKE, Cornwall
Ropers Walk Barns
Four star self-catering
- 01209 891632
- peterandliz@roperswalkbarns.co.uk

MYLOR, Cornwall
Mylor Yacht Harbour – Admiralty Apartments
Four star self-catering
- 0132 637 2121
- culum@mylor.com

NEWQUAY, Cornwall
The Park
Four and Five star self-catering
- 0163 7860 322
- info@mawganporth.co.uk
- www.mawganporth.co.uk

NORTHLEIGH, Devon
Smallicombe Farm
Four star guest accommodation
- 01404 831310
- maggie_todd@yahoo.com
- www.smallicombe.com

NR CREDITON, Devon
Creedy Manor
Four star self-catering
- 01363 772684
- sandra@creedymanor.com
- www.creedymanor.com

OKEHAMPTON, Devon
Beer Farm
Four star self-catering
- 01837 840265
- info@beerfarm.co.uk
- www.beerfarm.co.uk

PADSTOW, Cornwall
Arum House
Four star bed & breakfast
- 01841 532364
- emmathompson7@sky.com
- www.padstow-bed-and-breakfast.com

PENZANCE, Cornwall
Hotel Penzance
Four star Townhouse
- +44 01736 363117
- enquiries@hotelpenzance.com
- www.hotelpenzance.com

PILLATON, Cornwall
Kernock Cottages
Five star self-catering
- 0157 935 0435
- hughbeth@kernockcottages.com
- www.kernockcottages.com

POLZEATH, Cornwall
Manna Place
Four star self-catering
- 01208 863258
- anniepolzeath@hotmail.com
- www.mannaplace.co.uk

PORTHTOWAN, Cornwall
Rose Hill Lodges
Five star self-catering
- 01209 891920
- reception@rosehilllodges.com
- www.rosehilllodges.com

PORTHTOWAN, Cornwall
Arvor Holidays
Four star self-catering
- 01209 891611
- pat@arvorholidays.com

PORTREATH, Cornwall
Gwel an Mor Lodges
Self-catering holiday lodges
- 02380 251992
- sandy@landish.co.uk

PORTSCATHO, Cornwall
Pollaughan Cottages
Four and Five star self-catering
- +44 01872 580150
- holidays@pollaughan.co.uk

REDMOOR, Cornwall
Chark Country Holidays
Four star self-catering
- +44 01208 871118
- charkholidays@tiscali.co.uk

REDRUTH, Cornwall
Higher Laity Farm
Five star self-catering
- 0120 9842 317
- info@higherlaityfarm.co.uk
- www.higherlaityfarm.co.uk

RUAN HIGH LANES, Cornwall
Trelagossick Farm
Three and Four star self-catering
- 0187 250 1338
- enquiries@trelagossickfarm.co.uk
- www.trelagossickfarm.co.uk

Trenona Farm Holidays
Four star self-catering
- 0187 250 1339
- pam@trenonafarmholidays.co.uk

SANDFORD, Devon
Ashridge Farm
Four star bed & breakfast
- 01363 774292
- jill@ashridgefarm.co.uk
- www.ashridgefarm.co.uk/

ST CLETHER, Cornwall
Ta Mill
Three and Four star self-catering
- +44 01840 261797
- helen@tamill.co.uk
- tamill.co.uk

ST ENDELLION, Cornwall
Tolraggott Farm Cottages
Four star self-catering
- +44 01208 880927
- email@rock-wadebridge.co.uk
- www.rock-wadebridge.co.uk

ST MARTINS, Cornwall
Bucklawren Farm
Four and Five star self-catering
- 01503 240738
- bucklawren@btopenworld.com
- bucklawarren.com

ST MARYS, Isles of Scilly
The Atlantic
Three star hotel
- 0172 6627 191
- neil.roberts@staustellbrewery.co.uk

Isles of Scilly Country Guest House
Three star guest house
- 01720 422 440
- scillyguesthouse@hotmail.co.uk
- www.scillyguesthouse.co.uk

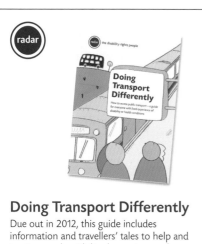

Doing Transport Differently

Due out in 2012, this guide includes information and travellers' tales to help and inspire people with lived experience of disability or health conditions to use public transport.

Available from Radar's online shop
www.radar-shop.org.uk

National Key Scheme Guide

Updated every year, this guide lists the location of almost 9,000 NKS toilets around the UK. It shows opening times, provider name and whether the toilet is unisex.

Available from Radar's online shop
www.radar-shop.org.uk

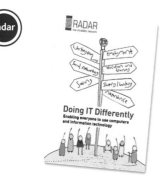

Doing IT Differently

Information to help everyone, regardless of disability, take advantage of information technology (IT) and computers. Includes advice on how to choose and use a computer, and how to adapt it to suit your needs.

Available from Radar's online shop
www.radar-shop.org.uk

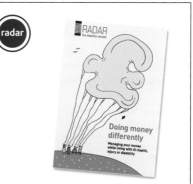

Doing Money Differently

Explores new ways of making, saving and looking after your money. This guide covers where your money comes from, where to keep it, where it goes and what to do if you are in debt.

Available from Radar's online shop
www.radar-shop.org.uk

ST VEEP, Cornwall
A Little Bit Of Heaven
Four star self-catering
- 01208 873295
- daphne@alittlebitofheaven.co.uk
- www.alittlebitiofheaven.co.uk

STRATTON, BUDE, Cornwall
Oak Lodge Bed and Breakfast
Four star bed & breakfast
- 0128 8354 144
- julie@oaklodgebude.com
- www.oaklodgebude.com

TORQUAY, Devon
Atlantis Holiday Apartments
Four star self-catering
- 01803 607929
- enquiry@atlantistorquay.co.uk
- www.atlantistorquay.co.uk

Crown Lodge
Four star guest accommodation
- 01803 298772
- stay@crownlodgehotel.co.uk
- www.crownlodgehotel.co.uk

WHITNAGE, Devon
West Pitt Farm
Three, Four and Five star self-catering
- +44 01884 820296
- susannewestgate@yahoo.com
- www.westpittfarm.co.uk

WIDECOMBE-IN-THE-MOOR, Devon
Wooder Manor Holiday Homes
Three and Four star self-catering
- 0136 4621 391
- angela@woodermanor.com
- www.woodermanor.com

About Eastern England

The East of England region includes Bedfordshire, Cambridgeshire, Essex, Hertfordshire, Norfolk and Suffolk. It stretches from the fringes of London and the Thames Estuary to the Wash and encompasses historic towns, varied countryside and a long coastline.

A string of coastal resorts, most with level promenades, cater for every taste of seaside holiday. Great Yarmouth, Clacton and Southend have a long

tradition of providing a range of lively entertainment for their visitors, whether staying in the area or on day trips. Quieter resorts include Hunstanton and Sheringham on the north Norfolk coast, Lowestoft and the old port of Southwold in Suffolk and Frinton in Essex. Harwich and Felixstowe are still important commercial ports as well as resorts.

The region is rich in historic houses and other buildings, including Colchester Castle in England's oldest town, Tilbury Fort, run by English Heritage where

Elizabeth I rallied her troops before the Spanish Armada, Melford Hall in Suffolk and Hatfield House in Hertfordshire. Ancient cathedrals and churches can be visited in Ely, Norwich, Peterborough, Bury St Edmunds and St Albans.

In Cambridge, visitors can join the regular walking tours to see the Colleges and other historic buildings. Norwich, which was once the 2nd largest town in the England has the largest collection of medieval buildings and street patterns in the country. Other notable towns in the area include Bedford, Huntingdon, Kings Lynn, Saffron Walden, Sudbury and Woodbridge. The countryside between Ipswich and Colchester was immortalised by painter John Constable.

The Norfolk Broads just inland from the coast on the Norfolk/Suffolk border is now a National Park and offers many opportunities for boating, bird watching and enjoying the unique scenery. Other sites of interest to country lovers include the Wildfowl & Wetlands Trust site at Welney near Peterborough, the National Trust's Wicken Fen near Ely and

Needham Lake in Suffolk. Country Parks with facilities for disabled visitors include Sandringham in West Norfolk and Aldenham at Elstree, Hertfordshire.

More formal gardens in the area include the Swiss Garden at Biggleswade in central Bedfordshire, the extensive Gardens of the Rose at St Albans and the University Botanic Garden at Cambridge. Near King's Lynn, Norfolk Lavender is a commercial lavender farm holding the national collection of the plant. Other outdoor attractions include the Museum of East Anglian Life at Stowmarket, Woburn Park in Bedfordshire and the Raptor Foundation near Huntingdon. The North Norfolk Railway, running between Sheringham and Holt has a restored coach equipped for wheelchair users. For an up-to-the-minute shopping experience the region has the Lakeside Shopping Centre at Thurrock.

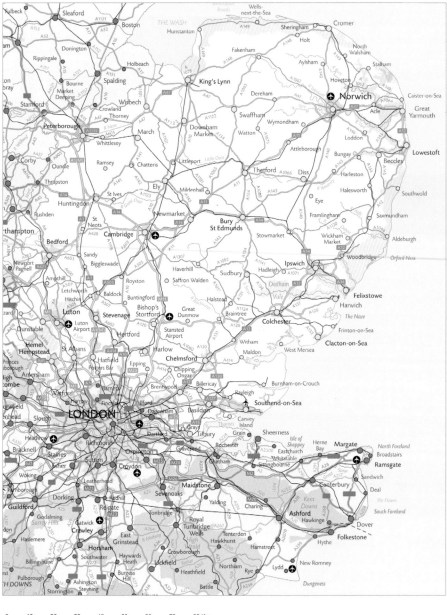

| 0 | 10 | 20 | 30 | 40 | 50 | 60 | 70 | 80 Km |

| 0 | 10 | 20 | 30 | 40 | 50 Miles |

Resources

Tourism

East of England Tourist Board

Bury St Edmunds Tourist Information
Centre, 6 Angel Hill, Bury St Edmunds,
Suffolk IP33 1UZ.

☎ 01284 764667

🌐 www.visiteastofengland.com

Official Tourist Board for the east England
region.

Travel

Awayadays

Stone Cottage, Front Road, Wood Dalling,
Norwich NR11 6RN.

☎ 01263 587005

✉ david@awayadays.com

🌐 www.awayadays.com

Operate day and package tours in Norfolk
and evening tours of Norwich in a 15-seat
coach equipped with a lift and that can
carry up to four passengers in wheelchairs.
Accessible refreshment and toilet stops can
be included. Pick-ups at railway stations
can be arranged, as can tailor-made tours
including the booking of accommodation.
Contact David McMaster.

Information & advice

Disability Essex

Moulsham Mill, Parkway, Chelmsford CM2 7PX.

☎ 084 4412 1771

✉ info@disabilityessex.org

🌐 www.disabilityessex.org

Provide holiday information to disabled
people in Essex as well as general
information on disability.

DIAL

Offer free, impartial and confidential
information and advice by telephone
to disabled people, their relatives and
professionals. Local branches of DIAL
are constantly changing but at the time
of writing, the following groups were
members of DIAL UK and may be able to
help visitors in their areas. Please call before
travelling to check whether the service and
organisation is still available:

DIAL Basildon

☎ 0845 450 3001/2

Optua Bury St Edmunds

☎ 01284 748800

Directions Plus, Cambridge

☎ 01223 569600
   Textphone 01223 569601

DRC Dunstable

☎ 01582 470900
   Textphone 01582 470959

DAS East Suffolk

☎ 01394 387070

Essex DPA

☎ 0870 873 6333
   Textphone 01245 253400

DIAL Great Yarmouth

☎ 01493 337651

DIS Huntingdonshire

☎ 01480 830036

Ipswich DAB

☎ 01473 217313

DIAL Lowestoft

☎ 01502 511333
   Textphone 01502 405453

Norfolk Coalition

☎ 01603 666951

DIAL Peterborough

☎ 01733 265551

DIAL Southend

☎ 0800 731 6372
   Textphone 01702 356031

Optua Stowmarket
- ☎ 01449 672781
  Textphone 01449 775999

West Norfolk DIS
- ☎ 01553 776177
  Textphone 01553 774766

Equipment Hire

SHOPMOBILITY

The National Federation of Shopmobility UK (NFSUK), PO Box 6641, Christchurch BH23 9DQ
- ☎ 0844 41 41 850
- ✉ Info@shopmobilityuk.org
- 🌐 www.shopmobilityuk.org

Hire manual and powered wheelchairs and scooters. Have a range of branches around the UK. You can find the nearest Shopmobility schemes to you on their on-line Directory. Access is obtained by clicking on the 'Shopmobility Directory' button on the top of the row to the left of their website and using the search criteria. You will need to contact a specific Shopmobility Scheme in order to make equipment bookings or find out detailed information. General and contact information is contained in their Directory.

The Disability Resource Centre

Poynters House, Poynters Road, Dunstable LU5 4TP.
- ☎ 01582 470900
- ✉ equipment@drcbeds.org.uk
- 🌐 www.drcbeds.org.uk

Have manual wheelchairs to hire on a short-term basis. They also have a number of small items of equipment for sale and can advise on local suppliers.

The HAND Partnership

Horning Road, West, Hoveton, NORWICH, NR12 8QJ.
- ☎ 01603784777
- 🌐 www.thpmobility.org.uk

Wheelchairs and scooters are available to hire for people living or on holiday in Norfolk. They also carry out scooter repairs.

Hertfordshire Action on Disability

The Woodside Centre, The Commons, Welwyn Garden City AL7 4DD.
- ☎ 01707 384260 (equipment hire)
  01707 375159 (transport)
- ✉ info@hadnet.org.uk
- 🌐 www.hadnet.org.uk

Operate a wheelchair hire scheme and an accessible transport service.

Maple Mobility DGT Services

Unit 7, Buckingham Court, Dairy Road, Dukes Park Industrial Estate, Chelmsford CM2 6XW.
- ☎ 01245 451514
- 🌐 www.maplemobility.co.uk

Manual and powered wheelchairs and scooters are available at weekly rates. Delivery and collection in the Chelmsford area.

Rainbow Services

2 Wych Elm, Harlow, Essex CM20 1QP.
- ☎ 01279 308151
- ✉ info@rainbowservices.org.uk
- 🌐 www.rainbowservices.org.uk

This community organisation has manual wheelchairs to hire for a moderate fee to residents and people visiting Harlow.

South East Mobility

49-51 Orsett Rd, Grays, Essex RM17 5HJ

🕾 0845 644 2892

📧 info@southeastmobility.co.uk

🌐 www.southeastmobility.co.uk

Company supplying a wide range of equipment for disabled people. Scooters, wheelchairs and some other equipment including a commode and bath lift are available for hire.

Publications

Access to Bedford

🕾 01234 221762 (for the access officer)

🌐 www.bedford.gov.uk

A range of leaflets giving information on accommodation, places to eat and transport. Produced by the Borough Council in association with Bedford Access Group. Available free from Bedford Tourist Information Centre, Town Hall, St Paul's Square, Bedford MK40 1SJ.

Accessible South Lincolnshire & West Norfolk

Written by John Killick and published by the Disabled Motorists Federation, this book provides information on the accessibility of places to visit and eat in the Fens. Available (price £3.50) from Mr J E Killick, 145 Knoulberry Road, Blackfell, Washington, Tyne & Wear NE37 1JN.

Accommodation

Norfolk Country Cottages

Carlton House, Market Place, Reepham NR10 4JJ.

🕾 01603 871872

📧 info@norfolkcottages.co.uk

🌐 www.norfolkcottages.co.uk

A leading provider of self-catering holiday accommodation in Norfolk. Their brochure indicates properties that have features for or may be suitable for disabled people.

CHIGWELL, Essex

Vitalise Jubilee Lodge

Grange Farm, High Road, Chigwell IG7 6DP.

🕾 020 8501 2331

Contact: Vitalise

🕾 0845 345 1970

📧 bookings@vitalise.org.uk

🌐 www.vitalise.org.uk

Centre on the edge of Epping Forest for breaks for people with disabilities.

CLACTON-ON-SEA, Essex

Groomshill

8 Holland Road, Clacton-on-Sea

Contact: Livability

🕾 08456 584478

📧 info@livability.org.uk

🌐 www.livability.org.uk

Holiday bungalow adapted for disabled people near town centre and seafront.

EAST HARLING, Norfolk

Berwick Cottage

School Lane, East Harling, Norfolk NR16 2LU.

🕾 01787 372343

📧 info@thelinberwicktrust.org.uk

🌐 www.thelinberwicktrust.org.uk

Purpose-built cottage in village between Thetford and Diss.

GREAT YARMOUTH, Norfolk
Scout Holiday Homes Trust Caravan
Seashore Holiday Park, North Denes, Great
Yarmouth, Norfolk, NR30 4HG.
Contact: Scout Holiday Homes Trust
- 020 8433 7290
Adapted unit in Great Yarmouth, Norfolk.

HOVETON, Norfolk
Broomhill
Station Road, Hoveton, near Wroxham.
Contact: Livability
- 08456 584478
- info@livability.org.uk
- www.livability.org.uk
Self-contained flats by Wroxham Broad,
owned by Livability, designed for wheelchair
users.

SANDRINGHAM, Norfolk
Park House
Sandringham, King's Lynn PE35 6EH.
- 01485 543000
- parkinfo@LCDisability.org
- www.parkhousehotel.org.uk
Country house hotel run by Leonard
Cheshire, for disabled people and their
companions.

SHERINGHAM, Norfolk
Rainbow Holiday Centre
15 Hooks Hill Road, Sheringham, Norfolk,
NR26 8NL.
- 01263 822161
- www.break-charity.org
Centre offering holidays, short breaks and
respite care for children and adults with
disabilities including those with high level
needs and challenging behaviour.

NAS ASSESSED ACCOMMODATION

ALDEBURGH, Suffolk
The Brudenell Hotel
Four star hotel
- 01728 452071
- manager@brudenellhotel.co.uk

ASHDON, Essex
Hill Farm Holiday Cottages
Three star self-catering
- 01799 584 881
- hillfarm-holiday-cottages@hotmail.
co.uk
- www.hillfarm-holiday-cottages.co.uk

AYLMERTON, Norfolk
Roman Camp Inn
Four star Inn
- 01263 838291
- enquiries@romancampinn.co.uk

BACTON, Norfolk
Primrose Cottage
Three star self-catering
- 01692 650667
- holiday@cablegap.co.uk
- www.ukparks.co.uk/cablegap

Castaways Holiday Park
Four star holiday park
- 01692 650 436 / 650418
- castaways.bacton@hotmail.co.uk
- www.castawaysholidaypark.co.uk

BECCLES, Suffolk
The Lodge
Four star self-catering
- 0150 2716 428
- karenrenilson@hotmail.com

BEESTON, Norfolk
Holmdene Farm
Three star self-catering
- 01328 701 284
- holmdenefarm@farmersweekly.net

BLAXHALL, Suffolk
YHA Blaxhall
Three star hostel
- 0870 7708 868
- neilbaldwin@yha.org.uk
- www.yha.org.uk

BOXFORD, Suffolk
Sherbourne Lodge Cottages
Four star self-catering
- +44 01787 210885
- enquiries@
  sherbournelodgecottages.co.uk
- www.sherbournecottages.co.uk

BURGH ST PETER, Norfolk
Waveney River Centre
Five star holiday park
- 01502 677343
- ruth@waveneyrivercentre.co.uk

CARLTON COLVILLE, LOWESTOFT, Suffolk
Ivy House Country Hotel
Hotel
- 01502 501353
- admin@ivyhousecountryhotel.co.uk

CHELMSFORD, Essex
Boswell House Hotel
Two star small hotel
- 0124 528 7587
- boswell118@aol.com

CRATFIELD, Suffolk
School Farm Cottages
Four star self-catering
- 01986 798844
- schoolfarmcotts@aol.com

CROMER, Norfolk
Incleborough House
Five star bed & breakfast
- 01263 515 939
- enquiries@incleboroughhouse.co.uk
- incleboroughhouse.co.uk

EAST HARLING, Norfolk
Berwick Cottage
Four star self-catering
- 01787 372343
- info@thelinberwicktrust.org.uk

EDGEFIELD, Norfolk
Wood Farm Cottages
Four star self-catering
- 01263 587347
- info@wood-farm.com

ELM, Cambridgeshire
The Elm Tree Inn
Four star Inn
- 0194 5587 009
- theelmtreeinn@mail.com
- www.elmtree-inn.com

FOXLEY WOOD, Norfolk
Moor Farm Stable Cottages
Three and Four star self-catering
- 0136 2688 523
- mail@moorfarmstablecottages.co.uk

FRITTON, Norfolk

Fritton Lake Lodges

Four star self-catering

- 01493 488666
- elaine@somerleyton.co.uk
- www.somerleyton.co.uk

GISSING, Norfolk

Norfolk Cottages Malthouse Farm

Four star self-catering

- 01379 674660
- bookings@norfolkcottages.net

GREAT BARTON, Suffolk

Wylene

Four star self-catering

- 0135 9271 130
- chriswhitton@aol.com

GREAT FINBOROUGH, Suffolk

Jack Bridge Cottage @ Jack Bridge Farm

Four star self-catering

- 01449 672177
- pembertons@jackbridgefarm.plus.com

GREAT SNORING, Norfolk

Vine Park Cottage

Four star farmhouse

- 01328 821016
- rita@vineparkcottagebandb.co.uk
- www.vineparkcottagebandb.co.uk

HAPPISBURGH, Norfolk

Church Farm Barns

Four star self-catering

- 0169 2650 137
- churchfarmbarns@hotmail.co.uk

HAPPISBURGH, Norfolk

Boundary Stables

Four star self-catering

- 01692 650 171
- bookings@boundarystables.co.uk
- boundarystables.co.uk

HAUGHLEY, Suffolk

Red House Farm

Three and Four star self-catering

- +44 01449 673323
- mary@redhousefarmhaughley.co.uk
- www.redhousefarmhaughley.co.uk

HEACHAM, Norfolk

Oakhill

Four star self-catering

- 0148 5534 267
- shohol@birdsnorfolk
  holidayhomes.co.uk
- www.norfolkholidayhomes-birds.co.uk

HENLEY, Suffolk

Damerons Farm Holidays

Four star self-catering

- 01473 832454
- info@dameronsfarmholidays.co.uk
- www.dameronsfarmholidays.co.uk

HITCHAM, Suffolk

The White Horse Inn

Four star Inn

- 0144 9740 981
- lewis@thewhitehorse.wanadoo.co.uk
- www.thewhitehorsehitcham.co.uk

HORNING, Norfolk

King Line Cottages

Three and Four star self-catering

- 01692 630297
- kingline@norfolk-broads.co.uk
- www.norfolk-broads.co.uk

HUNSTANTON, Norfolk
Foxgloves Cottage
Four star self-catering
- 01485 532 460
- deepdenehouse@btopenworld.com

KELLING, Norfolk
The Pheasant Hotel
Two star hotel
- +44 01263 588382
- enquiries@pheasanthotelnorfolk.co.uk

LITTLE DOWNHAM, Cambridgeshire
Wood Fen Lodge
Four star guest house
- +44 01353 862495
- info@woodfenlodge.co.uk

LITTLE SNORING, Norfolk
Jex Farm Barn and Stable
Four star self-catering
- 0132 887 8257
- farmerstephen@
  jexfarm.wanadoo.co.uk

MAUTBY, Norfolk
Lower Wood Farm Country Cottages
Four and Five star self-catering
- 0149 3722 523
- info@lowerwoodfarm.co.uk

METHWOLD, Norfolk
Next Door at Magdalen House
Four star self-catering
- 0136 6727 255
- k.cootes@btconnect.com
- www.magdalenhouse.co.uk

MICKFIELD, Suffolk
Read Hall Cottage
Five star self-catering
- 0144 9711 366
- info@readhall.co.uk

MIDDLEWOOD GREEN, Suffolk
Leys Farmhouse Annexe
Three star self-catering
- 01449 711 750
- hevtrev@btopenworld.com
- www.leysfarmhouseannexe.co.uk

MUNDESLEY, Norfolk
Overcliff Lodge
Four star guest house
- 01263 720 016
- overcliff.lodge@btinternet.com
- www.overclifflodge.co.uk

NAYLAND, Suffolk
Gladwins Farm
Four and Five star self-catering
- 0120 6262 261
- contact@gladwinsfarm.co.uk

NORWICH, Norfolk
Spixworth Hall Cottages
Four star self-catering
- +44 01603 898190
- hallcottages@btinternet.com

OLD HUNSTANTON, Norfolk
Caley Hall Hotel
Three star hotel
- +44 01485 533486
- mail@caleyhallhotel.co.uk

PAKEFIELD, Suffolk
Pakefield Caravan Park
Four star holiday park
- T +44 01502 561136
- E shelley@normanhurst.net

REYDON, SOUTHWOLD, Suffolk
Newlands Country House
Four star guest accommodation
- T 0150 272 2164
- E newlandssouthwold@tiscali.co.uk

SAINT OSYTH, Essex
Lee Wick Farm Holiday Cottages
Four star self-catering
- T 01255 823 031
- E info@leewickfarm.co.uk

SANDRINGHAM, Norfolk
Park House Hotel
Three star hotel
- T 0148 554 3000
- E tess.gilder@lcdisability.org

SHERINGHAM, Norfolk
Sheringham Cottages
Four star self-catering
- T 01263 577560
- E trevor.claydon@which.net
- W www.sheringhamcottages.com

YHA Sheringham
Three star hostel
- T 0870 7708 868
- E neilbaldwin@yha.org.uk
- W www.yha.org.uk

SHOTLEY, Suffolk
Orwell View Barns
Five star self-catering
- T 0147 3788 497
- E info@orwellviewbarns.co.uk
- W www.orwellviewbarns.co.uk

SIBTON, Suffolk
Park Farm Sibton
Four star self-catering
- T 0172 8668 324
- E annelawrence28@btinternet.com

SOUTH WALSHAM, Norfolk
Break-O-Day
Self-catering house
- T 0126 3715 779
- E info@norfolkcottages.co.uk

SWILLAND, Suffolk
Swilland Mill
Five star self-catering
- T 0147 3785 122
- E jamieprojoin@aol.com

THORPE-LE-SOKEN, Essex
Lifehouse Country Spa Resort
Four star hotel
- T 0125 5863 464
- E marco.t@lifehouse.co.uk
- W www.lifehouse.co.uk

TITCHWELL, Norfolk
Titchwell Manor Hotel
Three star hotel
- T +44 01485 210221
- E margaret@titchwellmanor.com

TRIMINGHAM, Norfolk
Woodland Leisure Park
Four star holiday and Touring park
- 0126 3579 208
- liz@woodland-park.co.uk
- www.woodland-park.co.uk

WALTON-ON-THE-NAZE, Essex
Bufo Villae Guest House
Four star guest accommodation
- 01255 672644
- www.bufovillae.co.uk

WATTISFIELD, Suffolk
Jayes Holiday Cottages
Three star self-catering
- 01359 251255
- info@jayesholidaycottages.co.uk
- www.jayesholidaycottages.co.uk

WATTISHAM, Suffolk
Wattisham Hall Holiday Cottages
Four star self-catering
- 01449 744288
- michellesquirrell212@btinternet.com

WELLS-NEXT-THE-SEA, Norfolk
YHA Wells-next-the-Sea Youth Hostel
Four star hostel
- 0870 7708 868
- neilbaldwin@yha.org.uk
- www.yha.org.uk

WENDLING, NEAR DEREHAM, Norfolk
Greenbanks and Three Palms Leisure Pool
Four star guest accommodation
- 1362 687742
- enquiries@greenbankshotel.co.uk

WEST RUDHAM, Norfolk
Oyster House
Four star bed & breakfast
- 01485 528327
- oyster-house@tiscali.co.uk

WISSETT, Suffolk
The Old Stables, Wissett Lodge
Four star self-catering
- 01986 873173
- mail@wissettlodge.co.uk

WORTHAM, Suffolk
Ivy House Farm
Four star self-catering
- +44 01379 898395
- prjsbrad@aol.com

About the East Midlands

This region, ranging from the wide, flat Fens to the mountainous Peak District, comprises the counties of Derbyshire, Leicestershire, Lincolnshire, Northamptonshire, Nottinghamshire and Rutland.

Around the Lincolnshire coast resorts such as Cleethorpes, Skegness and Mablethorpe provide the opportunity for seaside holidays with a level seafront and much traditional entertainment. Inland there is a choice between staying in historic towns or more rural localities.

Many important historic events took place and myths were formed in the area. You can learn more of Hereward the Wake in the Fens around Crowland or Robin Hood in Nottingham and Sherwood Forest. The Wars of the Roses ended at Bosworth in Leicestershire, where there is a Visitor Centre and Country Park, and the Civil War began at Nottingham Castle, now an art gallery and museum.

The two largest cities in the region are Leicester and Nottingham. Both provide opportunities to enjoy music, theatre and sporting events and have a variety of attractions depicting the history and industries of the area. Other important towns include Derby, Northampton and Lincoln, with its magnificent Cathedral towering over the surrounding countryside at the top of a steep hill.

Many smaller towns are also worth visiting. At Boston the church tower dominates the surrounding fenland. In nearby Spalding the Springfields Gardens are renowned, as befits a town that is the centre of Britain's major flower growing area. Another town proud of its parks is Buxton where the Museum has an exhibition on the surrounding Peak District. The twisted spire on the parish church of Chesterfield is another of the noted landmarks of the region.

Most of the Peak District National Park is in Derbyshire. Other countryside attractions include accessible trails in Grafton Park and Boughton Park near

Kettering, the Saltfleetby National Nature Reserve on the Lincolnshire Coast and the National Trust's Clumber Park in north Nottinghamshire. There are opportunities for water sports, birdwatching, fishing and many other activities at Rutland Water. Life on an Edwardian estate can be experienced at Elvaston Country Park near Derby.

The region is the home of a number of transport attractions including the Crich Tramways Village in Derbyshire, the Great Central Railway in Nottinghamshire and Leicestershire and the National Space Science Centre at Leicester. Those with literary interests can compare the background of D H Lawrence at the Durban House Heritage Centre at Eastwood with that of Lord Byron at Newstead Abbey only a few miles away in the outskirts of Nottingham.

203

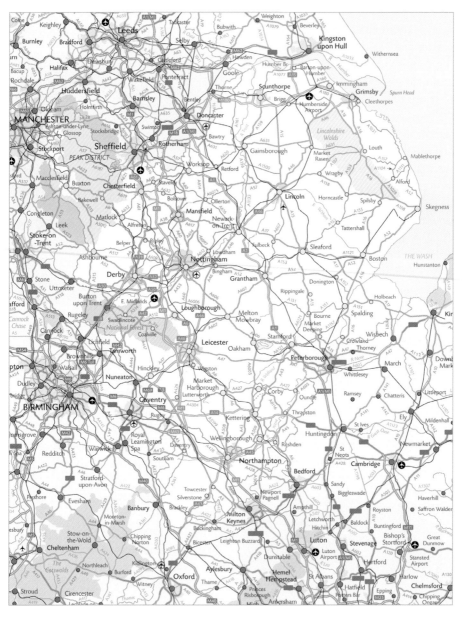

| 0 | 10 | 20 | 30 | 40 | 50 | 60 | 70 | 80 Km |

| 0 | 10 | 20 | 30 | 40 | 50 Miles |

Resources

Tourism

Tourist Information Centres

You can locate details of Tourist Information Centres throughout this region using the destination finder in the Enjoy England website. You will also find destination guides, ideas, events, attractions and accommodation:

- Ⓦ www.enjoyengland.com/ DestinationFinder

Information & advice

Mosaic: shaping disability services

2 Oak Spinney Park, Ratby Lane, Leicester Forest East LE3 3AW.

- Ⓣ 0116 2318720
- Ⓔ enquiries@mosaic1898.co.uk
- Ⓦ www.mosaic1898.co.uk

Voluntary organisation providing a range of services to disabled people, their families and carers. They have two accessible self-catering bungalows at Overstrand, North Norfolk. Bookings are always taken on a first come, first served basis. During high season bookings are only taken for one week at a time. At other times you can book for a fortnight.

Disability Lincs Ltd

Ancaster Day Centre, Boundary Street, Lincoln LN5 8NJ.

- Ⓣ 01522 870602
- Ⓔ enquiries@disabilitylincs.org.uk
- Ⓦ www.disabilitylincs.org.uk

Enquiries to the administrative officer.

DIAL

Offer free, impartial and confidential information and advice by telephone to disabled people, their relatives and professionals. Local branches of DIAL are constantly changing but at the time of writing, the following groups were members of DIAL UK and may be able to help visitors in their areas. Please call before travelling to check whether the service and organisation is still available:

Brigg Carers' Support Centre

- Ⓣ 01652 650585

Disability Direct, Derby

- Ⓣ 01332 299449: 01332 368585

Leicester CIL

- Ⓣ 0116 222 5005

DIAL Mansfield

- Ⓣ 01623 625891

DIAL Northants Corby

- Ⓣ 01536 204742

DIAL Northants Daventry

- Ⓣ 01327 701646

Equipment hire

SHOPMOBILITY

The National Federation of Shopmobility UK (NFSUK), PO Box 6641, Christchurch BH23 9DQ.

- Ⓣ 0844 41 41 850
- Ⓔ info@shopmobilityuk.org
- Ⓦ www.shopmobilityuk.org

Hire manual and powered wheelchairs and scooters. Have a range of branches around the UK. You can find the nearest Shopmobility schemes to you on their on-line Directory. Access is obtained by clicking on the 'Shopmobility Directory' button on the top of the row to the left of their website and using the search criteria. You will need to contact a specific Shopmobility

Scheme in order to make equipment bookings or find out detailed information. General and contact information is contained in their Directory. A few branches that we know are still in existence are listed below.

Scooter Serv
15 Moat Lane, Towcester, Northamptonshire NN12 6AD.
☎ 0845 612 1912
✉ service@scooterserv.com
🌐 www.scooterserv.com
This company can hire manual and powered wheelchairs and scooters for use on the UK mainland.

Publications

Access for All
☎ 01629 816200
✉ customer.service@peakdistrict.gov.uk
Guides giving information for disabled visitors to the Peak District including car parks, public transport, accessible trails, public toilets and guided walks. Available in print from Peak District National Park, Aldern House, Baslow Road, Bakewell DE45 1AE.
The information is also available on:
🌐 www.peakdistrict.org

Accommodation

BOSTON, Lincolnshire
Special Needs Activity Centre Lincolnshire
14 Croppers Way, Freiston, Boston PE22 0QT.
☎ 01205 761373
✉ info@snac.org.uk
🌐 www.snac.org.uk
Special Needs Activity Centre in Lincolnshire.

CHESTERFIELD, Derbyshire
Ashgate Holiday Bungalow
Ashgreen, Ashgate Road, Ashgate, Chesterfield S42 7JE.
☎ 0115 983 5731
✉ julie.harbottle@mencap.org.uk
Holiday bungalow owned by Mencap on outskirts of Chesterfield. Purpose-built for people with learning/physical disabilities and their companions
Contact: Julie Harbottle
Mencap, 96 Douglas Road, Long Eaton, Nottingham NG10 4BD.

MILFORD, Derbyshire
The Ebenezer Chapel
Derwent River Bridge, Milford.
☎ 01332 840564
✉ ann.wayne@derbyshire-holidays.com
🌐 www.derbyshire-holidays.com
Converted former chapel in riverside village of Milord.

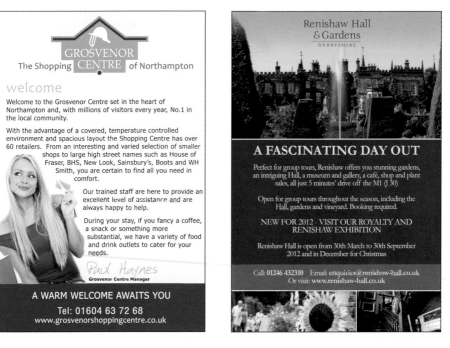

Derbyshire Holidays Ltd
PO Box 7649, Belper, Derbyshire DE56 9DT.
📞 01332 840564
✉ ann.wayne@derbyshire-holidays.com
🌐 www.derbyshire-holidays.com
Contact: Ann Wayne
This fine stone character building, in this attraction rich area, has been skillfully converted offering accommodation for up to 22 guests, with eight bedrooms and five bathrooms. There's an 38ft beamed & galleried lounge, a Finnish sauna-suite, fully-equipped kitchen, and an upper extra lounge, overlooking the River Derwent. The two stair-lifts (not full wheelchair lifts) and other helpful little touches make the two lower floors of the chapel suited to accompanied disabled guests.

SKEGNESS, Lincolnshire
37 Langton Court
Burgh Road, Skegness.
📞 01775 768433
Self-catering bungalow adapted for wheelchair users in Lincolnshire.

NAS ASSESSED ACCOMMODATION

ALDERWASLEY, Derbyshire
Wiggonlea Stable and Fletchers Barn
Four star self-catering
📞 01773 852344
✉ wiggonlea@uwclub.net

ALFORD, Lincolnshire
Half Moon Hotel and Restaurant
Three star small hotel
📞 0150 7463 477
✉ halfmoonalford25@aol.com
🌐 www.halfmoonalford.co.uk

ASHBY-CUM-FENBY, Lincolnshire
Hall Farm Hotel & Restaurant
Three star small hotel
📞 0147 2220 666
✉ info@hallfarmhotelandrestaurant.co.uk
🌐 www.hallfarmhotelandrestaurant.co.uk

BAMFORD, Derbyshire
Ladybower Apartments
Five star self-catering
📞 +44 01433 651361
✉ enquiries@ladybowerapartments.co.uk

BAMFORD, Derbyshire
Yorkshire Bridge Inn
Four star inn
📞 0143 3651 361
✉ info@yorkshire-bridge.co.uk
🌐 www.yorkshire-bridge.co.uk

BICKER, Lincolnshire
Supreme Inns
Three star hotel
📞 0120 5822 804
✉ sales@supremeinns.co.uk
🌐 www.supremeinns.co.uk

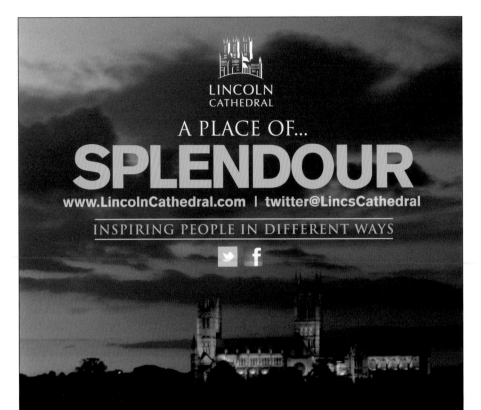

LINCOLN CATHEDRAL

A PLACE OF...
SPLENDOUR

www.LincolnCathedral.com | twitter@LincsCathedral

INSPIRING PEOPLE IN DIFFERENT WAYS

One of the greatest Gothic buildings in Europe | Marvel at the Great West Front | Visit the medieval and Wren libraries | Discover the famous Lincoln Imp | View the Dean's Eye window dating from 1220 See the shrine of St.Hugh and the tomb of Katherine Swinford Visit the Chapter House and enjoy the atmosphere captured on the Da Vinci Code | Be inspired by architecture almost a 1000 years old | Experience The View from St Hugh!

The Cloisters Refectory is available for light refreshments and the Cathedral Shop for gifts. Open daily for floor and roof tours or join us for worship at one of our daily services

Check before you visit as restrictions may apply, Call **01522 561600** Email **visitors@lincolncathedral.co.uk**

BLYTH, Nottinghamshire

The Courtyard at Hodsock Priory

Five star guest accommodation

- 1909591204
- lj@hodsockpriory.com

BLYTON, Lincolnshire

Blyton Ponds

Three star bed & breakfast

- 01427 628240
- blytonponds@msn.com
- www.blytonponds.co.uk

BRASSINGTON, Derbyshire

Hoe Grange Holidays

Four star self-catering

- 0162 9540 262
- info@hoegrangeholidays.co.uk
- www.hoegrangeholidays.co.uk

BURGH ON BAIN, Lincolnshire

Bainfield Lodge

Four star self-catering

- 0150 7313 540
- enquiries@bainfieldholidaylodge.co.uk
- www.bainfieldholidaylodge.co.uk

BUXTON, Derbyshire

Alpine Lodge Guest House

Four star guest house

- 0129 8261 55
- jean@jeangreenwaycole.plus.com
- www.alpinelodgebuxton.co.uk

CASTLE DONNINGTON, Leicestershire

Spring Cottage

Four star bed & breakfast

- 0133 2814 289
- enquiries@springcottagebb.co.uk
- www.springcottagebb.co.uk

CHURCH BROUGHTON, Derbyshire

Oaklands Country Lodges

Four star self-catering

- 01283 730283
- redfern751@btinternet.com
- www.oaklandscountrylodges.co.uk

CLEETHORPES, Lincolnshire

Tudor Terrace Guest House

Four star guest house

- 1472 600800
- tudor.terrace@ntlworld.com
- www.tudorterrace.co.uk

CLUMBER PARK, WORKSOP, Nottinghamshire

Clumber Park Hotel & Spa

Hotel

- jh@clumberparkhotel.com

COVENHAM ST BARTHOLOMEW, Lincolnshire

The Thomas Centre

Four and Five star self-catering

- 01507 363 217
- enquiries@thethomascentre.co.uk
- www.thethomascentre.co.uk

DISEWORTH, Leicestershire

Lady Gate Guest House

Four star guest house

- 01332 811565
- enquiries@ladygateguesthouse.co.uk
- www.ladygateguesthouse.co.uk

EARL STERNDALE, Derbyshire

Wheeldon Trees Farm

Four star self-catering

- 01298 83219
- stay@wheeldontreesfarm.co.uk

EAST BARKWITH, Lincolnshire
The Grange Holiday Cottages
Four star self-catering
- 01673 858670
- sarahstamp@farmersweekly.net
- www.thegrange-lincolnshire.co.uk

EDWINSTOWE, Nottinghamshire
YHA Sherwood Forest
Four star hostel
- 0870 7708 868
- neilbaldwin@yha.org.uk
- www.yha.org.uk

GLOOSTON, Leicestershire
Old Barn Inn Ltd
Four star inn
- 0185 854 5215
- mail@oldbarninn.co.uk

GOULCEBY, LOUTH, Lincolnshire
Bay Tree Cottage
Four star self-catering
- 0150 734 3230
- info@goulcebypost.co.uk

GRAINTHORPE, Lincolnshire
Canal Farm Cottages
Four star self-catering
- 01472 388 825
- r-ma@canalfarmcottages.co.uk
- www.canalfarmcottages.co.uk

Kents Farm Cottages
Three star self-catering
- 0147 238 8264
- sandracarr500@msn.com

GUILSBOROUGH, Northamptonshire
Coton Lodge
Five star farmhouse
- 0160 4740 215
- jo@cotonlodge.co.uk
- www.cotonlodge.co.uk

HALLGATES, CROPSTON, Leicestershire
Horseshoe Cottage Farm
Five star bed & breakfast
- 0116 2350038
- lindajee@ljee.freeserve.co.uk
- www.horseshoecottagefarm.com

HARDSTOFT, Derbyshire
Whitton Lodge
Four star guest accommodation
- 0177 3875 614
- pjohnthestud@aol.com
- www.whittonlodge.co.uk

HAREBY, Lincolnshire
Meridian Retreats
Four star self-catering
- 01205 870210
- office@ewbowser.com
- www.meridianretreats.co.uk

HARPSWELL, Lincolnshire
The Old Stables
Four star self-catering
- 0142 7668 412
- marktatam@hall-farm.co.uk
- ww.hall-farm.co.uk

HARTINGTON, Derbyshire
Ash Tree Cottage – PK763
Four star self-catering
- 01298 84247
- nettletorfarm@btconnect.com

HELSEY, NR HOGSTHORPE, Lincolnshire
Helsey House Cottages
Four star self-catering
- 01754 872 927
- eaepcs@yahoo.co.uk

HINCKLEY, Leicestershire
Sketchley Grange Hotel
Hotel
- 0145 5251 133
- conference@sketchleygrange.co.uk
- www.sketchleygrange.co.uk

HOLBEACH, Lincolnshire
Stennetts Farm Cottages
Three and Four star self-catering
- 01406 380 408
- info@stennettsfarmcottages.co.uk
- www.stennettsfarmcottages.co.uk

HORNCASTLE, Lincolnshire
Best Western Admiral Rodney Hotel
Three star hotel
- 01507 523131
- alisondavis@admiralrodney.net

HUBBERTS BRIDGE, NR BOSTON, Lincolnshire
Elms Farm Cottages
Four and Five star self-catering
- 0120 5290 840
- carol@elmsfarmcottages.co.uk
- www.elmsfarmcottages.co.uk

INGOLDMELLS, Lincolnshire
Ingoldale Park
Four star self-catering
- 01754 872335
- ingoldalepark@btopenworld.com
- www.ingoldmells.net

LEICESTER, Leicestershire
Belmont Hotel
Hotel
- 0116 254 4773
- info@belmonthotel.co.uk
- www.belmonthotel.co.uk

LEVERTON, NR BOSTON, Lincolnshire
Crewyard Cottages
Four star self-catering
- 01205 871389
- gina@gina31.wanadoo.co.uk

LOUGHBOROUGH, Leicestershire
Imago at Burleigh Court
Four star hotel
- 01509 633 007
- g.hodge@burleigh-court.co.uk

Leys Guest House
Three star guest house
- 0150 9646 440
- leysab2@msn.com

LOUTH, Lincolnshire
Nursery Cottage, The Granary, Millhouse & The Stables
Four star self-catering
- 0150 7358 256
- nurserycottage@hotmail.co.uk
- www.mealsfarm.com

LOUTH, Lincolnshire
Brackenborough Hall Coach House Holidays
Four and Five star self-catering
- 01507 603 193
- paulandflora@brackenboroughhall.com
- www.brackenboroughhall.com

MABLETHORPE, Lincolnshire
Colours Guest House
Four star guest house
- 01507 473 427
- donna@coloursguesthouse.co.uk
- www.coloursguesthouse.co.uk

MARKET HARBOROUGH, Leicestershire
The Angel Hotel & Restaurant
Three star hotel
- 01858 462 702
- d.barton@theangel-hotel.co.uk
- www.theange-lhotel.co.uk

MARTIN, Lincolnshire
The Manor House Stables
Four star self-catering
- 01526 378 717
- sherryforbes@hotmail.com
- www.manorhousestables.co.uk

MARTON, Lincolnshire
Black Swan Guest House
Guest house
- 01427 718878
- info@blackswanguesthouse.co.uk

MINTING, Lincolnshire
Greenfield Farm
Bed & breakfast
- 01507 578457
- greenfieldfarm@farming.co.uk
- www.greenfieldfarm.net

MOIRA, Leicestershire
YHA National Forest
Four star hostel
- 0870 7708 868
- neilbaldwin@yha.org.uk
- www.yha.org.uk

NEWARK, Nottinghamshire
Dairy Cottage
Four star self-catering
- 0194 9850 309
- william-baird@btconnect.com

NEWHAVEN, Derbyshire
Old House Farm Cottages
Four star self-catering
- 01629 636268
- s.flower1@virgin.net
- www.oldhousefarm.com

NORTH CARLTON, Lincolnshire
Cliff Farm Cottage
Four star self-catering
- 01522 730475
- info@cliff-farm-cottage.co.uk
- www.cliff-farm-cottage.co.uk

NORTH WILLINGHAM, Lincolnshire
The Old Dairy Cottage
Self-catering cottages
- 0167 3838 272
- carole.wright394@btinternet.com

OAKHAM, Leicestershire
Lodge Trust Country Park
Three star self-catering
- 01572 768073
- carolyn@lodgetrust.org.uk
- www.lodgecountrypark.org.uk

OLD BRAMPTON, Derbyshire
Chestnut Cottage and Willow Cottage
Four star self-catering
- 01246 566159
- patricia_green@btconnect.com

OUNDLE, Northamptonshire
Oundle Cottage Breaks
Three and Four star self-catering
- +44 01832 275508
- richard@simmondsatoundle.co.uk

PARTNEY, NR SPILSBY, Lincolnshire
The Red Lion Inn
Four star Inn
- 01790 752 271
- enquiries@redlioninnpartney.co.uk
- www.redlioninnpartney.co.uk

SALMONBY, Lincolnshire
Grange Farm Holiday Cottages
Three star self-catering
- 0150 7534 101
- info@grangefarmholidaybreaks.co.uk
- www.grangefarmholidaybreaks.co.uk

SKEGNESS, Lincolnshire
Chatsworth
Three star guest accommodation
- 01754 764177
- lynne@chatsworthhotel.co.uk
- www.chatsworthskegness.co.uk

SOUTH SCARLE, Nottinghamshire
Greystones Guest Accommodation
Four star bed & breakfast
- 01636 893 969
- sheenafowkes@greystonesguests.co.uk
- www.greystonesguests.co.uk

STAINFIELD, Lincolnshire
Rural Roosts
Four star self-catering
- 01526 398 492
- katie@ruralroosts.co.uk
- www.ruralroosts.co.uk

SWADLINCOTE, Derbyshire
Forest Lodges
Three and Four star self-catering
- 0128 356 3483
- debbie@roslistonforestrycentre.co.uk

SWEPSTONE, Leicestershire
Church View Barn
Three star self-catering
- 0153 0272 481
- wendydavis39@hotmail.com

THORGANBY, Lincolnshire
Thorganby Hall Farm Cottages, Little Walk and Marris
Three and Four star self-catering
- 01472 398 270
- emma@thorganby.plus.com
- www.thorganbyhall.co.uk

THORPE ST PETER, Lincolnshire
Ings Barn
Self-catering cottage
- 0152 2595 164
- manorbarnlincs@tiscali.co.uk

THRUSSINGTON, Leicestershire
Walton Thorns Farm Cottages
Four star self-catering
- 01509 880315
- liz@waltonthorns.co.uk
- www.waltonthorns.co.uk

WIGSTHORPE, Northamptonshire
Nene Valley Cottages
Five star self-catering
- 01832 720488
- burnetts@gotadsl.co.uk
- www.nenevalleycottages.co.uk

Doing Transport Differently

Due out in 2012, this guide includes information and travellers' tales to help and inspire people with lived experience of disability or health conditions to use public transport.

Available from Radar's online shop
www.radar-shop.org.uk

National Key Scheme Guide

Updated every year, this guide lists the location of almost 9,000 NKS toilets around the UK. It shows opening times, provider name and whether the toilet is unisex.

Available from Radar's online shop
www.radar-shop.org.uk

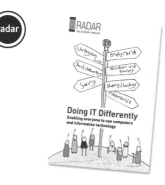

Doing IT Differently

Information to help everyone, regardless of disability, take advantage of information technology (IT) and computers. Includes advice on how to choose and use a computer, and how to adapt it to suit your needs.

Available from Radar's online shop
www.radar-shop.org.uk

Doing Money Differently

Explores new ways of making, saving and looking after your money. This guide covers where your money comes from, where to keep it, where it goes and what to do if you are in debt.

Available from Radar's online shop
www.radar-shop.org.uk

WILBARSTON, Northamptonshire

The Fox Inn
Three star Inn
- 0153 6771 270
- jessie7@ntlworld.com
- www.thefoxinnwilbarston.com

WOODHALL SPA, Lincolnshire

Village Limits Country Pub, Restaurant and Motel
Four star guest accommodation
- 01526 353312
- info@villagelimits.co.uk
- www.villagelimits.co.uk

Petwood Hotel
Three star hotel
- 01526 352411
- Jon@petwood.co.uk
- www.petwood.co.uk

WORKSOP, Nottinghamshire

Browns
Five star bed & breakfast
- 01909 720659
- browns.holbeck@btconnect.com

WYCOMB, Leicestershire

Stonepits Farm Bed & Breakfast
Four star farmhouse
- 0166 444 4597
- stay@stonepitsfarm.co.uk
- www.stonepittsfarm.co.uk

About the West Midlands

The Heart of England region comprises Herefordshire, Shropshire, Staffordshire, Warwickshire, West Midlands and Worcestershire. It is an area that combines a major urban centre, a rich historic and industrial heritage and some of England's most typical and unspoilt countryside.

The rivers Severn and Wye flow through Shropshire, Worcestershire and Herefordshire on the Welsh border. Fruit

blossom attracts visitors to the Vale of Evesham in the spring. To the north, Staffordshire shares the Peak District with its neighbouring counties.

Birmingham, the country's second largest city, provides the full range of urban attractions and has more miles of canals than Venice. Recent developments in the city centre include the Symphony Hall and a rebuilt shopping area around the Bullring. There is also a wide range of museums, shops, parks, sporting venues and other activities. Outside the city centre the National Exhibition Centre and Arena hosts a full programme of concerts, exhibitions and other events.

Ironbridge in Shropshire, the birthplace of the Industrial Revolution, is a World Heritage Site supporting a cluster of museums that are largely accessible. The Black Country Living Museum at Dudley is a large open-air site depicting life and industry in the area. The pottery industry can be explored at visitor centres and factory shops in Stoke-on-Trent and Worcester. In Birmingham, a late 19th century jewellery factory has been recreated as the Jewellery Quarter Discovery Centre. The development of the motor industry can be experienced at the Heritage Motor Centre at Gaydon near Warwick and the Coventry Transport Museum.

For other tastes there are museums devoted to beer in Burton-on-Trent and cider in Hereford, Cadbury World in

Birmingham and the Ryton Organic Gardens near Coventry.

The literary and artistic heritage of the area is considerable. Pride of place must go to Stratford-upon-Avon, birthplace of William Shakespeare, and home to the fully accessible Shakespeare Centre. The hills of Shropshire and Worcestershire were immortalised by A E Houseman. Other notables include Dr Johnson from Lichfield, George Elliot from Nuneaton and Edward Elgar from Worcester.

At Britain's first major theme park, Alton Towers in Staffordshire, the grounds and many of the attractions are accessible and help can be provided in getting onto rides. Dedicated holiday shoppers can visit the Merryhill Centre near Dudley.

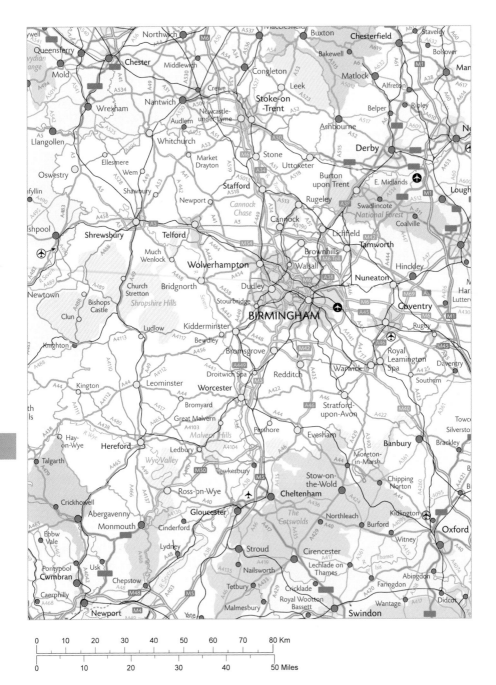

0   10   20   30   40   50   60   70   80 Km

0   10   20   30   40   50 Miles

Resources

Tourism

Heart of England Tourist Board

The official tourist board for the 'Heart of England'. Their website includes suggested attractions, places to stay and events.

Ⓦ www.visitheartofengland.com

Information & advice

DIAL

Offer free, impartial and confidential information and advice by telephone to disabled people, their relatives and professionals. Local branches of DIAL are constantly changing but at the time of writing, the following groups were members of DIAL UK and may be able to help visitors in their areas. Please call before travelling to check whether the service and organisation is still available:

Liseux Trust Birmingham

Ⓣ 0121 382 6660
   Textphone 0121 350 8182

ABLE Herefordshire

Ⓣ 01432 277770

DIAL North Worcestershire

Ⓣ 0800 970 7202
   Textphone 01562 68248

DIAL Nuneaton & Bedworth

Ⓣ 024 7634 9954

CARES Sandwell

Ⓣ 0121 558 7003 (also Textphone)

DIAL Shropshire, Telford & Wrekin

Ⓣ 0845 602 5561

DIAL Solihull

Ⓣ 0121 770 0333 (also Textphone)

DIAL South Worcestershire

Ⓣ 01905 27790
   Textphone 01905 22191

Disability Solutions, Stoke

Ⓣ 01782 683100
   Textphone 01782 683804

Walsall DIAL

Ⓣ 01922 635588

CDP Warwickshire & Coventry

Ⓣ 01926 889349 (also Textphone)

Equipment Hire

SHOPMOBILITY

The National Federation of Shopmobility UK (NFSUK), PO Box 6641, Christchurch, BH23 9DQ.

Ⓣ 0844 41 41 850
Ⓔ info@shopmobilityuk.org
Ⓦ www.shopmobilityuk.org

Hire manual and powered wheelchairs and scooters. Have a range of branches around the UK. You can find the nearest Shopmobility schemes to you on their on-line Directory. Access is obtained by clicking on the 'Shopmobility Directory' button on the top of the row to the left of their website and using the search criteria. You will need to contact a specific Shopmobility Scheme in order to make equipment bookings or find out detailed information. General and contact information is contained in their Directory.

DIAL Nuneaton & Bedworth

New Ramsden Centre, School Walk, Attleborough, Nuneaton CV11 4PJ.

Ⓣ 024 7634 9954

In addition to their information service they run a short-term wheelchair loan service, with a small refundable deposit, for periods of up to 6 weeks. There is a 15 stone weight limit.

Leamington Spa Shopmobility

Warwick District Mobility Ltd, Level 4,
Royal Priors Car Park, Park St, Leamington
Spa CV32 4XT
- ☎ 01926 470450
- ✉ info@leamingtonshopmobility.org.uk
- 🌐 www.leamingtonshopmobility.org.uk

Boston Community Transport

The Len Medlock Centre, St Georges Road,
Boston PE21 8TY.
- ☎ Dial A Ride 01205 315934
  Voluntary Car Scheme 01205 315935
  Shopmobility 01205 314936
- ✉ transport@southlincscvs.org.uk

As part of a Shopmobility Scheme, scooters
and both powered and manual wheelchairs
are available for hire for both residents
for use elsewhere and people visiting the
area. Users have to be members of the
scheme for insurance purposes. Vehicles
can be delivered, at an additional charge, to
addresses within 10 miles of Boston.

Publications

Getting Around Access Guide
- ☎ 0121 214 7214
- ✉ customerrelations@centro.org.uk
- 🌐 www.centro.org.uk

A guide to accessible public transport in
the West Midlands PTA area. Published
each April, it includes information on the
accessible Midland Metro light rail service
between Birmingham and Wolverhampton
and lists local public toilets for disabled
people. Available in standard or large print,
Braille or on tape or CD from CENTRO
Customer Relations, 16 Summer Lane,
Birmingham B19 3SD.

Wheelchair User's Guide to Accessible Tourist Attractions & Accommodation for Shropshire
- 🌐 www.disabledholidayinfo.org.uk

*Wheelchair User's Guide to Accessible
Countryside Sites & Trails in Shropshire &
the Borderlands* 2007/8 and *Wheelchair
User's Guide to Accessible Activities in &
around Shropshire* (both researched by
a wheelchair user). Send a A5 addressed
envelope with a first class stamp for each
title to: Disabled Holiday Information, PO
Box 186, Oswestry SY10 1AF. They can be
also be downloaded from:

Online resources

www.stratford-upon-avon.co.uk
Detailed information on access at tourist
attractions and other facilities is given on
this site.

Accommodation

ILAM, Staffordshire
The Cottage by the Pond
Beechenhill Farm, Ilam, Ashbourne DE6 2BD.
Contact: Sue & Terry Prince
- ☎ 01335 310274
- ✉ info@beechenhill.co.uk
- 🌐 www.beechenhill.co.uk
Cottage on organic farm in the south Peak
District.

MALVERN, Worcestershire
Hidelow House Cottages
Acton Green, Acton Beauchamp, near
Malvern WR6 5AH.
- ☎ 01886 884658
- ✉ info@hidelow.co.uk
- 🌐 www.hidelow.co.uk

'Hidelow Lodge' is a single storey rural self-catering cottage between Malvern and Bromyard.

ROSS-ON-WYE, Herefordshire
Merton House Hotel
Edde Cross Street, Ross-on-Wye HR9 7BZ.
- 01989 563252
- merton.house@clara.co.uk
- www.themertonhotel.co.uk
Hotel in own grounds specially adapted for disabled and elderly guests.

Luxury Pine Lodge
14 Astbury Falls, Bridgnorth, Shropshire WV16 6AT.
- the-smiths-lodge@hotmail.co.uk
- www.luxurypinelodge.vpweb.co.uk
Contact: Yvonne Smith
This luxurious log cabin was specifically built to be fully accessible for disabled holidaymakers and their families and friends. The design of the lodge is contemporary and suited to modern living. We have made every effort to ensure that you enjoy a comfortable holiday in the pleasant surroundings of Shropshire. Facilities for disabled guests include ramped access, wide doorways, an electric profiling bed and a Hi-Trac overhead hoist system.

NAS ASSESSED ACCOMMODATION

BAGNALL, Staffordshire
Cordwainer Cottage
Three star self-catering
- 0178 2302 575
- enquires@cordwainercottage.co.uk
- www.cordwainercottage.co.uk

BIRMINGHAM, West Midlands,
SACO Livingbase
Four star serviced apartments
- 0121 643 8585
- janejones@sacoapartments.co.uk
- www.sacoapartments.co.uk

BROMYARD, Herefordshire
Durstone Cottage
Three star self-catering
- 0188 5400 221
- sarah.mulroy@btconnect.com

CHADDESLEY CORBETT, Worcestershire
Brockencote Hall Country House Hotel
Three star hotel
- 01562 777876
- alison@brockencotehall.com
- www.brockencotehall.com

COALPORT, Shropshire
YHA Coalport
Three star hostel
- 0870 7708 868
- neilbaldwin@yha.org.uk
- www.yha.org.uk

CRAVEN ARMS, Shropshire
Swallows Nest and Robin's Nest
Four star self-catering
- 01588 672383
- strefford@gmail.com
- www.streffordhall.co.uk

DIDDLEBURY, Shropshire
Goosefoot Barn Cottages
Four star self-catering
- ☎ 01584 861326
- ✉ info@goosefootbarn.co.uk
- 🌐 www.goosefootbarn.co.uk

DILHORNE, Staffordshire
Little Summerhill Cottages
Four star self-catering
- ☎ 0178 2550 967
- ✉ info@holidaycottagesstaffordshire.com
- 🌐 www.holidaycottagesstaffordshire.com

EATON-UNDER-HEYWOOD, Shropshire
Eaton Manor
Four and Five star self-catering
- ☎ 0169 4724 814
- ✉ nichola@eatonmanor.co.uk

HEREFORD, Herefordshire
Anvil Cottage, Apple Bough and Cider Press
Four star self-catering
- ☎ +44 01432 268689
- ✉ jennielayton@ereal.net

Penblaith Barn
Five star self-catering
- ☎ 0198 9730 210
- ✉ stay@trevasecottages.co.uk
- 🌐 www.trevasecottages.co.uk

HINDLIP, Worcestershire
The Manor Coach House
Four star guest accommodation
- ☎ 01905 456457
- ✉ info@manorcoachhouse.co.uk

ILAM, Staffordshire
The Orchards
Four star self-catering
- ☎ 01538 308205
- ✉ rushley.farm@btopenworld.com

Beechenhill Cottage and The Cottage by the Pond
Four star self-catering
- ☎ +44 01335 310274
- ✉ info@beechenhill.co.uk

YHA Ilam Hall
Four star hostel
- ☎ 0870 7708 868
- ✉ neilbaldwin@yha.org.uk
- 🌐 www.yha.org.uk

KNIGHTCOTE, Warwickshire
Knightcote Farm Cottages
Five star self-catering
- ☎ 0129 5770 637
- ✉ fionawalker@farmcottages.com
- 🌐 www.farmcottages.com

LEDBURY, Herefordshire
The Old Kennels Farm
Three and Four star self-catering
- ☎ 01531 635024
- ✉ info@oldkennelsfarm.co.uk

LEOMINSTER, Herefordshire
YHA Leominster
Four star hostel
- ☎ 0870 7708 868
- ✉ neilbaldwin@yha.org.uk
- 🌐 www.yha.org.uk

LIGHTHORNE, Warwickshire
Church Hill Farm B&B
Four star farmhouse
- 01926 651251
- sue@churchhillfarm.co.uk
- www.churchhillfarm.co.uk

LUDLOW, Shropshire
Sutton Court Farm Cottages
Three and Four star self-catering
- 01584 861305
- enquiries@suttoncourtfarm.co.uk
- www.suttoncourtfarm.co.uk

MALVERN, Herefordshire
Hidelow House Cottages
Four and Five star self-catering
- 01886 884547
- stay@hidelow.co.uk

MICHAELCHURCH ESCLEY, Herefordshire
Holt Farm
Four star self-catering
- 01981 510238

NR BRIDGENORTH, Shropshire
The Malthouse
Self-catering cottage
- 0845 2681 870
- www.cottages4you.co.uk

NR HEREFORD, Herefordshire
Poston Mill Park
Four star self-catering
- 01981 530225
- info@poston-mill.co.uk
- www.postonmillholidays.co.uk

NR LUDLOW, Herefordshire
Mocktree Barns Holiday Cottages
Three star self-catering
- 01547 540441
- mocktreebarns@care4free.net

ROSS ON WYE, Herefordshire
Trevase Granary
Five star self-catering
- 01989 730210
- pursey.trevase@btconnect.com
- www.trevasecottages.co.uk

Tump Farm
Three star self-catering
- 01600 891029
- clinwilcharmaine@hotmail.com

SHREWSBURY, Shropshire
Lyth Hill House
Five star bed & breakfast
- 0174 3874 660
- bnb@lythhillhouse.com
- www.lythhillhouse.com

STANSHOPE, Staffordshire
Church Farm Cottage & Ancestral Barn
Four and Five star self-catering
- 01335 310243
- enquiries@dovedalecottages.co.uk
- www.dovedalecottages.co.uk

WHITCHURCH, Herefordshire
Portland House Guest House
Guest house
- 01600 890757
- info@portlandguesthouse.co.uk
- www.portlandguesthouse.co.uk

WOLVERHAMPTON, West Midlands

Boningale Manor

Four star self-catering

- 01902 373376
- www.boningalemanor.com

WROXETER, NR SHREWSBURY,
Shropshire

Wroxeter Hotel

Three star country house hotel

- +44 01743 761256
- info@thewroxeterhotel.co.uk

WALTHAM CROSS, Herefordshire

YHA Lee Valley Village

Four star hostel

- 0870 7708 868
- neilbaldwin@yha.org.uk
- www.yha.org.uk

About North West England

The North West region of England is a wide and varied place – Cheshire, Cumbria, Greater Manchester, Lancashire and Merseyside all feature including the spectacular Lake District National Park. Whether you are looking for urban or rural scenery, the North West can offer whatever you need for a relaxing break or a full-on adventure holiday.

The North West is a region of contrast ranging from the style and contemporary environment of Manchester to the cultural and architectural grandeur of Liverpool, the Roman and medieval heritage of Chester to the rolling hills of Lancashire and the stunning scenery around the Lake District.

The leading seaside resort in the North is Blackpool with miles of redeveloped level promenade, piers, entertainment of all kinds and, of course, the famous

Blackpool Tower and Pleasure Beach, at which many rides can be enjoyed by disabled visitors.

Former City of Culture, Liverpool boasts a wide array of visitor opportunities including the redeveloped Albert Dock Centre which houses a variety of shops, restaurants, museums and galleries including Tate Liverpool, the International Slavery Museum and the Beatles Museum. Other attractions include the Walker Art Gallery, the World Museum, Liverpool One shopping centre and Mersey Ferries.

A short distance away is Manchester offering top class theatre, music and sport with a wide range of shops and restaurants. In the redeveloped Castlefields area you can visit the Museum of Science & Industry housed in the world's first passenger railway station. Away from the city centre, waterside developments include The Lowry and Imperial War Museum North at Salford Quays and the Trafford Centre for out-of-town shopping. You can also visit Manchester United football ground and take an accessible tour.

Historic towns of the region include Carlisle, Lancaster and Chester where the original city walls surround picturesque shopping streets and the cathedral. Advice on accessible sight-seeing routes can be obtained from the Tourist Information Centre.

Parks and gardens in the area include Liverpool University's Botanic gardens at Ness on the Wirral, the Topiary Gardens at Levens Hall near Kendal in the Lake District and Tatton Park near Knutsford in Cheshire. A large number of country parks have been established including the award winning Wyre Estuary Country Park in Lancashire. If wildlife is your thing you can choose from attractions including Chester Zoo and the Wildfowl & Wetlands Trust's Martin Mere near Ormskirk. In the Lake District a number of scenic paths have been developed for disabled people including the National Trust's Friars Crag Walk beside Derwentwater and the Ridding Wood Sculpture Trail in Grizedale Forest.

Throughout the area are displays of the local industrial heritage. Inland waterway transport is explored at the National Waterways Museum at Ellesmere Port and the silk industry at Macclesfield. The craft of glassmaking is on display at The World of Glass in St Helens. Small Pennine mill towns can be visited by the restored, award-winning East Lancashire Railway.

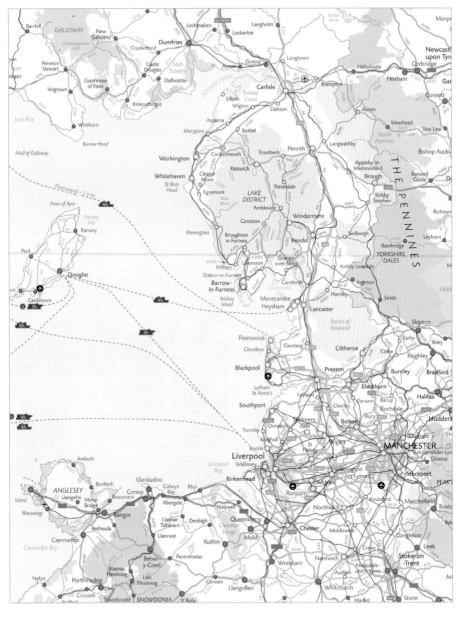

| 0 | 10 | 20 | 30 | 40 | 50 | 60 | 70 | 80 Km |
| 0 | 10 | | 20 | | 30 | | 40 | 50 Miles |

Resources

Tourism

The North West of England does not have a single regional tourism organisation.

Visit Chester & Cheshire

Chester Railway Station, 1st Floor, West Wing Offices, Station Road, Chester CH1 3NT.
- 01244 405600
- www.visitchester.com

Provide general information on Chester and Chesire.

Cumbria Tourism

Windermere Road, Staveley, Cumbria LA8 9PL.
- 01539 822222
- info@cumbriatourism.org
- www.golakes.co.uk

Provide general information and a number of free publications about the county.

Lancashire & Blackpool Tourist Board

Farington House, Lancashire Enterprise Business Park, Centurion Way, Leyland, PR26 6TW.
- 01772 426450
- info@visitlancashire.com
- www.visitlancashire.com

Provide general information on the area to visitors.

Marketing Manchester

Manchester Visitor Information Centre, 45-50 Piccadilly Plaza, Portland Street M1 4AJ.
- 0871 222 8223
- touristinformation@visitmanchester.com
- www.visitmanchester.com

Offers a selection of general tourist information on Manchester and its accommodation and attractions.

Blackpool Pleasure Beach

525 Ocean Boulevard, Blackpool FY4 1EZ.
- 0871 2221234
- info@bpbltd.com
- www.blackpoolpleasurebeach.com/facilities.php

Various facilities for disabled are available at the Pleasure Beach.

Information & advice

Disabled Living

Redbank House, 4 St Chad's Street, Cheetham, Manchester M8 8QA.
- 0870 777 4714
- information@disabledliving.co.uk
- www.disabledliving.co.uk

Charity which provides impartial information about equipment and services for disabled adults, children, older people and the professionals who support them.

Disability Stockport

23 High Street, Stockport SK1 1EG.
- 0161 480 7248
- email@disabilitystockport.org.uk
- www.disabilitystockport.org.uk

Offer an information service to disabled people in Stockport.

Cheshire Centre for Independent Living

Oakwood Lane, Barnton, Cheshire CW8 4HE.
- 01606 872760
- office@cheshirecil.org

'User-led' group of information providers in Cheshire providing information, training, information, practical help, direct payments and advocacy to assist disabled people throughout Cheshire.

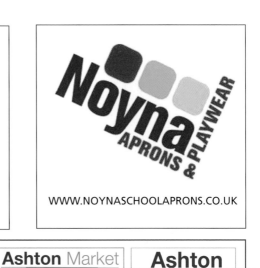

DIAL

Offer free, impartial and confidential information and advice by telephone to disabled people, their relatives and professionals. Local branches of DIAL are constantly changing but at the time of writing, the following groups were members of DIAL UK and may be able to help visitors in their areas. Please call before travelling to check whether the service and organisation is still available:

DI&S Blackpool, Fylde & Wyre
- 01253 625553

DIAL Chester
- 01244 4345655
  Textphone 01244 342472

Halton Disability Services
- 01928 717222
  Textphone 01928 718999

DIS Hyndburn
- 01254 397979

Access Lancashire
- 01772 621633

Macclesfield DIB
- 01625 501759

Preston DISC
- 01772 558863

DAI St Helens
- 01744 453053 (also Textphone)

Vale Royal Disability Services
- 01606 888400

Warrington Disability Partnership
- 01925 240064
  Textphone 01925 240853

West Lancashire Disability Helpline
- 0800 220676
  Textphone 01695 51512

Paveways, Wigan
- 01942 519909

Park Tours & Travel

The Mountain Goat Office, Victoria Street, Windermere, Cumbria LA23 1AD.
- 015394 45161
- www.mountain-goat.com

Offer full and half-day tours in the Lake District using mini-buses with experienced driver guides. Facilities for wheelchair users, with folding wheelchairs, who can mount steps and walk a few steps can be provided with prior notice.

Equipment hire

SHOPMOBILITY

The National Federation of Shopmobility UK (NFSUK), PO Box 6641, Christchurch, BH23 9DQ.
- 0844 41 41 850
- info@shopmobilityuk.org
- www.shopmobilityuk.org

Hire manual and powered wheelchairs and scooters. Have a range of branches around the UK. You can find the nearest Shopmobility schemes to you on their on-line Directory. Access is obtained by clicking on the 'Shopmobility Directory' button on the top of the row to the left of their website and using the search criteria. You will need to contact a specific Shopmobility Scheme in order to make equipment bookings or find out detailed information. General and contact information is contained in their Directory.

Age Concern Bolton

72/74 Ashburner Street, Bolton BL1 1TN.
- 01204 382411
- http://www.ageconcernbolton.org.uk/

Manual wheelchairs can be supplied for periods of up to 3 weeks to Bolton residents and people, over 50, visiting the area.

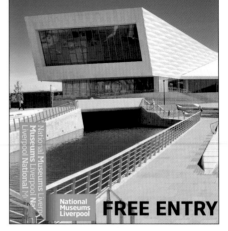

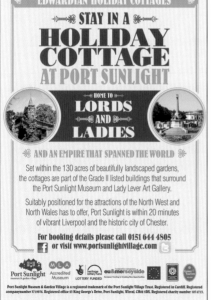

Blackpool Wheelchair Hire

183 Lytham Road, Blackpool FY1 6EU.
📞 01253 408453
🌐 www.blackpoolwheelchairs.co.uk
Manual and electric wheelchairs and scooters are available for hire on daily or weekly rates. Delivery to hotels in the area can be arranged.

Blackpool Shopmobility

52 Clifton Street, Blackpool FY1 1JP.
📞 01253 476451
Can hire manual wheelchairs and scooters for use in and around Blackpool and operate a door-to-door community transport service available for outings in the area. NKS toilet keys are also available.

The Helpful Hand

6/8 Chester Road, Macclesfield SK11 8DG.
📞 01625 424438
🌐 www.thehelpfulhand.co.uk
Manual and powered wheelchairs, scooters and a range of electric beds, chairs, stairlifts, commodes and incontinence equipment are available for sale and hire.

Fred Walton Mobility Products

308 Mosley Common Road, Worsley, Manchester M28 1DA.
📞 0808 108 5678
🌐 www.fredwalton.co.uk
In addition to selling a wide range of equipment, manual wheelchairs are available to hire at weekly rates. Delivery can be arranged throughout the country.

The Wheelchair Centre

229 Droylsden Road, Audenshaw, Manchester M34 5ZT.
📞 0161 370 2661/5949
📧 invalidaids@btconnect.com
🌐 www.thewheelchaircentre.co.uk
Manual wheelchairs are available for hire on daily or weekly basis and lightweight scooters available by the week.

Publications

The Access Guide to Blackpool

Published by Blackpool Tourism. Available from Jubilee Tourist Information Centre, Festival House, Promenade, Blackpool FY1 1AP.
📞 01253 478222
📧 tourism@blackpool.gov.uk
🌐 www.visitblackpool.com

Accessible Travel on Merseyside

📞 0151 227 5181
Information on public transport services for disabled people in the Merseyside PTA area is available, and updated, on www.merseytravel.gov.uk. Copies in alternative formats can be obtained from Merseytravel, PO Box 1976, Liverpool L69 3HN

Online resources

Accessible Lake District

🌐 www.nationalparks.gov.uk/visiting/outdooractivities/accessforall/accessible-lakedistrict.htm
Site describes a series of 39 routes, suitable for people with limited mobility, throughout the Lake District.

Accessible countryside for Everyone

🌐 www.accessiblecountryside.org.uk/northwest/cheshire/
Contains information on disabled access and wheelchair walks across the countryside and green spaces of Cheshire.

Miles Without Stiles

Ⓦ www.lake-district.gov.uk

An on-line guide to 41 routes in the Lake District National Park that are considered accessible for people with limited mobility. They are classified into three standards of surface and gradient as well as the distance and other features of the area. Comprehensive information on parking and toilets is also given in the 'Accessible for all' section of their website. There is also a link to a list of shorter paths and approaches to viewpoints that may be accessible to wheelchair users.

Accommodation

AMBLESIDE, Cumbria

Nationwide Bungalow

Borrans Road, Ambleside, Cumbria, LA22 0EN.

Ⓣ 08456 584478

Ⓔ info@livability.org.uk

Ⓦ www.livability.org.uk

Holiday bungalow specially adapted for disabled people close to Lake Windermere.

BLACKPOOL, Lancashire

Century Hotel

406 North Promenade, Blackpool FY1 2LB.

Ⓣ 01253 354598

Ⓦ www.centuryhotel.co.uk

Family owned hotel on the seafront in Blackpool.

Elizabeth Frankland Moore Home

539 Lytham Road, Blackpool FY4 1RA.

Ⓣ 01253 343313

Ⓔ headquarters@blesma.org

Ⓦ www.blesma.org

BLESMA nursing and residential care home for ex-service men and women on southern edge of town.

BOWNESS-ON-WINDERMERE, Cumbria

Windermere Manor

Rayrigg Road, Windermere LA23 1ES.

Ⓣ 0845 603 0051

Ⓔ windermere.manor@ actionforblindpeople.org.uk

Ⓦ www.visionhotels.co.uk

Hotel with adaptations and facilities for visually impaired people and their families and friends.

BROUGHTON-IN-FURNESS, Cumbria

The Kepplewray Centre

Broughton-in-Furness LA20 6HE.

Ⓣ 01229 716936

Ⓔ web1@kepplewray.org.uk

Ⓦ www.kepplewray.org.uk

Activity Centre in southern Lake District also open to people not taking part in organised programmes.

LYTHAM ST ANNES, Lancashire

St Annes Hotel

69-71 South Promenade, St Annes on Sea FY8 1LZ.

Ⓣ 01253 713108

Ⓦ www.st-annes-hotel.com

Hotel on seafront designed for disabled guests in Lancashire.

NANTWICH, Cheshire

The Wingate Centre

Wrenbury Hall Drive, Wrenbury, Nantwich CW5 8ES.

Ⓣ 01270 780456

Ⓦ www.wingatecentre.co.uk

Group accommodation for children and adults owned by Wingate Special Children's Trust in rural area.

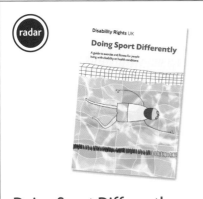

Doing Sport Differently

Available early 2012, this guide will support and encourage people with lived experience of disability or health conditions to participate in or become involved in fitness and sport.

Available from Radar's online shop
www.radar-shop.org.uk

Doing Careers Differently

Packed with useful information, this guide includes stories from disabled people who have built satisfying careers, from part-time flexible work to a first-time management role and beyond.

Available from Radar's online shop
www.radar-shop.org.uk

The Blackpool Tower

We want all our guests to have an amazing experience every time they visit us. To view our Guide for Guests with a Disability visit:
www.theblackpooltower.com/plan-your-visit/disabled-policy.aspx
www.theblackpooltower.com

SOUTHPORT, Merseyside
Salfordian Hotel
37 Park Crescent, Southport PR9 9LT.
- ☎ 01704 538810
- ✉ salfordian@salford.gov.uk
- 🌐 www.salford.gov.uk/salfordian
Hotel owned by a charity in own grounds.

Vitalise Sandpipers
Fairway, Southport PR9 0AL.
- ☎ 0845 345 1970
Centre on shore of Marine Lake, a mile from town centre. Purpose-built for breaks for disabled people.

NAS ASSESSED ACCOMMODATION

ACTON BRIDGE, Cheshire
Wall Hill Farm Guest House
Five star guest accommodation
- ☎ 0160 685 2654
- ✉ info@wallhillfarmguesthouse.co.uk
- 🌐 www.wallhillfarmguesthouse.co.uk

AINSDALE, SOUTHPORT, Merseyside
Willowbank Holiday Home and Touring Park
Five star holiday and touring park
- ✉ info@willowbankcp.co.uk
- 🌐 www.willowbankcp.co.uk

ALSTON, LONGRIDGE, Lancashire
Proven House
Four star self-catering
- ☎ 01772 782653
- ✉ kenglish56@hotmail.co.uk

AMBLESIDE, Cumbria
Rothay Manor
Three star hotel
- ☎ 015394 30892
- ✉ anne-marie@rothaymanor.co.uk
- 🌐 www.rothaymanor.co.uk

ARNSIDE, Cumbria
YHA Arnside
Three star hostel
- ☎ 0870 7708 868
- ✉ neilbaldwin@yha.org.uk
- 🌐 www.yha.org.uk

ASHTON WITH STODDAY, Lancashire
Ashton Hall Cottages
Four star self-catering
- ☎ 0152 4751 325
- ✉ ashtonhallcottages@googlemail.com
- 🌐 www.ashtonhallcottages.co.uk

BASSENTHWAITE, Cumbria
Sandhills Farm
Four star farmhouse
- ☎ 0176 877 6307
- ✉ helen.langcake974@btinternet.com

BLACKPOOL, Lancashire
Ashley Victoria
Four star guest accommodation
- ☎ 0125 3348 787
- ✉ info@theprincess-blackpool.co.uk
- 🌐 www.blackpoolfamily
  accommodation.com

Beachwood Guest House
Three star guest accommodation
- ☎ 01253 401951
- ✉ beachwood.guesthouse@virgin.net
- 🌐 www.beachwoodhotel.co.uk

Big Blue Hotel
Four star hotel
- ☎ 01253 400 045
- ✉ martin.jackson@bigbluehotel.com
- 🌐 www.bigbluehotel.com

Coast Apartments
Four star self-catering
- T 01253 351377
- E enquiries@coastapartments.co.uk
- W www.coastapartments.co.uk

Holmsdale
Three star guest house
- T 01253 621008
- E office@holmsdalehotel-blackpool.com
- W www.holmsdalehotel-blackpool.com

The Address
Three star guest accommodation
- T 0125 3624 238
- E stay@theaddressblackpool.co.uk

The Beach House
Five star self-catering
- T 0125 335 2699
- E info@thebeachhouseblackpool.co.uk
- W www.thebeachhouseblackpool.co.uk/

The Berkeley
Three and Four star self-catering
- T 01253 351244
- E info@selfcatering.tv
- W www.selfcatering.tv

The Lawton
Three star guest accommodation
- T 01253 753471
- E thelawtonhotel@gmail.com

The Willow Tree House
Two star guest house
- T 0125 331 8613
- E thebristol.guesthouse@gmail.com
- W www.willowtreehouseblackpool.co.uk

BOSLEY, Cheshire
Strawberry Duck Cottage
Three star self-catering
- T 01260 223591
- E emonthemove@hotmail.com
- W www.strawberryduckcottage.co.uk

BOWNESS ON SOLWAY, Cumbria
The Old Chapel
Three star bed & breakfast
- T 01697 351126
- E oldchapelbowness@hotmail.com
- W www.oldchapelbownessonsolway.com

BURSCOUGH, Lancashire
Martin Lane Farmhouse Holiday Cottages
Four and Five star self-catering
- T 0170 489 3527
- E cottages@btinternet.com

CARLISLE, Cumbria
Mount Farm B&B
Four star farmhouse
- T 01228 674 641
- E judith.wilson11@btinternet.com
- W www.mount-farm.co.uk

Old Brewery Residences
Three star self-catering
- T 01228 597352
- E deec@impacthousing.org.uk
- W www.impacthousing.org.uk

CASTLE CARROCK, BRAMPTON, Cumbria
Tottergill Farm Cottages
Four and Five star self-catering
- T 01228 670615
- E stephen@tottergill.co.uk
- W www.tottergill.co.uk

CASTLEFIELD, MANCHESTER,
YHA Manchester
Four star hostel
- ☎ 0870 7708 868
- ✉ neilbaldwin@yha.org.uk
- 🌐 www.yha.org.uk

CATLOWDY, LONGTOWN, Cumbria
Bessiestown Farm Country Guesthouse
Five star guest accommodation
- ☎ 01228 577219
- ✉ info@bessiestown.co.uk
- 🌐 www.bessiestown.co.uk

CATON, Lancashire
4 The Croft Ground Floor Apartment
Four star self-catering
- ✉ suebrierly@hotmail.com
- 🌐 www.holiday-rentals.com/10721

CHESTER, Cheshire
Brookside Hotel
Three star Small hotel
- ☎ 0124 4381 943
- ✉ mariongilfoyle@btinternet.com

CHIPPING, Lancashire
The Gibbon Bridge Hotel
Four star hotel
- ☎ 0199 561 456
- ✉ marketing@gibbon-bridge.co.uk

CONGLETON, Cheshire
Sandhole Farm
Four star guest accommodation
- ☎ 01260 224419
- ✉ veronica@sandholefarm.co.uk
- 🌐 www.sandholefarm.co.uk

CROOK, Cumbria
Lake District Disabled Holidays
Four star self-catering
- ☎ 015394 47421

DOWNHOLLAND, Lancashire
Cross Farm Cottages
Four star self-catering
- ☎ 0151 5261 576
- ✉ ns.harrison@virgin.net

EDGWORTH, Lancashire
Meadowcroft Barn B&B
Five star farmhouse
- ☎ 0120 4853 270
- ✉ meadowcroftbarn@btinternet.com

Clough Head Farm
Four star self-catering
- ☎ 01254 704758
- 🌐 www.cloughheadfarm.co.uk

GARSTANG, Lancashire
Barnacre Cottages
Five star self-catering
- ☎ 0199 5600 918
- ✉ sue@barnacre-cottages.co.uk
- 🌐 www.barnacre-cottages.co.uk

GRANGE OVER SANDS, Cumbria
Netherwood Hotel
Three star hotel
- ☎ 015395 32552
- ✉ chris@netherwood-hotel.co.uk

GRASMERE, Cumbria
Rothay Lodge & Rothay Lodge
Apartment
Four star self-catering
- ☎ 0115 923 2618
- ✉ enquiries@rothay-lodge.co.uk
- 🌐 www.rothay-lodge.co.uk

ISEL, COCKERMOUTH, Cumbria
Linskeldfield Tarn Holiday Cottages
Four star self-catering
- 0190 0822 136
- info@linskeldfield.co.uk
- www.linskeldfield.co.uk

KENDAL, Cumbria
Meadowcroft Country Guest House
Four star guest house
- 01539 821 171
- info@meadowcroft-guesthouse.com
- www.meadowcroft-guesthouse.com

Top Thorn Farm
Three star self-catering
- 0153 9824 252
- info.barnes@btconnect.com

KIRKOSWALD, Cumbria
Howscales
Four star self-catering
- 01768 898666
- liz@howscales.co.uk
- www.howscales.co.uk

LANGHO, Lancashire
Best Western Mytton Fold Hotel and
Golf Complex
Three star hotel
- 0125 424 0662
- barbara@myttonfold.co.uk

LIVERPOOL, Merseyside
Ibis Hotel
Hotel
- 0151 7069 800
- www.ibishotel.com

YHA Liverpool
Four star hostel
- 0870 7708 868
- neilbaldwin@yha.org.uk
- www.yha.org.uk

LONGTHWAITHE, BORROWDALE, Cumbria
YHA Borrowdale
Four star hostel
- 0870 7708 868
- neilbaldwin@yha.org.uk
- www.yha.org.uk

LORTON, COCKERMOUTH, Cumbria
Southwaite Green
Five star self-catering
- 0190 0821 055
- info@southwaitegreen.co.uk
- www.southwaitegreen.co.uk

LOWER FAIRSNAPE FARM, BLEASDALE, Lancashire
Bleasdale Cottages
Four star self-catering
- 01995 61343
- info@bleasdalecottages.co.uk
- www.bleasdalecottages.co.uk

LYTHAM ST ANNES, Lancashire
Avondale
Four star self-catering
- 0125 378 9190
- alvinperkins2@totalise.co.uk

The Chadwick Hotel
Three star hotel
- 0125 3720061
- sales@thechadwickhotel.com
- www.thechadwickhotel.com

The Langdales Hotel
Three star hotel
📞 0125 3721 342
📧 info@langdaleshotel.co.uk
🌐 www.langdaleshotel.co.uk

MACCLESFIELD, Cheshire
The Old Byre
Two star self-catering
📞 01260 223293
📧 dotgilman@hotmail.co.uk

MANCHESTER, Greater Manchester
Hilton Manchester Deansgate
Accredited hotel
📞 020 7856 8380
📧 bernadette.gilligan@hilton.com
🌐 www.hilton.co.uk/
manchesterdeansgate

Park Inn Manchester Victoria
Four star hotel
📞 0161 837 8301
📧 neil.raw@rezidorparkinn.com
🌐 www.manchester-victoria.parkinn.co.uk

Atrium Apartments by Bridge Street
Worldwide
Four star serviced apartments
📞 0161 235 2000
📧 martin.jones@bridgestreet.com
🌐 www.atriummanchester.com

Bewleys Hotel, Manchester Airport
Hotel
📧 sales.ManchesterAirport@
BewleysHotels.co.uk

Lancashire County Cricket Club & Old
Trafford Lodge
Three star guest accommodation
📧 lodge@lccc.co.uk
🌐 www.lccc.co.uk

The Midland
Four star hotel
📞 0161 236 3333
📧 PBayliss@qhotels.co.uk
🌐 www.qhotels.co.uk

SACO Manchester
Four star serviced apartments
📞 0845 1220 405
📧 janejones@sacoapartments.co.uk
🌐 www.sacoapartments.co.uk

MORECAMBE, Lancashire
Eden Vale Luxury Holiday Flats
Three star self-catering
📞 0152 441 5544
📧 jicoombs@talktalk.net
🌐 www.edenvalemorecambe.co.uk

MUNGRISDALE, Cumbria
Bannerdale
Self-catering cottage
📞 0176 8779 678
📧 enquiries@nearhowe.co.uk
🌐 www.nearhowe.co.uk

NEAR CONGLETON, Cheshire
Ladderstile Retreat
Five star farmhouse
📞 0126 0223 338
📧 rose@ladderstileretreat.co.uk
🌐 www.ladderstileretreat.co.uk

NEWTON-IN-BOWLAND, Lancashire
Stonefold Holiday Cottage
Four star self-catering
- stonefoldholidaycottage.co.uk

PULFORD, Cheshire
Grosvenor Pulford Hotel and Spa
Four star hotel
- 01244 570560
- sue@nelsonnorthwest.co.uk
- www.grosvenorpulfordhotel.co.uk

QUERNMORE, LANCASTER, Lancashire
Knotts Farm Holiday Cottages
Four star self-catering
- 01524 63749
- stay@knottsfarm.co.uk
- www.knottsfarm.co.uk

RAINOW, Cheshire
Kerridge End Holiday Cottages
Five star self-catering
- 01625 424220
- info@
  kerridgeendholidaycottages.co.uk

REDMAIN, NEAR COCKERMOUTH, Cumbria
Redmain Hall Farm
Four star self-catering
- 0122 8599 950
- sheena@cumbrian-cottages.co.uk
- www.cumbrian-cottages.co.uk

RIBCHESTER, Lancashire
Riverside Barn Bed & Breakfast
Five star guest accommodation (room only)
- 0125 4878 095/0125 4721 000
- sarah.brotherton@btconnect.com
- www.riversidebarn.co.uk

Pinfold Farm
Four star self-catering
- 01254 820 740
- info@pinfoldfarm.co.uk
- www.pinfoldfarm.co.uk

ROCHDALE, Lancashire
Fernhill B&B
Three star guest accommodation - Room Only
- 0170 6355 671
- info@fernhillbreaks.co.uk
- www.fernhillbreaks.co.uk

SALFORD, MANCHESTER,
The Lowry Hotel
Hotel
- 0161 827 4082
- jobrien@roccofortehotels.com

SCALES, Cumbria
Scales Farm Country Guest House
Four star guest house
- +44 017687 79660
- scales@scalesfarm.com
- www.scalesfarm.com

SCORTON, Lancashire
Cleveley Mere Boutique Lodges
Four and Five star self-catering
- rogerburnside@aol.com
- www.cleveleymere .com

SKELTON, PENRITH, Cumbria
Salutation Yard T/A Sojourn North
Four star self-catering
- 0176 8484 940
- bookings@sojourn-north.co.uk

SOUTHPORT, Lancashire

Sandy Brook Farm

Three star farmhouse and
Three star self-catering

- 01704 880337
- sandybrookfarm@gmail.com
- www.sandybrookfarm.co.uk

ST BEES, Cumbria

Springbank Farm Lodges

Four star self-catering

- 01946 822 375
- stevewoodman@talk21.com
- www.springbanklodges.co.uk

STAVELEY, Cumbria

Avondale

Three star self-catering

- 015394 45713
- enquiries@avondale.uk.net
- www.avondale.uk.net

THURSTONFIELD, Cumbria

The Tranquil Otter & The Lough
Apartment

Five star self-catering

- 01228 576 661
- info@thetranquilotter.co.uk
- www.thetranquilotter.co.uk

WEST KIRBY, Merseyside

Herons Well

Five star self-catering

- glynis.lavelle@btinternet.com

WINDERMERE, Cumbria

The Bowering

Four star self-catering

- 0125 3890 070
- helen@thebowering.co.uk

Hawksmoor Guest House

Four star guest house

- 0153 9442 110
- enquiries@hawksmoor.com
- www.hawksmoor.com

Linthwaite House Hotel

Four star country house hotel

- 015394 88600
- handmade@linthwaite.com
- www.linthwaite.com

About Yorkshire

The broad acres of England's largest county stretch from the River Tees to the Humber, from the top of the Pennines to the North Sea. Within its borders are attractions for all types of holiday or short break including an increasing number of accessible accommodation and attractions.

The Yorkshire Dales is justifiably famous with deep valleys criss-crossed with limestone dry walls. Contrasting are the wild heather and bracken moors and hump-backed peaks such as Ingleborough and Whernside. One of the best ways to see the Dales is to take a ride on the Settle to Carlisle Railway, an unforgettable journey through some fine landscapes.

The other National Park, the North Yorkshire Moors, is quieter; England's largest expanse of heather moorland. Where the moors meet the sea are some

of Britain's highest cliffs, rich in fossils from the Jurassic times. Little fishing villages lay in gaps between the cliffs:

Robin Hoods Bay, Staithes and Runswick Bay. Whitby is amongst them: still a working fishing port, with the smell of kipper smoking, in the shadow of the cliff top abbey.

Further down the coast is Scarborough. Two fine bays separated by a castle-topped headland; amusement arcades compete with cockle stalls and donkey rides. South of Scarborough are the Bempton cliffs; owned by the RSPB, that have some of the richest colonies of seabirds in England; make sure you go when the puffins are at home!

Yorkshire's first golden age was in the middle ages, when Cistercian monks built splendid monasteries. Most impressive is Fountains Abbey, just north of Ripon. In the 18th century its grounds were landscaped, with lakes, woods and hidden temples.

Also in this region is York; home to an impressive cathedral and a complete circle of 13th century walls. Within the walls you can find narrow streets of half-timbered houses and interesting shops. Outside the walls is the national Railway Museum: paradise for the train spotter and still fascinating for everybody else.

Should York be a little crowded for your taste, Beverley to the south west is a smaller and much quieter version. It too has a Minster and its other church, St Mary's, has a 13th Century carving: of a rabbit, believed to be Lewis Carroll's

inspiration for the white rabbit in Alice in Wonderland.

The Southern part of Yorkshire was the heart of the industrial revolution. You will find dark mills and cobbled streets, as well as some of the countries grandest Victorian architecture. Not only in the big cities of Leeds and Bradford, but in smaller towns like Todmorden and Hebden Bridge. The cities now sport more than their fair share of galleries and museums, often filled with art treasures from local lads and lasses made good: Henry Moore at Leeds, Barbara Hepworth at Wakefield and David Hockney at Saltaire.

But if you prefer gloomy and moody, head for Haworth, home to the Bronte sisters. You can get there by travelling by steam train on the Keighley and Worth valley railway. You can still feel the presence of the three writers in the dark vicarage where they lived with their father and wayward brother, or on the wild moors where they played as children and made up their first tales.

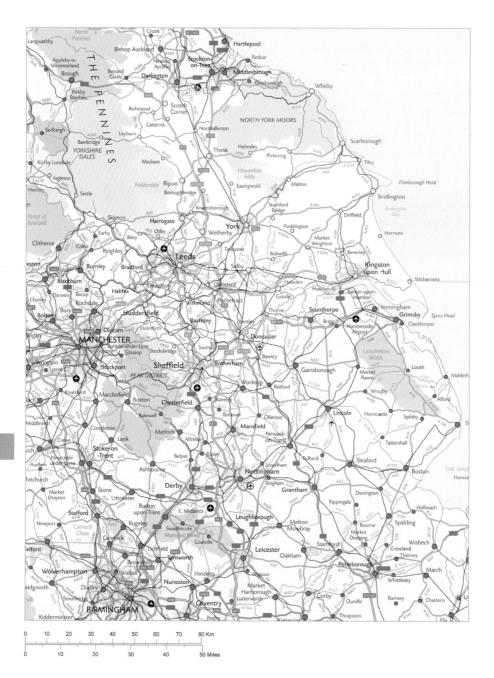

Resources

Tourism

Welcome to Yorkshire

Dry Sand Foundry, Foundry Square,
Holbeck, Leeds, LS11 5D.
- 01904 707961
- info@yorkshire.com
- www.yorkshire.com

Information & advice

DIAL

Offer free, impartial and confidential
information and advice by telephone
to disabled people, their relatives and
professionals. Local branches of DIAL
are constantly changing but at the time
of writing, the following groups were
members of DIAL UK and may be able to
help visitors in their areas. Please call before
travelling to check whether the service and
organisation is still available:

DIAL Barnsley
- 01226 240273

Disability Advice Bradford
- 01274 594173
  Textphone 01274 530951

Calderdale DART
- 01422 346040

DIAL Doncaster
- 01302 327800
  Textphone 01302 768297

Choices & Rights, Hull
- 01482 878778
  Textphone 01482 370986

DIAL Leeds
- 0113 214 3630
  Textphone 0113 214 3627

Rotherham DIS
- 01709 373658

Scarborough DAG
- 01723 379397 (also Textphone)

DIAL Selby
- 01757 210495

DIAL Wakefield
- 01977 723933/4
  Textphone 01977 724081

DIAC York
- 01904 638467

Equipment hire

SHOPMOBILITY

The National Federation of Shopmobility
UK (NFSUK), PO Box 6641, Christchurch
BH23 9DQ.
- 0844 41 41 850
- info@shopmobilityuk.org
- www.shopmobilityuk.org

Hire manual and powered wheelchairs
and scooters. Have a range of branches
around the UK. You can find the nearest
Shopmobility schemes to you on their online Directory. Access is obtained by clicking
on the 'Shopmobility Directory' button
on the top of the row to the left of their
website and using the search criteria. You
will need to contact a specific Shopmobility
Scheme in order to make equipment
bookings or find out detailed information.
General and contact information is
contained in their Directory.

Bayliss Mobility Ltd

Enterprise Complex, Walmgate, York YO1
9TT.
- 01904 611516
- www.livingindependent.co.uk

Provide second hand, but not a wide
choice of wheelchairs for hire as well as
selling a wide range of mobility and other
equipment.

Skipton & Craven Action for Disability
46/48 Newmarket Street, Skipton BD23 2DB.
- ☎ 01756 701005
- ✉ information@scad.eclipse.co.uk
- 🌐 www.scad.org.uk

Operate a hire service for manual wheelchairs, an accessible minibus service and have a specially adapted canal boat for day trips. Available for groups.

Whitby & District Disablement Action Group
Church House Centre, Flowergate, Whitby YO21 3BA.
- ☎ 01947 821001
- ✉ whitbydag@btconnect.com
- 🌐 www.whitbydag.org.uk

Offer a wheelchair hire scheme and have manual wheelchair and scooters. Deposits and hire charges payable in advance. All-terrain wheelchairs are available to hire for use on Whitby beach.

Online resources

www.yorkshire.com/disabled-go
Hosts a wide range of information in the 'disabled go' and 'accessible yorkshire' sections.

The North York Moors National Park Authority
- 🌐 www.moors.uk.net
- ☎ 01439 770657

Produced by the North York Moors National Park Authority, this website has a good list of 'easy going' walking routes, to be found under their 'Accessible Trails' section on the site, as well as a comprehensive 'Access for All' guide on accommodation, toilets and attractions.

Accommodation

BEAMSLEY, North Yorkshire

The Beamsley Project
Harrogate Road, Beamsley, Skipton BD23 6JA.
- ☎ 01756 710255
- ✉ info@beamsleyproject.org.uk
- 🌐 www.beamsleyproject.org.uk

Holiday centre in Yorkshire Dales for groups of disabled people and their companions.

The Lodge @ Birkby Hall
Birkby Hall, Birkby Lane, Bailiff Bridge, Brighouse, West Yorkshire HD6 4JJ.
- ☎ 01484 400321
- ✉ thelodge@birkbyhall.co.uk
- 🌐 www.birkbyhall.co.uk

Contact: Janet & Steven Wild
Luxury bed & breakfast accommodation created with one purpose in mind – your comfort. Relax in the oak floored guest lounge or on the balcony, and enjoy the views over acres of farmland before retiring to your own en-suite bedroom for a restful night's sleep. We offer a twin or double bedroom with all the amenities expected to accommodate disabled guests, and are committed to providing access for everyone. Extra time and consideration will be given to anybody with mobility, hearing or visual restrictions.

BEVERLEY, East Yorkshire
Rudstone Walk Country Cottages
South Cave, Brough, near Beverley HU15 2AH.
- 01430 422230
- admin@rudstone-walk.co.uk
- www.rudstone-walk.co.uk
Cottages designed for disabled people overlooking The Wolds and Humber.

SKIPSEA, East Yorkshire
Scout Holiday Homes Trust Caravan
Low Skirlington Leisure Park, Skipsea YO25 8SY.
Contact: Scout Holiday Homes Trust
- 020 8433 7290
Unit on family owned site near Driffield.

Linden Tree
Carlton Road, Carlton Miniott, Thirsk, North Yorkshire YO7 4LX.
- 01845 523765
- ptearall@btinternet.com
- www.visitlindentree.co.uk
We offer family run holiday cottages and bed & breakfast accommodation in an ideal location for exploring the Yorkshire Dales and the North Yorkshire Moors, with opportunities for walks and fishing nearby. Our bed & breakfast accommodation is on ground level, and we offer wide doors and a shower room fitted for wheelchair access. Start your day with a hearty traditional breakfast, with continental and vegetarian options available on request. York, Harrogate and Teeside are easily accessible. A warm welcome awaits you at Linden Tree.

YORK, North Yorkshire
Woodlands Respite Care Centre
120 Thief Lane, Hull Road, York YO10 3HU.
- 01904 430600
- enquiries@woodlands.org.uk
- www.woodlands.org.uk
Purpose-built centre to meet the needs of people with multiple sclerosis. Located in own grounds to the east of the city of York.

NAS ASSESSED ACCOMMODATION

BALIFF BRIDGE, BRIGHOUSE, Yorkshire
The Lodge at Birkby Hall
Four star bed & breakfast
- 01484 400 321
- Thelodge@birkbyhall.co.uk
- www.birkbyhall.co.uk

BRIDLINGTON, Yorkshire
Providence Place
Four star guest house
- 01262 603 840
- enquiries@providenceplace.info

BRIDLINGTON, Yorkshire
Marina Holiday Apartments
Two star self-catering
- 0148 2629 063
- marinaholidays@hotmail.co.uk

Pride-N-Joy
Three star self-catering
- 0114 3601 145
- peter@pride-n-joy.co.uk

BROUGH, Yorkshire
Rudstone Walk Country Accommodation
Four star guest accommodation
- 0143 0422 230
- office@rudstone-walk.co.uk
- www.rudstone-walk.co.uk

BUCKDEN, Yorkshire
9 Dalegarth and Heron Ghyll
Four star self-catering
- 01756 760877
- info@dalegarth.co.uk

EASINGWOLD, Yorkshire
Thornton Lodge Farm
Four star farmhouse
- 01347 821306
- enquiries@thorntonlodgefarm.co.uk

EBBERSTON, Yorkshire
Cow Pasture Cottage & Swallowtail Cottage
Three and Four star self-catering
- 01723 859285
- brendagreen@yorkshireancestors.com
- www.studleyhousefarm.co.uk

ELLERBY, Yorkshire
The Ellerby
Four star Inn
- 01947 840342
- dra12@live.co.uk
- www.ellerbyhotel.co.uk

FELLBECK, Yorkshire
Brimham Rocks Cottages
Four star self-catering
- 0176 5620 284
- brimhamrockscottages@yahoo.com

FILEY, Yorkshire
5 Leys Holiday Accommodation
Five star self-catering
- 0148 263 8300
- info@5leys.co.uk
- www.5leys.co.uk

FLAMBOROUGH, Yorkshire
Flamborough Rock Cottages
Three and Four star self-catering
- 0126 2605 957
- jannicegeraghty@hotmail.co.uk

HARWOOD DALE, Yorkshire
The Grainary
Four star farmhouse
- 0172 3870 026
- grainary@btopenworld.com
- www.grainary.co.uk

HELMSLEY, Yorkshire
YHA Helmsley
Four star hostel
- 0870 7708 868
- neilbaldwin@yha.org.uk
- www.yha.org.uk

HIGH CATTON, STAMFORD BRIGDE, Yorkshire
The Courtyard & Ruxpin Cottage
Four and Five star self-catering
- 01759 371 374
- foster-s@sky.com
- www.highcattongrange.co.uk

ILKLEY, West Yorkshire
Ilkley Moor Cottages and Apartments at Westwood Lodge
Four and Five star self-catering
- 01943 433430
- welcome@westwoodlodge.co.uk
- www.westwoodlodge.co.uk

KELFIELD, Yorkshire
The Dovecote Barns York
Five star self-catering
- 01757 248 331
- info@dovecotebarnsyork.co.uk

KIRKBYMOORSIDE, Yorkshire

The Cornmill
Four star guest house
📞 0175 1432 000
📧 cornmill@kirbymills.co.uk
🌐 www.kirbymills.co.uk

Partridge Cottage
Four star self-catering
📞 01751 430500
📧 jeffreyhlee@aol.com
🌐 www.lowhaggfarm.com

LEEDS, West Yorkshire

Weetwood Hall
Four star hotel
📞 0113 2306000
📧 peter.chubb@weetwood.co.uk
🌐 www.weetwood.co.uk

LOCKTON, Yorkshire

YHA Lockton
Four star hostel
📞 0870 7708 868
📧 neilbaldwin@yha.org.uk
🌐 www.yha.org.uk

LOVESOME HILL, Yorkshire

Lovesome Hill Farm
Four star farmhouse
📞 01609 772311
📧 lovesomehillfarm@btinternet.com
🌐 www.lovesomehillfarm.co.uk

MIDDLETON, PICKERING, Yorkshire

The Hawthornes Lodges
Four star self-catering
📞 0175 1474 755
📧 info@thehawthornes.co.uk
🌐 www.thehawthornes.co.uk

Mel House Cottage
Newton-on-Rawcliffe, Pickering, North
Yorkshire YO18 8QA.
📞 01751 475396
🌐 www.letsholiday.com
📧 holiday@letsholiday.com
🅒 Contact John & Penny Wicks
Four comfortable, well-equipped, four
star properties with indoor pool/
spa/sauna. Located in an attractive
'level' village in the North York Moors
National Park (with pub, duck pond
and children's play area nearby) four
miles from the busy market town of
Pickering. Ideal for access to the Moors,
Cropton & Dalby forests, the East
Yorkshire coast, the City of York and a
nostalgic ride on the North York Moors
Steam Railway. Accompanied, children,
dogs and horses are welcome! You
won't be disappointed!

 'Mallard' is 'wheelchair accessible' (NAS accredited as Level 'M3 Assisted')

 'Swift' is 'wheelchair accessible' (NAS accredited as Level 'M3 independent')

 'Owl' is suitable for people with mobility impairment (NAS accredited as Level 'M1').

PICKERING, Yorkshire
Sunset Cottage
Four star self-catering
- 01751 472172
- bookings@boonhill.co.uk
- www.boonhill.co.uk

Keld Head Farm Cottages
Four star self-catering
- 01751 473974
- julian@keldheadcottages.com
- www.keldheadcottages.com

Eastgate Cottages
Four and Five star self-catering
- 01751 476653
- info@northyorkshirecottages.co.uk

PONTEFRACT, West Yorkshire
Tower House Executive Guest House
Five star guest house
- +44 1977 699988
- towerhouse.guesthouse@virgin.net

PRESTON, HULL, Yorkshire
Little Weghill Farm
Four star farmhouse
- 0148 2897 650
- info@littleweghillfarm.co.uk
- www.littleweghillfarm.co.uk

RICCALL, YORK, Yorkshire
Pound Cottage, Copper Cottage & Crown Cottage
Four star self-catering
- 01757 248203
- info@southnewlandsfarm.co.uk
- www.southnewlandsfarm.co.uk

SANDSEND, Yorkshire
Sandsend Bay Cottages
Four star self-catering
- 01947 893331
- info@sandsendbaycottages.co.uk

SCARBOROUGH, Yorkshire
Inglenook Guest House
Five star guest house
- 0172 3369 454
- inglenookguesthouse@live.co.uk

Scarborough Travel and Holiday Lodge
Three star guest accommodation
- 0172 3363 537
- enquiries@scarborough-lodge.co.uk
- www.scarborough-lodge.co.uk

SEWERBY, Yorkshire
Field House Farm Cottages
Four and Five star self-catering
- 01262 674932
- john.foster@
  fieldhousefarmcottages.co.uk
- www.fieldhousefarmcottages.co.uk

STAITHES, Yorkshire
Dale House Farm Cottages
Four star self-catering
- 0194 7840 377
- em.welford@btinternet.com
- www.dalehousefarmcottages.co.uk

STANNINGTON, Yorkshire
The Cart Shed
Four star self-catering
- 0114 2302 122
- moorwoodequine@googlemail.com

STAPE, Yorkshire
Rawcliffe House Farm
Four star self-catering
- 01751 473292
- stay@rawcliffehousefarm.co.uk
- www.rawcliffehousefarm.co.uk

Practical advice about how to do everyday things differently

Each guide is packed with practical advice and includes real-life stories to inspire people to take control of different aspects of their lives, with maximum choice and independence.

Doing Careers Differently

Whatever your aspirations and wherever you are in your career, this guide will help you both take the first step or plan longer term to make a success of your career while living with a disability or health condition.

Doing IT Differently

Provides information and assistance to allow everyone the opportunity to take advantage and overcome the barriers of Information Technology (IT) and computers regardless of disability.

Doing Work Differently

Explores practical solutions to real questions related to work and provides real life examples of how people have started a job, found a new career, or found a way to keep doing their current job if their circumstances change.

Doing Money Differently

Looks at new ways of making, saving and looking after your money. It is a toolkit to help you understand money better and lessen the amount of time you spend thinking and worrying about it.

Download your free copy from: www.radar.org.uk/publications

Telephone: 020 7250 3222
Textphone: 18001 020 7250 3222
Email: radar@radar.org.uk
www.radar.org.uk

 the disability rights people

SUMMERBRIDGE, Yorkshire
Helme Pasture
Four star self-catering
- 01423 780279
- info@helmepasture.co.uk
- www.helmepasture.co.uk

SWINTON, MALTON, Yorkshire
Walnut Garth
Four star self-catering
- 01653 691293
- cas@walnutgarth.co.uk
- www.walnutgarth.co.uk

THORPE BASSETT, Yorkshire
The Old Post Office
Four star self-catering
- 01944 758047
- ssimpsoncottages@aol.com

WHITBY, Yorkshire
Captain Cook's Haven
Three and Four star self-catering
- 01947 893573

Groves Dyke
Three star self-catering
- 01947 811404
- relax@grovesdyke.co.uk
- www.grovesdyke.co.uk

Whitby Holiday Park
Four star holiday and Touring park
- 01947 602664
- shelley@normanhurst.net
- www.coastdaleparks.co.uk

YHA Whitby
Four star hostel
- 0870 7708 868
- neilbaldwin@yha.org.uk
- www.yha.org.uk

WRELTON, Yorkshire
Beech Farm Cottages
Four and Five star self-catering
- 01751 476612
- holiday@beechfarm.com
- www.beechfarm.com

YAPHAM, Yorkshire
Wolds View Holiday Cottages
Four and Five star self-catering
- 01759 302172
- info@woldsviewcottages.co.uk
- www.woldsviewcottages.co.uk

YORK, Yorkshire
Best Western Monkbar Hotel
Three star hotel
- 01904 638086
- june@monkbarhotel.co.uk
- www.monkbarhotel.co.uk

About North East England

The North East region covers the area between the Tees Valley and the Scottish border including County Durham, Northumberland and Tyne & Wear. Within its boundaries are the natural wild areas of the northern Pennines, the dramatic Northumberland Coast, the Tyne valley and the extensive Northumberland National Park.

Much of Britain's history was moulded in this Region. Hadrian's Wall, now a World Heritage Site, was for centuries the northern boundary of the Roman Empire. The Wall and its associated areas can be explored at many sites including Corbridge and Segedunum Fort in Wallsend. Britain's early Christian heritage is represented by Lindisfarne Priory on Holy Island near Berwick-on-Tweed and in this region you can also visit the majestic Durham Cathedral and the historic Bede's World Anglo-Saxon museum at Jarrow. Evidence of the turbulent Middle Ages can be seen at castles such as Bamburgh and Barnard. A more peaceful feature of Barnard Castle is the Bowes Museum housing the North's greatest collection of fine and decorative art.

With its extensive coastline, the area has a long seafaring tradition. Captain Cook was born near Middlesbrough where his life and achievements are depicted at the Captain Cook Birthplace Museum. A replica of his ship, 'Endeavour' can be seen at Stockton-on-Tees and a 1800's quayside has been reconstructed at Hartlepool.

The Industrial Revolution brought pioneering developments in mining, engineering, shipbuilding and other heavy industry to the region as depicted at the Discovery Museum in Newcastle. The world's first public railway ran between Stockton and Darlington and the railway heritage is widely displayed including at Locomotion, the National Railway Museum's new centre at Shildon in County Durham.

As to the present and future, one of the country's most prominent works of art, the Angel of the North, greets travellers approaching Gateshead where, on the southern bank of the Tyne, the Baltic Centre for Contemporary Art and the

Sage music performance centre were built to mark the Millennium. Across the river in the lively regional capital of Newcastle-upon-Tyne, another Millennium project, the Life Science Centre focuses on the science of genetics. Holiday shoppers can choose between Newcastle's city centre shops around Eldon Square or the out-of-town MetroCentre in Gateshead.

There are many opportunities for countryside recreation and outdoor activities in the region. Kielder Forest, Europe's largest man-made woodland, has a visitor centre at Kielder Castle and a wide range of water sports are available on Kielder Water as well as trips on an accessible cruiser. The Wildfowl & Wetlands Trust has a centre at Washington near Sunderland. At Alnwick in Northumberland, the Gardens of the Castle are being recreated – try the accessible treetop walkway. The Castle itself has frequently appeared on large and small screens, most notably in the first two Harry Potter films.

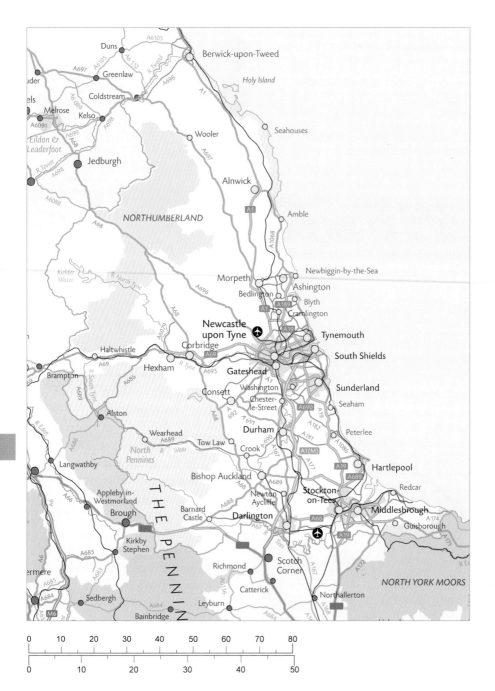

Resources

Tourism

North East England Tourism

🌐 www.visitnortheastengland.com

This website hosts links to numerous tourist offices in the North East and general information on what to do when visiting.

Information & advice

Disability North

Castles Farm Road, Newcastle upon Tyne NE3 1PH.

☎ 0191 284 0480

✉ reception@disabilitynorth.org.uk

🌐 disabilitynorth.org.uk

The Information & Advisory Service can offer advice on holiday accommodation for people with a disability.

DIAL

Offer free, impartial and confidential information and advice by telephone to disabled people, their relatives and professionals. Local branches of DIAL are constantly changing but at the time of writing, the following groups were members of DIAL UK and may be able to help visitors in their areas. Please call before travelling to check whether the service and organisation is still available:

Blyth Valley Disabled Forum

☎ 01670 364657

Darlington Assn on Disability

☎ 01325 489999

   Textphone 01325 245061

Hartlepool Access Group

☎ 01429 861777

BLISS-Ability, South Shields

☎ 0191 427 1666 (also Textphone)

Equipment hire

Adapt-ABILITY

Sanderson Street, Coxhoe, Durham DH6 4DF.

☎ 0800 0925092

✉ info@adapt-ability.co.uk

🌐 www.adapt-ability.co.uk

This company has manual and powered wheelchairs and scooters and a range of other equipment for hire from the above address and also from a branch in Hartlepool.

Adapt-ABILITY

We are a comprehensive healthcare resource situated in Durham, providing an array of facilities; from aids for disabled people to the testing of eyes and dispensing of spectacles. We have a sound financial base and an enviable reputation, so you can buy or hire from us with complete confidence. We operate a home delivery service to most parts of Northumbria, Durham and Cleveland, and are proud to have been providing healthcare to the people of the Northeast of England for over 75 years.

SHOPMOBILITY

The National Federation of Shopmobility UK (NFSUK), PO Box 6641, Christchurch BH23 9DQ.

☎ 0844 41 41 850

✉ Info@shopmobilityuk.org

🌐 www.shopmobilityuk.org

Hire manual and powered wheelchairs and scooters. Have a range of branches around the UK. You can find the nearest Shopmobility schemes to you on their on-line Directory. Access is obtained by clicking

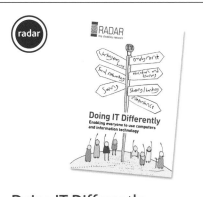

on the 'Shopmobility Directory' button on the top of the row to the left of their website and using the search criteria. You will need to contact a specific Shopmobility Scheme in order to make equipment bookings or find out detailed information. General and contact information is contained in their Directory.

Publications

County Durham Access Directory

📞 0191 383 3337

A booklet published regularly, giving information for people with disabilities about transport services in the county. Available in print, Braille or on tape by post from Passenger Transport, Durham County Council, Environment & Technical Services, County Hall, Durham DH1 5UQ.

Accommodation

BERWICK-UPON-TWEED, Northumberland

Ord House Country Park

East Ord, Berwick-upon-Tweed TD15 2NS.

📞 01289 305288

📧 enquiries@ordhouse.co.uk

🌐 www.ordhouse.co.uk

Park for touring caravans in village near Berwick.

KIELDER, Northumberland

Calvert Trust Kielder

Kielder Water, Hexham NE48 1BS.

📞 01434 250232

Purpose-built chalets in Northumberland.

Cornriggs Cottages

Low Cornriggs Farm, Cornriggs, Cowshill, Bishop Auckland, Co Durham DL13 1AQ.

📞 01388 537600

📧 cornriggsfarm@btconnect.com

🌐 www.cornriggsfarm.co.uk

Contact: Janet Elliott

Luxury cottages, spectacular views. Central location to Durham, Beamish and The Lakes. Three large bedrooms, accessible WC and shower, bathroom, kitchen diner, lounge with satellite TV, outside seating, and garden. Open all year. Payment by credit/debit card, cash or cheque. Nearest shop is 1.50 miles away, and nearest pub is 0.90 miles away.

NAS ASSESSED ACCOMMODATION

BAMBURGH, Northumberland
Outchester & Ross Farm Cottages
Four and Five star self-catering
- 01668 213228
- jbs@rossfarm.f2s.com
- www.rosscottages.co.uk

BARDON MILL, Northumberland
Coach House B&B
Four star bed & breakfast
- 01434 344 779
- mail@bardonmillcoachhouse.co.uk
- www.bardonmillcoachhouse.co.uk

Old High Shield
Four star self-catering
- 0143 434 4791
- highshield@btinternet.com

BELFORD, Northumberland
Elwick Farm Cottages
Four star self-catering
- 01668 213259
- w.r.reay@talk21.com
- www.elwickcottages.co.uk

BELLINGHAM, Northumberland
Brownrigg Lodges
Three star self-catering
- 01434 220 272
- mac.kent@virgin.net
- www.brownrigglodges.com

BERWICK-UPON-TWEED, Northumberland
Fenham Farm, Coastal Bed & Breakfast
Four star guest accommodation
- 0128 9381 245
- gillcurry@hotmail.com

Meadow Hill Guest House
Four star guest house
- 01289 306325
- christineabart@aol.com
- www.meadow-hill.co.uk

West Ord Holiday Cottages
Three and Four star self-catering
- +44 01289 386631
- stay@westord.co.uk
- www.westord.co.uk

BINGFIELD, HEXHAM, Northumberland
The Hytte
Five star self-catering
- 01434 672321
- srgregory@thehytte.com
- www.thehytte.com

BOWES, Durham
Mellwaters Barn
Four star self-catering
- 01833 628181
- mellwatersbarn@aol.com
- www.mellwatersbarn.co.uk

BUTTERKNOWLE, Durham
Little Owl Lodge
Four star self-catering
- 0138 8710 749
- yvonne@alpacas-easthowle.co.uk
- www.alpacas-easthowle.co.uk

CHATHILL, Northumberland
Doxford Hall Hotel & Spa
Four star country house hotel
- 0166 5589 700
- info@doxfordhall.com
- www.doxfordhall.com

COCKFIELD, BISHOP AUCKLAND, Durham
Stonecroft and Swallows Nest
Four star self-catering
- 01388 718251
- info@farmholidaysuk.com
- www.farmholidaysuk.com

CORNHILL ON TWEED, Northumberland
The Collingwood Arms Hotel
Three star hotel
- 01890 882424
- enquiries@collingwoodarms.com
- www.collingwoodarms.com

CORNRIGGS, COWSHILL, Durham
Cornriggs Cottages
Five star self-catering
- 0169 7746 777
- enquiries@northumbria-byways.com
- www.northumbria-byways.com

CRAMLINGTON, NORTHUMBERLAND, Northumberland
Burradon Farm Cottages and Houses
Four and Five star self-catering
- 0191 447 4616
- judy@burradonfarm.co.uk
- www.burradonfarm.co.uk

CRASTER, Northumberland
Craster Pine Lodges
Four star self-catering
- 01665 576286
- info@crasterholidays.co.uk
- www.crasterpinelodges.co.uk

DARLINGTON, Durham
River Cottage
Five star self-catering
- 01325 730 059
- sarahrutter@me.com

DOXFORD ESTATE, Northumberland
Doxford Cottages
Five star self-catering
- 01665 589 393
- alun@doxfordcottages.co.uk
- www.doxfordcottages.co.uk

EDLINGHAM, Northumberland
Lumbylaw Cottages
Four star self-catering
- 0166 5574 277
- holidays@lumbylaw.co.uk
- www.lumbylaw.co.uk

EGGLESTON, Durham
Stable Court
Four star self-catering
- 01263 862500
- www.stablecourt.co.uk

GAINFORD, Durham
East Greystone Farm Cottages
Four and Five star self-catering
- 01325 730236
- sue@holidayfarmcottages.co.uk
- www.holidayfarmcottages.co.uk

GRINDON FARM, HAYDON BRIDGE, Northumberland
The Old Farmhouse
Four star self-catering
- 0143 468 4273
- chris@grindonfarm.co.uk
- www.grindonfarm.co.uk

HAYDON BRIDGE, Northumberland
Grindon Cartshed
Four star bed & breakfast
- 📞 01434 684273
- ✉ cartshed@grindon.force9.co.uk
- 🌐 www.grindonfarm.co.uk

Shaftoe's
Four star guest house
- 📞 0143 4600 533
- ✉ bookings@shaftoes.co.uk
- 🌐 www.shaftoes.co.uk

HIGH HESLEDEN, Durham
The Ship Inn
Four star Inn
- 📞 01429 836 453
- ✉ sheila@theshipinn.net

INGLETON, Durham
Mill Granary Cottages
Five star self-catering
- 📞 +44 01325 730339
- ✉ info@millgranary.co.uk

KIELDER, Northumberland
Calvert Trust Kielder
Four star self-catering
- 📞 0143 4250 232
- ✉ tara.martin@calvert-kielder.com
- 🌐 www.calvert-trust.org.uk

Falstone Barns
Five star self-catering
- 📞 01434 240251
- ✉ info@falstonebarns.com
- 🌐 www.falstonebarns.com

KIRKNEWTON, Northumberland
Crookhouse
Four star self-catering
- 📞 01668 216 113
- ✉ stay@crookhousecottages.co.uk
- 🌐 www.crookhouse.co.uk

LAMBLEY, NEAR BRAMPTON, Northumberland
Clover Hill Cottage
Four star self-catering
- ✉ erringtonfarms@live.com
- 🌐 www.cloverhillcumbria.co.uk

LONGHORSLEY, Northumberland
Linden Hall Golf & Country Club
Four star country house hotel
- 📞 01670 500000
- ✉ seamus.coen@macdonald-hotels.co.uk
- 🌐 www.macdonaldhotels.co.uk

Beacon Hill Farm
Four and Five star self-catering
- 📞 01670 780900
- ✉ alun@beaconhill.co.uk
- 🌐 www.beaconhill.co.uk

LUCKER, NORTHUMBERLAND, Northumberland
Lucker Hall Steading
Four and Five star self-catering
- 📞 0166 8219 941
- ✉ jane@nehc.co.uk
- 🌐 www.alnwickcastleholiday
  cottages.co..uk

NEWBROUGH, HEXHAM, Northumberland
Carr Edge Farm
Four star farmhouse
- 📞 01434 674788
- ✉ stay@carredge.co.uk
- 🌐 www.carredge.co.uk

NEWCASTLE UPON TYNE, Tyne & Wear
Euro Hostel Newcastle
Four star hostel
- 0845 4900 371
- stevem@euro-hostels.co.uk
- www.euro-hostels.co.uk

Hilton Newcastle Gateshead
Accredited hotel
- 0191 4909 700
- wendy.bryant@hilton.com
- www.hilton.com

NORTH CHARLTON, Northumberland
The Reading Rooms
Four star self-catering
- 0166 5589 434
- enquiries@
  northumberlandcottages.com
- www.northumberlandcottages.com

QUEBEC, Durham
Hamsteels Hall Cottages
Four star self-catering
- 01207 520388
- june@hamsteelshall.co.uk
- www.hamsteelshall.co.uk

ROCHESTER, NR OTTERBURN, Northumberland
Redesdale Arms
Four star Inn
- 0183 0520 668
- info@redesdale-hotel.co.uk
- www.redesdale-hotel.co.uk

RUFFSIDE VILLAGE, Durham
Hadrian & Derwent Country Escapes
Four star self-catering
- 01207 588100/508001
- helen@hadriananddderwent.co.uk

SHILBOTTLE, Northumberland
Village Farm
Three, Four and Five star self-catering
- 01665 575591
- crissy@villagefarmcottages.co.uk
- www.villagefarmcottages.co.uk

SLALEY, NR HEXHAM, Northumberland
The Old Byre Rye Hill Farm
Four star self-catering
- 01434 673259
- info@ryehillfarm.co.uk
- www.ryehillfarm.co.uk

SUNNISIDE, NR NEWCASTLE, Tyne & Wear
Hedley Hall Country Cottages
Four star self-catering
- 0120 7231 835
- hedleyhall@aol.com
- www.hedleyhall.com

THORNTON, BERWICK UPON TWEED, Northumberland
Skylark Cottage
Four star self-catering
- 0128 9382 223
- laura@lcsmales-son.co.uk

WINSTON, Durham
Alwent Mill Cottage
Four star self-catering
- 01325 730479
- libby@alwentmill.co.uk

WOOLER, Northumberland
Fenton Hill Farm Cottages
Four star self-catering
- 01668 216228
- stay@fentonhillfarm.co.uk
- www.fentonhillfarm.co.uk

" *2012 is the ideal time to experience
fantastic events and festivals, and
discover Scotland's inspirational
natural and built landscapes.* "

Scotland

"
Scotland offers an amazing range of landscapes, from gentle rolling hills to breathtaking peaks, rugged coastlines and lochs to sub-tropical gardens.
"

Visit Scotland

As a place to visit for a wonderful holiday, Scotland is hard to beat. We have great places to stay, warm, friendly people, inspiring scenery, superb food and drink, a fascinating culture and history, plus a vast range of things to see and do.

The drama and sheer variety of Scotland's natural features never fails to impress visitors. Though small, the country offers an amazing range of landscapes, from the gentle rolling hills of Dumfries and Galloway to the breath-taking peaks of the Cairngorms, and from the rugged coastlines of the north east to the sub-tropical gardens of Wester Ross. Explore Scotland's lochs and mountains, its interesting geography and its gloriously unpredictable climate.

Discover the different historical and culture elements that can be rightly claimed to be unique to this country. Whatever you want from your holiday, Scotland is waiting to be discovered. We're proud of our beautiful country, proud of our traditions and our history and we look forward to sharing them with you.

2012: Creative Scotland

From rock to opera, Scottish arts and culture has the power to enthrall, challenge, provoke and inspire. Scotland has fired imagination, encouraged invention and inspired creation for

generations. In 2012, the Year of Creative Scotland, experience Scotland's cultural and creative vibrancy at first hand.

A celebration of Scotland's creative assets and contribution to the world, 2012 is the ideal time to experience fantastic events and festivals and discover Scotland's inspirational natural and built landscapes. For more information visit www.visitscotland.com/creative

Year of Creative Scotland 2012

Accessible Scotland
If you are planning a holiday in Scotland and have a mobility impairment, then there are a number of ways to choose accommodation and activities that are suitable to your needs. Visit www.visitscotland.com/guide/where-to-stay/accessible-scotland and use the links at the foot of the page to check

for accommodation that can meet your requirements. Or contact us directly at info@visitscotland.com to let VisitScotland.com advisors not only help find the right place – but also book it for you.

Surprise yourself!

Find out more information about Scotland at:
www.visitscotland.com

About Scotland

Scotland has something for everyone – dramatic and attractive scenery in the countryside and around the coast, historic towns, a well-established arts scene, seaside resorts, attractions, wilderness areas for solitude and the bustle of major cities.

The historic core of capital city Edinburgh is on the Royal Mile between the Castle and the Palace of Holyroodhouse – the new home of the Scottish Parliament contrasting with the elegant Georgian terraces in the New Town, north of Princes Street. Attractions include the Museum of Scotland, the National Gallery of Scotland and the Scottish National Portrait Gallery as well as the Scotch Whisky Heritage Centre and Our Dynamic Earth (exploring the evolution of our planet. In August the Edinburgh Festival attracts arts lovers to a wide range of events at a variety of venues. In the hills of this area, you'll find the small towns of Peebles, Selkirk and Hawick and small fishing ports such as Eyemouth. Sir Walter Scott's home at Abbotsford near Melrose is closed for restoration until 2013, but the gardens and a new visitor centre are due to open during 2012.

South west

Glasgow's major growth in the 19th Century has been followed by recent regeneration of the city centre and waterfront. The newly-opened Riverside, houses a museum of transport and travel. On the outskirts, you'll find the Burrell Art Collection at its purpose-built gallery in Pollok Country Park. Other attractions include Greenbank Gardens at Clarkston (National Trust for Scotland), the David Livingstone Centre at Blantyre, Flotterstone (a Countryside Centre in the Pentland Hills) and the Falkirk Wheel, the only revolving boat lift in the world. Further west is the picturesque south-facing coast and countryside of Dumfries and Galloway, and the resorts of Ayr and Largs on the Ayrshire coast. Attractions here include Burns Cottage at Alloway, Culzean Castle and Country Park near Maybole, Drumlanrig Castle in Dumfriesshire, the World Heritage Site of New Lanark and Viking history centre Vikingar! at Largs.

East

North of the Forth are the major centres of Dundee, Perth and Aberdeen. History devotees can visit the Bannockburn Heritage Centre at Stirling, while country lovers can choose from many sites around the Perthshire towns of Pitlochry and Dunkeld, and the Grampians and perhaps visit one of the many local whisky distilleries. Visitor centres displaying the historic life of the area include the Grampian Transport Museum at Alford, the Aberdeenshire Farming Heritage Centre in Aden Country Park, the Angus Folk Museum and the British Golf Museum at St Andrews in Fife.

Highlands & Islands

Outside Inverness (the city centre in this area) is the Culloden Battlefield (National Trust for Scotland). Travelling inland, you reach Loch Ness in the Great Glen (sightings of the monster are not guaranteed!). You'll find dramatic wild countryside and many small towns and villages. The world-famous Inverewe Gardens are at Poolewe in Wester Ross and there are displays of crafts and farming at the Highlands Folk Museum in Kingussie. The Islands have their own attractions. Some, off the west coast can be reached by short ferry trips or, in the case of Skye, by bridge. Highland life 100 years ago is depicted at the Skye Museum of Island Life. Visiting Orkney, Shetland and the Western Isles will need more planning, but all are worth a visit for their distinctive lifestyle and reminders of their prehistoric and Nordic past.

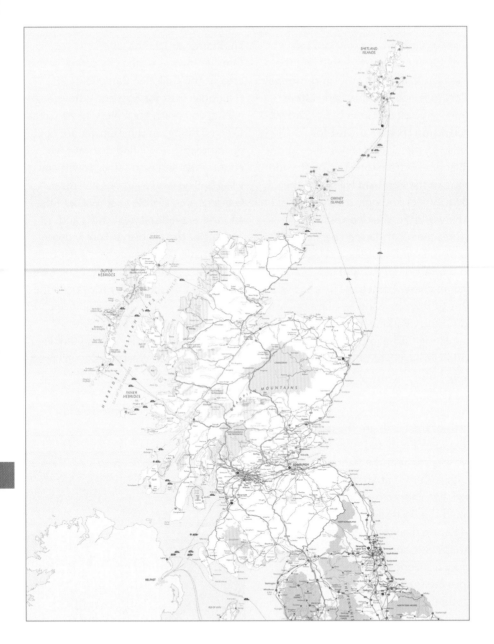

Resources

Tourism

VisitScotland

Quality & Standards, Thistle House, Beechwood Park North, Inverness IV2 3ED.
ⓦ www.visitscotland.com
Operate an Accessibility Scheme for places to stay and attractions that are inspected against specific criteria for three levels of impaired mobility Search their site for 'Accessible Scotland' to find out more.

Transport

The three largest airports in Scotland are operated by BAA Scotland. For information on the services at each contact:

Aberdeen Airport
ⓣ 0844 481 6666
ⓦ www.aberdeenairport.com

Edinburgh Airport
ⓣ 0844 481 8989
ⓦ www.edinburghairport.com

Glasgow Airport
ⓣ 0844 481 5555
ⓦ www.glasgowairport.com

They share a Textphone enquiry number:
ⓣ 0844 571 7410

Highlands & Islands Airports Ltd

Inverness Airport, Inverness IV2 7JB.
ⓣ 01667 462445
ⓦ www.hial.co.uk
Operate 11 airports in northern Scotland providing commercial, tourist and emergency services. Facilities at some of the smaller airports are limited but all have basically accessible terminals and most have lifts for passengers who cannot use steps into aircraft.

CalMac Ferries

The Ferry Terminal, Gourock PA19 1QP.
ⓣ 0800 066 5000 (enquiries)
ⓔ reservations@calmac.co.uk
ⓦ www.calmac.co.uk
Operate a wide range of routes off the west coast of Scotland. Facilities for disabled passengers vary depending on the vessel used on the route; information is included on their website under 'The Fleet'. Anyone who may need assistance should notify the company when booking and checking in. Fare concessions for disabled drivers are available on production of appropriate documents.

NorthLink Ferries

Stromness Ferry Terminal,Ferry Road,Stromness,Orkney, KW16 3BH.
ⓣ Reservations 0845 6000 449
    Administration 01856 885500
ⓔ info@northlinkferries.co.uk
ⓦ www.northlinkferries.co.uk
Operate ferry services to Orkney and Shetland from Aberdeen and between Scrabster in Caithness and Stromness on Orkney, using three modern vessels. Each has toilets for disabled passengers and lifts between decks. Those used for overnight sailings have four cabins designed for disabled people of which two have enhanced facilities including hoists. Concessionary rates and special boarding arrangements are available for disabled people. There are toilets for disabled people at each of Northlink's terminals. Advance notice of passengers requiring assistance is appreciated.

Pentland Ferries

Pier Road, St Margaret's Hope, South Ronaldsay, Orkney KW17 2SW.

☎ 01856 831226

🖥 www.pentlandferries.co.uk

Operate car ferries on the 1-hour crossing between Gill's Bay in Caithness and the southern Orkney island of South Ronaldsay. No specific facilities are available for disabled passengers.

Highland Adventure Safaris

Drumdewan, Aberfeldy PH15 2JQ.

☎ 01887 820071

✉ info@highlandsafaris.net

🖥 www.highlandsafaris.net

From its base at an accessible visitor centre, between Aberfeldy and Tummel Bridge, Highland Adventure Safaris use a long wheelbase Land Rover to explore the Perthshire Highlands going to areas that would otherwise be inaccessible to many people. Assistance with getting on and off the vehicle can be provided.

Mobility Assist

98 High street, Galashiels, TD1 1SQ.

☎ 01896 757075

✉ mobilityassist@aol.com

Operate a taxi service in the Scottish Borders area using vehicles with rear lifts.

Information & advice

Orkney Disability Forum

Power Station Offices, Great Western Road, Kirkwall KW15 1AN.

☎ 01856 871515

🖥 www.orkneycommunities.co.uk/ODF

Offer a Dial-a-Bus and Shopmobility service and can provide information on access in Orkney.

DIAL

Offer free, impartial and confidential information and advice by telephone to disabled people, their relatives and professionals. Local branches of DIAL are constantly changing but at the time of writing, the following groups were members of DIAL UK and may be able to help visitors in their areas. Please call before travelling to check whether the service and organisation is still available:

Contact Point in East Dunbartonshire

☎ 0141 578 0183 (also Textphone)

Disability Resource Centre, Clydesdale

☎ 01555 770123

Three Eyes Project Glasgow

☎ 0141 954 8432

Wellbeing Glasgow

☎ 0141 248 1899

Textphone 01983 525424

South Lanark Disability Forum

☎ 01698 307733 (also Textphone)

Equipment hire

SHOPMOBILITY

The National Federation of Shopmobility UK (NFSUK), PO Box 6641, Christchurch BH23 9DQ.

☎ 0844 41 41 850

✉ info@shopmobilityuk.org

🖥 www.shopmobilityuk.org

Hire manual and powered wheelchairs and scooters. Have a range of branches around the UK. You can find the nearest Shopmobility schemes to you on their on-line Directory. Access is obtained by clicking on the 'Shopmobility Directory' button on the top of the row to the left of their website and using the search criteria. You will need to contact a specific Shopmobility Scheme in order to make equipment

bookings or find out detailed information. General and contact information is contained in their Directory.

Publications

Historic Scotland: Access Guide
Provides information on facilities and highlights possible difficulties, for disabled people at over 70 historic buildings and sites throughout Scotland. Available free from Historic Scotland, Longmore House, Salisbury Place, Edinburgh EH9 1SH.
☎ 0131 668 8800
🌐 www.historic-scotland.gov.uk

Countryside Visits: Places to visit in the Scottish Borders with some access for wheelchair users
A free booklet by the Scottish Borders Council Rangers Service with the Borders Disability Forum. Available from the. Scottish Borders Council Countryside Ranger Service, Council HQ, Newtown St Boswells, Melrose TD6 0SA
☎ 01835 826750
Updated information can be found on
🌐 www.bordersdisabilityforum/ news/rangers

Online resources

Shetland Access Guide
🌐 www.shetlandcommunities.org/ disability-shetland
Site with detailed information on facilities for disabled people on inter-island ferries and some premises in Lerwick on their website.

Accommodation

CRATHIE, Aberdeenshire
Crathie Opportunity Holidays
The Manse Courtyard, Crathie, Ballater AB35 5UL.
☎ 01339 742100
📧 info@crathieholidays.org.uk
🌐 www.crathieholidays.org.uk
Set within the restored Manse Courtyard of historic Crathie Kirk. Four wheelchair accessible self-catering holiday cottages. Each cottage has been carefully designed and furnished. Offer a unique range of facilities so that disabled people can enjoy a relaxing holiday in accessible accommodation.
Surrounded by a fenced play area and with the protection of a security gate this facility is ideal for families which include disabled people.

CRIEFF, Perthshire
Ancaster BLESMA Home
Alligan Road, Crieff PH7 3JU.
☎ 01764 652480
📧 blesma.crieff@btconnect.com
🌐 www.blesma.org
BLESMA nursing and residential home for disabled ex-servicemen and women set on a south-facing slope of the Grampian foothills. 24 hour nursing, respite and residential care provided. Single rooms and twin bedded rooms, all have en-suite facilities and colour television. Sky television is available in lounges and communal areas, as well as a full size snooker table in a games room which goes out into our 2.5 acre garden. There is entertainment in the evenings and an itinerary of up to five excursions a week is available to those who enjoy the active life. Electronic buggies

and wheelchairs are available for added independence. Weekly swimming trips and sailing, fishing, water sports, riding, flying and parachuting are available all with disabled facilities.

DIRLETON, East Lothian
Denis Duncan House
Manse Road, Dirleton.
📞 01787 372343
📧 info@thelinberwicktrust.org.uk
🌐 www.thelinberwicktrust.org.uk
Purpose built cottage in village west of North Berwick run by a registered charity, the Lin Berwick Trust. Lin Berwick is blind, has cerebral palsy and is a wheelchair user. As a result of her own inability to find holiday accommodation suitably adapted for her disabilities, she and her husband, Ralph, founded the Trust in 1989, with the aim of filling this gap in the holiday accommodation market. This cottage opened its doors to vistors in 2006.

DRUMNADROCHIT, Inverness-shire
Lochletter Lodges
Balnain, Drumnadrochit, Inverness IV63 6TJ.
📞 01456 476313
📧 info@lochletter.com
🌐 www.lochletter.com
Chalet lodges west of Loch Ness in Glenurquhart. Drumnadrochit is a nearby quiet village where there are shops and restaurants. Inverness city is about half an hours drive and has a large shopping centre, cinemas, swimming pool and other recreational facilities. There are 4, high quality, accessible wooden lodges, built so that each has its own view. They are

accessed via a private road which crosses the River Enrick as it leaves Loch Meiklie, a small loch close to the lodges.

FORGIE, Moray
Garden Cottage
Forgie, Near Forgie.
Contact: The Cobweb Foundation, 37-39 Bruce Street, Dunfermline KY11 7AG.
📞 01358 724145
🌐 www.cobwebfoundation.org
Converted cottage for wheelchair users overlooking Spey Forest. Applications for grant funding towards holiday costs are accepted from applicants from within Scotland.

KEITH, Moray
Parkhead Croft
Drummuir, Near Keith.
Contact: The Cobweb Foundation, 37-39 Bruce Street, Dunfermline KY11 7AG.
📞 01383 733849
📧 enquiries@cobwebfoundation.org
🌐 www.cobwebfoundation.org
Single storey cottage designed for disabled people between Keith and Dufftown. Applications for grant funding towards holiday costs are accepted from applicants from within Scotland.

NORTH BERWICK, East Lothian
Leuchie House MS Respite Centre
North Berwick EH39 5NT
📞 01620 892864
📧 enquiries@leuchie.com
Now an independent charity, this specially adapted holiday home in East Lothian provides respite care and breaks for people with Multiple Sclerosis.

"

At its best, Wales is the most beguiling part of the British Isles.

Rough Guide

"

Wales

A place that becomes obsessive, beckoning back its visitors year after year.

Lonely Planet

Wales
Cymru

Visit Wales

We'd love to have you visit us in Wales. But then you'd expect us to say that. For travel author Mike Parker, the man given the job of compiling *The Rough Guide to Wales*, the experience of being in Wales changed his life – so much so that he upped sticks and moved to live in a Welsh valley.

"Just how much I loved the place shook me to my bones." Parker says. "It was like falling in love with a person rather than a place, with all the dizzy disorientation and heart-thumping joy and awe that accompanies it."

So what do you need to know about a country that inspires such strong feelings? Although Wales is not that far from London, it is a completely different place. Just how different can often takes first-time visitors by surprise.

Green and hilly, Wales has its own language, a distinct Celtic culture and heritage plus a self-belief that gives Wales a national spirit that resonates more strongly than ever.

Then there is the landscape. At around 8,000 square miles (close to 21,000 square kilometres) Wales is smaller than the US state of Massachusetts, but if you were to roll it out flat, it would be bigger than Texas.

Boasting plenty of open space, Wales is around half the size of The Netherlands but compared to The Netherlands which is home to 16 million people, Wales has only 3 million.

In 2012 Wales becomes the first country in the world to open a dedicated path running along its entire coast – all 870 miles of it.

Wales is a country on a human-scale - somewhere where you will find more than enough space to enjoy yourself but is also a place with plenty of variety. Visitors will find something different and special around every corner. Boasting three National Parks and five Areas of Outstanding Natural Beauty the outdoors is one of Wales' greatest draws.

Not that it's just countryside. The towns and cities should definitely be on the itinerary too. There are a wide range of arts and music festivals staged in Wales throughout the year and the country has a growing reputation as a mouth-watering destination for food lovers. With 641 castles, there are countless opportunities to explore the history and heritage of this ancient land.

Travel
Many visitors come straight to Wales by air or sea, while others travel by road or train from England. It takes just two hours by train to get from London to Cardiff.

Other English cities are closer still. For example, you can drive into North Wales from Manchester Airport in less than an hour.

Visit our website
For up-to-date information on short breaks and proper holidays in Wales, go to the official Visit Wales website at: **www.visitwales.co.uk**

About Wales

Wales has a tourist industry that is both well established and rapidly modernising, providing opportunities for staying in traditional resorts, large cities, country towns or at more rural locations.

Well-established resorts with attractions for families and a largely level terrain are found around much of the coast. In the north these include Rhyl, Colwyn Bay and Llandudno. Aberdovey, Barmouth and Towyn are on the west coast and Tenby and Porthcawl in the south. The hillier sections of the coast have many historic towns, some with castles such as Harlech, Caernarfon and Conwy or with attractive harbours like New Quay.

Wales has three contrasting National Parks. The one covering the Pembrokeshire Coast contains some of

Britain's most dramatic coastal scenery and provides a thriving and varied wildlife habitat. The Snowdonia National Park in the north west has impressive mountains. It is possible to get to the top

of Wales' highest mountain on the Snowdon Mountain Railway with advance notice. The Brecon Beacons, stretching from the top of the once industrial valleys into mid-Wales, are not as high as Snowdonia but have a countryside which feels just as remote. Facilities for disabled visitors have been developed by each of the National Park Authorities.

Rural areas with attractive scenery can be found in other parts of Wales and there are many opportunities for countryside activities. Water sports of all kinds are available on many reservoirs. The Wildfowl & Wetlands Trust has a centre near Llanelli and country parks have been developed in many areas including Ty Mawr near Wrexham and Caldicot Castle in Monmouthshire. The National Botanic Garden of Wales, including the spectacular Great Glasshouse, is at Llanarthe near Carmarthen.

Machynlleth is the home of the Centre for Alternative Technology. Elsewhere there are re-creations of local industrial heritage, be it slate mining in Snowdonia,

quarrying in Anglesey, the National Wool Museum near Newcastle Emlyn in Carmarthenshire or coal mining and heavy industry at the Rhondda Heritage Centre. Wales is notable for the number of preserved steam railways, several of which, including the Llanberis Lake Railway, can carry disabled passengers.

All the facilities expected of a major modern capital city can be found in Cardiff – shops, music, sports including the Millennium Stadium, museums, night life and much more. The regenerated Cardiff Bay area is the home of the Welsh Assembly and the Wales Millennium Centre. A similarly wide range of attractions can be found in Swansea including the Dylan Thomas Centre and the National Waterfront Museum. Smaller towns worth visiting include the Victorian spa town of Llandrindod Wells in mid-Wales, St David's with the country's smallest Cathedral, the university town of Aberystwyth on the west coast and the county towns of Cardigan, Carmarthen and Monmouth.

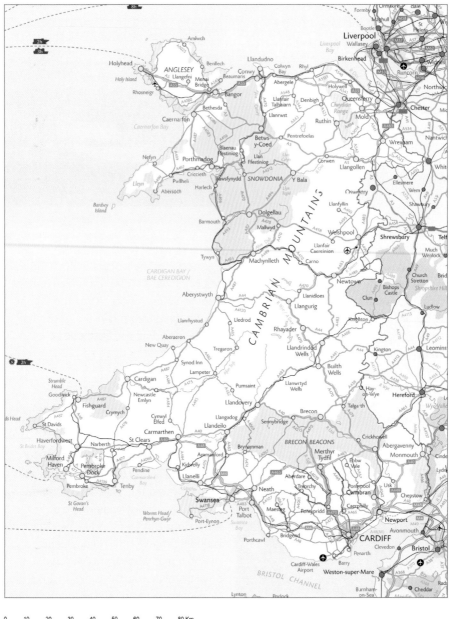

Resources

Tourism

Visit Wales

Visit Wales, QED Centre, Main Avenue, Trefforest Industrial Estate, Trefforest, Pontypridd, Rhondda, Cynon Taff CF37 5YR.

- ☎ 08708 300 306
- ✉ info@visitwales.co.uk
- 🌐 www.visitwales.co.uk

Produce a range of general tourist literature, which indicates accommodation suitable for disabled guests.

Information & advice

Disability Wales/Anabledd Cymru

Bridge House, Caerphilly Business Park, Van Road, Caerphilly CF83 3GW.

- ☎ 029 2088 7325
- 🌐 www.disabilitywales.org

Can answer enquiries by letter or phone, Freephone Helpline: 0800 731 6282 (Monday-Friday 10am-1pm).

DIAL

Offer free, impartial and confidential information and advice by telephone to disabled people, their relatives and professionals. Local branches of DIAL are constantly changing but at the time of writing, the following groups were members of DIAL UK and may be able to help visitors in their areas. Please call before travelling to check whether the service and organisation is still available:

Taran Information Service, Anglesey

- ☎ 01248 750077
  Textphone 01248 750095

Disablement Welfare Rights, Bangor

- ☎ 01248 352227

Cerebra, Carmarthen

- ☎ 0800 328 1159

Denbighshire Disability Forum

- ☎ 01745 354445

Connect DRA, Pembrokeshire

- ☎ 01348 873884

DIAL Swansea, Neath, Port Talbot

- ☎ 01792 583322

DAP Torfaen

- ☎ 001495 763778

Equipment hire

SHOPMOBILITY

The National Federation of Shopmobility UK (NFSUK), PO Box 6641, Christchurch BH23 9DQ.

- ☎ 0844 41 41 850
- ✉ info@shopmobilityuk.org
- 🌐 www.shopmobilityuk.org

Hire manual and powered wheelchairs and scooters. Have a range of branches around the UK. You can find the nearest Shopmobility schemes to you on their on-line Directory. Access is obtained by clicking on the 'Shopmobility Directory' button on the top of the row to the left of their website and using the search criteria. You will need to contact a specific Shopmobility Scheme in order to make equipment bookings or find out detailed information. General and contact information is contained in their Directory.

Bridgend Wheelchair Hire

Unit 23 St Theodores Way Brynmenyn Industrial Estate Bridgend CF32 9TZ.

- ☎ 01656 661579
- ✉ info@bridgendwheelchairhire.co.uk
- 🌐 www.bridgendwheelchairhire.co.uk

Manual and electric wheelchairs and scooters with a range of attachments and other equipment for hire. Repair service also offered.

CYMROD Clwb Teithio Dwyfor Travel Club
Sgwar yr Orsaf, PO Box 60, Pwllheli LL53 5WT.
☎ 01758 614311
Wheelchairs and scooters are available for hire for disabled people on holiday in the area around Pwllheli on daily and weekly rates. They also have wheelchair accessible vehicles for use in the area that can be hired on a mileage basis. Advance enquiries requested.

Mobility Freedom Direct
Trem-Y-Gorwel, Cwmcou, Newcastle Emlyn, Ceredigion SA38 9PE.
☎ 01239 710061
✉ enquiries@mobility-freedom-direct. com
🌐 www.mobility-freedom-direct.com
Scooters and powered wheelchairs are available to hire with delivery available at additional cost.

Physically Impaired People of Pembrokeshire Association
Information Service, The Basement, Haverfordwest Registry Office, Tower Hill, Haverfordwest, Pembrokeshire SA61 1SS.
☎ 01437760665
✉ pippapembs@btconnect.com
Offer a hire service for wheelchairs, scooters and bathroom equipment for visitors. Daily and weekly hire rates available. Advance bookings accepted in high season.

Publications

Places to Visit with Disabled and Easier Access
☎ 01874 6220451
A guide listing over 60 short trails, sites of historic, landscape or wildlife interest suitable for disabled people and anyone who just wants a nice and easy, hassle-free stroll in the Brecon Beacons. Available from National Park Information Centres, by post from Brecon Beacons National Park Authority, Plas y Ffynnon, Cambrian Way, Brecon LD3 7DP. Or view it online at:
🌐 www.breconbeacons.org/visit-us/ easy-access

Snowdonia for All
Information on trails, local towns and facilities for disabled people. This is available to view online in the 'Snowdonia for all' section of their website.
☎ 01766 770274
✉ parc@eryri-npa.gov.uk
🌐 www.eryri-npa.gov.uk

Walks for All
National Park Centre, South Parade, Tenby, Pembrokeshire SA70 7DL.
☎ 01834 845040
✉ tenby.centre@pembrokeshirecoast.org.uk
🌐 www.pembrokeshirecoast.org.uk
The 'Walks for all' section on this website provides information on accessible trails, beaches and viewpoints. Also available is an A5 bilingual guide folder that features 17 removable easy access walks around Pembrokeshire. Includes basic maps and B&W photographs. At the rear of the booklet are sections on easy access beaches and viewpoints. Prices: from the address above.

Cornerstone Cottage

Christine Neve, 2 Pound Cottages, Castlemartin
Pembroke SA71 5HN

Tel: 01646 661 369
Email: christine.gneve@mypostoffice.co.uk

Single-storey detached stone conversion with disabled access.
Two bedrooms.

Bank Farm Leisure
Camping and caravan site
With self-catering bungalows to let

Bank Farm Leisure
Horton, Gower,
Swansea SA3 1LL
Tel: 01792 390228
bankfarmleisure@aol.com
www.bankfarmleisure.co.uk

Get Caravanning
A guide to helping you explore caravanning from
a disabled person's point of view.

Available from Radar's online shop
www.radar-shop.org.uk

Flintshire County Council

For more information on Public Conveniences
within Flintshire please phone us on

01352 703 350

CYNGOR
Sir y Fflint
Flintshire
COUNTY COUNCIL

BARLOWS
—— Caravan Park ——

Pen-y-Cefn Road, Caerwys
North Wales CH7 5BH

Telephone 01352 720625

Accommodation

ABERAERON, Ceredigion
Ty Glyn Holiday Centre
Ciliau Aeron, Near Lampeter SA48 8DE.
Contact: Louise Hutchins, Hafod, Llanarth,
Ceredigion SA47 0QB.
☏ 0845 0944364
ⓦ www.tyglyndavistrust.co.uk
Purpose-built centre set in the countryside
for self-catering groups of children and
young people with disabilities.

ABERDOVEY, Gwynedd
Wrekin
Corbett Avenue, Tywyn, near Aberdovey.
Contact: Mr C Hayes, 21 Belvedere Walk,
Shrewsbury SY2 5LT.
☏ 01743 240058
Adapted bungalow owned by Shropshire
Scope offering holidays for disabled people
and in particular those with learning
disabilities.

BONCATH, Pembrokeshire
Clynfyw Countryside Centre
Abercych, Boncath SA37 0HF.
☏ 01239 841236
ⓦ www.clynfyw.co.uk
Contact: Jim Bowen.
Cottages designed for disabled people
based on a 200 acre family-run organic
farm and woodland. There are four
cottages, each of which have their own
distinctive character. Two of the cottages
are on a single level with flat access from
outside and the cottages aim to make
anyone's stay as accessible as possible.

BRECON BEACONS, Powys
Brecon Beacons Holiday Cottages
Brynoyre, Talybont-on-Usk, Brecon,
Powys LD3 7YS.
☏ 01874 676446
Ⓔ enquiries@breconcottages.com
ⓦ www.breconcottages.com
Offer a large selection of disability-friendly
properties that have been designed with
accessibility in mind. All offer stunning
views of the National Park and are located
in convenient places. Many properties have
ramps, walk-in shower rooms, wet rooms,
lifts and beds with electronic hoists and lifts
for baths. The section of the website that
lists accessible cottages can be found at:
ⓦ www.breconcottages.com/accessible

COWBRIDGE, Glamorgan
**Jane Hodge Respite Care & Holiday
Centre**
Trerhyngyll, Cowbridge CF71 7TN.
☏ 01446 772608
Respite care centre, owned by the Livability
Charity, designed for disabled people with
high dependency needs.

KIDWELLY, Carmarthenshire
Scout Holiday Homes Trust Chalet
Contact: Scout Holiday Homes Trust (see
voluntary organisations in Useful resources)
☏ 020 8433 7290
Adapted unit in Kidwelly, Carmarthenshire
suitable for people with all levels of
impairment.

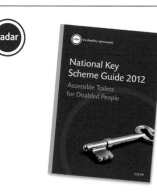

LLANDUDNO, Conwy

Belmont Hotel

21 North Parade, Llandudno LL30 2LP.

☎ 01492 877770

✉ belmonthotel@tiscali.co.uk

🌐 www.royalblindsociety.org

Hotel owned by Royal Blind Society in a seafront location overlooking Llandudno Bay on the North Wales coast. Ideally situated within easy reach of Llandudno's promenade, and local tourist attractions. Provides specialist holiday accommodation for visually impaired people and their families and friends. Also an ideal base for an activity holiday, being within easy reach of Llandudno's dry ski slope and the magical mountains of the Snowdonia National Park. Excursions with descriptive commentary are arranged and volunteers are available to accompany guests on outings.

West Shore Hotel

West Parade, Llandudno LL30 2BB.

☎ 01492 876833

✉ westshore@livability.org.uk

Hotel specially adapted for disabled holiday makers run by the charity Livability.

PENALLY, Pembrokeshire

The Wheelabout

The Ridgeway, Penally, Near Tenby SA70 7RL.

Contact: The Harriet Davis Trust, Tenby Observer Offices, Warren Street, Tenby SA70 7JY.

☎ 01834 845197

✉ helen@harriet-davis-trust.freeserve.co.uk

🌐 www.penally.org.uk

Purpose-designed and equipped house for families with disabled children in a quaint village in West Wales.

PRESTATYN, Denbighshire

The Boulevard

Prestatyn.

Contact: Mr C Hayes, 21 Belvedere Walk, Shrewsbury SY2 5LT.

☎ 01743 240058

Adapted bungalow owned by Shropshire Scope suitable for guests with a range of disabilities or impairments.

TENBY, Pembrokeshire

Giltar View

Southcliffe Street, Tenby

Contact: The Harriet Davis Trust, Tenby Observer Offices, Warren Street, Tenby SA70 7JY.

☎ 01834 845197

✉ helen@harriet-davis-trust.freeserve.co.uk

House adapted for families with disabled children in Pembrokeshire.

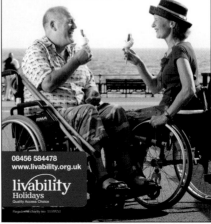

Harriet's House
Castle Square, Tenby.
Contact: The Harriet Davis Trust, Tenby
Observer Offices, Warren Street, Tenby
SA70 7JY.
☎ 01834 845197
✉ helen@harriet-davis-trust.freeserve.
co.uk
Flat adapted for families with disabled
children in Tenby.

Cornerstone Cottage
Castlemartin, Pembroke.
☎ 01646 661369
Nestled in the quiet village of
Castlemartin in the Pembrokeshire
National Park, our modern yet cosy
cottage has been carefully designed
with disabled guests in mind whilst
retaining the original charms and
character of the building. Originally
a Smithy, the cottage dates back to
1860 and has exposed beams, original
stone walls and natural stone flooring
throughout. Pembroke with its historical
castle, mill pond, cafe and shops is just
6 miles away and the coast is just a
short drive away too. The single storey
detached cottage has two bedrooms
(a double and a single with extra guest
bed if required) sleeping up to four
people. The cottage also features a fully
accessible wetroom.

Homeleigh Country Cottages
Homeleigh Country Cottages, Red
Roses, Whitland, Carmarthenshire SA34
0PN.
☎ 01834 831765
✉ enquiries@homeleigh.org
🌐 www.homeleigh.org
Homeleigh Country Cottages are ideally
situated in the peaceful Pembrokeshire
countryside within a few minutes drive
to many blue flag beaches including
Amroth, Saundersfoot, Tenby and many
more. They offer a warm welcome to
guests who need a little extra help to
make their holiday perfect. All doors
are extra wide with level entry. Shower
rooms are laid out for carefree use in
the wetroom style. Disabled aids include
electric beds, hoists, shower chairs,
commodes etc. Call or email to request
a brochure.

"

Our coastal beauty is the stuff of legends, with shorelines trimmed by golden sands and rocky outcrops.

"

Ireland

"

Just go where the island of Ireland takes you. Guaranteed, you'll return home with memories that will last a lifetime.

"

Ireland

Visit the Island of Ireland

Historically, Ireland is divided into four ancient provinces, Leinster, Munster, Connacht and Ulster. Politically, it is divided between the Republic of Ireland, which covers just under five-sixths of the island, and Northern Ireland, part of the United Kingdom, which covers the remainder and is located in the northeast of the island.

Perched on the northwest tip of Europe, this is the one place in the world where even time getting lost will be worthwhile... With ancient myths and legends to uncover, amazing landscapes to explore and locals who will be more than happy to reveal our hidden gems, just go where the island of Ireland takes you. Guaranteed, you'll return home with memories that will last a lifetime.

Ireland has over 1,448km of spectacular coastline, surrounded by the Atlantic on the west and the Irish Sea on the east. As well as towering cliffs, clear fresh waters, pristine sandy beaches, and an abundance of opportunities for the watersports

enthusiast, the coastline enjoys lively fishing villages with some of the best seafood in the world. Our coastal beauty is the stuff of legends, with shorelines trimmed by golden sands and rocky outcrops.

Inland, the lakelands and rural idylls are equally as varied as they are tranquil. You see, it's not just green on our island, it's much, much more than that.

From bizarre lunar landscapes and the mighty Atlantic to labyrinthine caves and crystal clear waterways, come and discover Ireland's breathtaking beauty.

For more information about Ireland:

The Island of Ireland
www.discoverireland.com
www.ireland.com

The Republic of Ireland
www.discoverireland.ie

When you cross that line on the map between the Republic and Northern Ireland, the first thing you're likely to notice is that you don't notice anything different: The landscape is green, and the people are friendly.

Northern Ireland
www.discovernorthernireland.com

The Fun Starts Here
DISCOVER IRELAND.IE

About Northern Ireland

The six counties of Northern Ireland, Fermanagh, Antrim, Down, Tyrone, Armagh and Derry provide varied countryside, dramatic coastlines, historic towns and attractive villages.

The six counties of Northern Ireland, Fermanagh, Antrim, Down, Tyrone, Armagh and Derry provide varied countryside, dramatic coastlines, historic towns and attractive villages.

Among the most notable landscapes are the Mourne Mountains on the southern coast of County Down, the Glens of Antrim on the north east coast and the Sperrin Mountains spanning Counties Londonderry and Tyrone. However the most famous natural feature is the Giant's Causeway on the north Antrim coast. A new Visitor Centre is due to

open during 2012 and meanwhile an accessible bus serves this World Heritage Site from the nearby town of Bushmills.

There are two major inland lakes, Lough Neagh and, in Co. Fermanagh, the extensive Lough Erne. Both offer many opportunities for angling and birdwatching. Boating is very popular on Lough Erne and there is the option of cruising south of the border along the re-opened Shannon-Erne waterway. The almost landlocked Strangford Lough in Co. Down is another mecca for birdwatchers. Near its mouth at Portaferry a modern accessible aquarium, Exploris, displays the natural history of both the Lough and the Irish Sea.

and Newcastle on the east. Tourists can learn about the linen industry at a visitor centre and factory tour in Banbridge and visit the Ulster-American Folk Park near Omagh.

The capital city of Northern Ireland, Belfast has a city centre with an array of facilities including theatres, shops, restaurants, bars and many other features including the Botanic Gardens, the Waterfront Concert Hall and W5 a state of the art centre to explore science. The Ulster Folk & Transport Museum, outside the city, has reconstructed buildings, one of Europe's widest ranging collections of transport history and an exhibition about the Titanic, which was built in Belfast's shipyards. Other attractions on the outskirts of the city include Colin Glen Forest Park and Belfast Zoo.

The National Trust owns several properties in Northern Ireland including Rowallane Gardens outside Belfast, Castle Ward overlooking Strangford Lough, the elegant Florence Court in Co. Fermanagh and the ornate Crown Bar in central Belfast. There are opportunities to enjoy and learn about the countryside at several of the country parks and countryside centres run by Northern Ireland Environment Agency including Roe Valley Park near Limavady and Crawfordsburn outside Bangor.

Other historic towns include the walled City of Derry, Armagh with its two Cathedrals and Georgian townscape, and Downpatrick which has a centre devoted to the life of St Patrick. There are great castles at Enniskillen and Carrickfergus. Seaside resorts include Ballycastle and Portrush on the north coast and Bangor

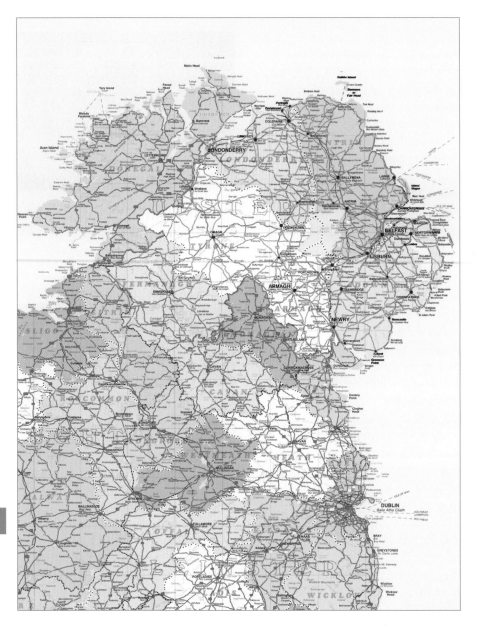

0	10	20	30	40	50	60	70	80 Km

0	10	20	30	40	50 Miles

Resources

Tourism

Northern Ireland Tourist Board
St Anne's Court, 59 North Street, Belfast
BT1 1NB.
☏ 028 9023 1221
    Textphone 028 9089 5512
✉ info@nitb.com
🌐 www.discovernorthernireland.com
All Northern Ireland Tourist Board
publications, including guides to hotels, bed
& breakfast, self-catering accommodation
and attractions are available in alternative
formats and can be downloaded from the
website.

Transport

P & O Ferries
☏ 08716 64 20 20
🌐 www.poferries.com
Operate both fast craft and conventional
ferries between Larne and Cairnryan and
fast craft on a summer seasonal service
between Larne and Troon. On board there
are lifts between car and passenger decks
and toilets for disabled passengers. Advice
on the suitability of vessels is available when
booking and at least 48 hours notice is
requested for any assistance that may be
required.

Stena Line
Stena House, Station Approach, Holyhead,
Anglesey LL65 1DQ.
☏ 08447 707070
🌐 www.stenaline.co.uk
Operate traditional ferry and fast-ferry
services on a number of routes to
Ireland. For Northern Ireland the routes

are Liverpool to Belfast and Cairnryan
to Belfast. These vessels are accessible
to wheelchair users. Assistance can be
provided at ports and on board although
as much notice as possible is requested.
For more information on their routes and
services see their website.

Translink
Central Station, Belfast BT1 3PB.
☏ 028 9066 6630
    Textphone 028 9035 4007
🌐 www.translink.co.uk
Translink can provide information on the
accessibility of train and bus transport
throughout Northern Ireland. Information
on access at rail and bus stations is given on
their website.

Information & advice

Disability Action
Portside Business Park, 189 Airport Road
West, Belfast BT3 9ED.
☏ 028 9029 7880
    Textphone 028 9029 7882
✉ hq@disabilityaction.org
🌐 www.disabilityaction.org
Disability Action can provide general
information on holiday accommodation
and transport in Northern Ireland.

Diabetes UK Northern Ireland
Bridgewood House, Newforge Lane, Belfast
BT9 5NW.
☏ 028 9066 6646
✉ n.ireland@diabetes.org.uk
🌐 www.diabetes.org.uk/northernireland
An annual support holiday for children aged
8-11 years and a youth support holiday,
for ages 12-17 are arranged, to help young
people manage their diabetes in a holiday

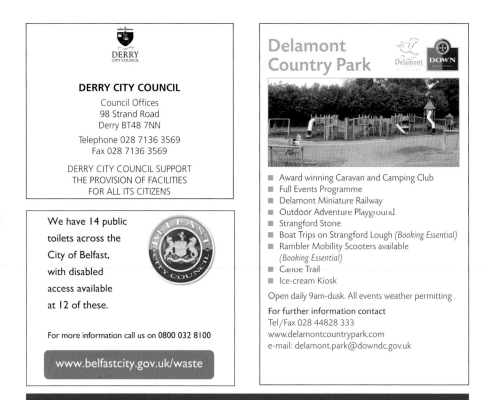

environment at which there is an organised programme of events and activities. The holiday is staffed by volunteers including healthcare professionals. Weekends for adults and families are also arranged.

Equipment hire

SHOPMOBILITY

The National Federation of Shopmobility UK (NFSUK), PO Box 6641, Christchurch, BH23 9DQ.
- 0844 41 41 850
- info@shopmobilityuk.org
- www.shopmobilityuk.org

Hire manual and powered wheelchairs and scooters. Have a range of branches around the UK. You can find the nearest Shopmobility schemes to you on their on-line Directory. Access is obtained by clicking on the 'Shopmobility Directory' button on the top of the row to the left of their website and using the search criteria. You will need to contact a specific Shopmobility Scheme in order to make equipment bookings or find out detailed information. General and contact information is contained in their Directory.

McElmeel Mobility Services

15 Ballyscandal Road, Armagh BT61 8BL.
- 028 3752 5333
- info@mobility-services.com
- www.mobility-services.com

Vehicle adaption company that has for hire both cars fitted with hand controls and those that can carry passengers in wheelchairs.

Accommodation

KILKEEL, Co. Down

Mourne Activity Centre

42 Ballinran Road, Kilkeel BT34 4JA.
- 028 4176 5727
- tina.kenmuir@inclusionmatters.org

Holiday & Conference Centre near the Mourne Mountains. Special interest tours, festival breaks, craft and traditional skills courses are available. Offer multi-activity breaks, such as walking, cycling, horse riding, golf, falconry, fishing, adventure outdoor activities, team building & painting breaks many of which are suitable for disabled visitors.

LISNASKEA, Co. Fermanagh

Share Holiday Village

Smith's Strand, Lisnaskea BT92 0EQ.
- 028 6772 2122
- www.sharevillage.org

Holiday and Activity Centre designed for use by disabled people based on Smith's Strand near Lisnaskea in County Fermanagh – Northern Ireland. Waterside location. Accommodates people from all backgrounds in large numbers.

Share is a charity that works for the inclusion of disabled and non-disabled people by providing opportunities for all to participate in a wide range of creative, educational and recreational programmes through over 30 different arts, land and water activities.

About the Republic of Ireland

The 26 counties of the Republic: Carlow, Cavan, Clare, Cork, Donegal, Dublin, Galway, Kerry, Kildare, Kilkenny, Laois, Leitrim, Limerick, Longford, Louth, Mayo, Meath, Monaghan, Offaly, Roscommon, Sligo, Tipperary, Waterford, Westmeath, Wexford and Wicklow provide a varied and rich holiday opportunity.

The ancient heritage is all around and the Republic is full of myths and legends. Turn off a motorway and you'll find standing stones, fairy forts, stone circles, burial mounds and dolmens that have intrigued travellers for centuries. The Celtic love of arts and song is alive in modern Ireland, where a taste for theatre, music, literature and history are key to the national identity.

You could spend days in the Boyne Valley, visiting Brú na Bóinne and the Hill of Tara. Or take a trip to an island: the Iron Age fort, Dun Aengus, has survived on Inis Mór for 2000 years, while Skellig

Michael, off the Kerry coast, dates from the 7th century. This monastic complex perched on a rock is also a UNESCO world heritage site. You could check out the Bronze Age stone circles in Cork and Kerry or the Céide Fields in North Mayo, the most extensive Stone Age site in the world. Or visit the National Museum in Dublin to see the greatest collection of prehistoric gold objects in Western Europe. The sun shining through the passage tomb at Newgrange at the winter solstice was one of the wonders of the ancient world. Now it is a UNESCO world heritage site.

The capital city, Dublin, offers an eclectic mix of city, countryside and coastline. Temple Bar, on the south bank of the River Liffey is Dublin's cultural quarter, with a medieval street pattern and narrow cobbled streets. It has many pubs, a regular book market, a lively nightlife, a popular shopping area and is the location of many Irish cultural institutions, including the Irish Photography Centre, the Ark Children's Cultural Centre, the Irish Film Institute, incorporating the Irish Film Archive, the Temple Bar Music Centre, the Arthouse Multimedia Centre, as well as the Irish Stock Exchange and the Central Bank of Ireland.

Visit Kilmainham Gaol, one of the largest unoccupied gaols in Europe. Or Dublin castle, originally built on the orders of King John of England in 1204 on a site previously settled by the Vikings. For fun, try the National Wax Museum at Foster Place.

Resources

Tourism

Tourism Ireland Ltd

Head Office, 5th Floor, Bishop's Square, Redmond's Hill, Dublin 2.

📞 +353 (0)1 476 3400

🌐 www.tourismireland.com

UK Office: Nations House, 103 Wigmore Street, London W1U 1QS.

📞 0800 039 7000

📧 info.gb@tourismireland.com

Tourism Ireland hold some information on accessible accommodation. Suitable properties are indicated in their annual *Guide to Guest Accommodation* and *Guide to Self-Catering Accommodation* and on their website although the information is not readily searchable.

Office of Public Works

Visitor Services, Office of Public Works,Unit 20, Lakeside Retail Park,Claremorris,Co. Mayo.

📞 + 353 1 647 6592

📧 info@heritageireland.ie

🌐 www.heritageireland.ie

Manage a wide range of heritage sites including monuments and historic buildings throughout the country. Their annual visitor Information leaflets include an indication of the extent of access for disabled visitors.

Transport

Irish Ferries

Contact Centre, PO Box 19, Alexandra Road, Ferryport, Dublin 1.

📞 0818 300400

📧 info@irishferries.com

📧 disabilityofficer@irishferries.com

🌐 www.irishferries.com

UK office: Corn Exchange, Brunswick Street, Liverpool L2 7TP.

📞 08705 171717

Operate car ferry services on the Holyhead-Dublin and Pembroke-Rosslare routes and also a fast ferry service between Holyhead and Dublin. All vessels have facilities for disabled passengers and at all four ports terminals have been built to be accessible. Advance notification at the time of booking is requested if passengers feel they have specific requirements. Much information for disabled passengers can be found on their website under 'special needs' and anyone with more specific information should contact the Disability Officers through the Contact Centre or via the disability officer email address above.

Irish Railways – Iarnród Eireann

📞 +353 (0)1 703 2634

📧 access@irishrail.ie

🌐 www.iarnrodeireann.ie
   www.irishrail.ie

General information on access and services for disabled passengers as well as information on the accessibility of individual stations is available on the website. Choose 'Travel and Station Information' and then 'Accessibilty'. Requests for assistance should be made in advance, preferably at least 24 hours, to the station from which the journey is starting

Cuan Na Mara

Self-catering cottage and house on the Inishowen peninsula of County Donegal, Ireland. Our two-storey house is designed with the needs of the disabled community in mind.

Contact:
Mrs Sarah Lafferty
Tel: 07493 79121 or
00353 749379121
info@inishowen
cottage.com
www.inishowen
cottage.com

Visit Radar's online shop

For a range of products to promote independent living.

www.radar-shop.org.uk

or to the Mobility Liaison Office, Iarnród Eireann, Connolly Station, Dublin 1.

P & O Ferries
☎ 08716 64 20 20
🌐 www.poferries.com
Car ferry services are operated to Dublin from Liverpool however the vessels used do not have lifts between the car deck and the main passenger areas. Advice on the suitability of vessels is available when booking and at least 48 hours notice is requested for any assistance that may be required.

Stena Line
Stena House, Station Approach, Holyhead, Anglesey LL65 1DQ.
☎ 08705 707070
   Textphone 08795 421127
🌐 www.stenaline.co.uk
Operate ferry services between Holyhead and Dun Laoghaire and Dublin and between Fishguard and Rosslare using vessels that are accessible to wheelchair users. Assistance can be provided at both port and on board although as much notice as possible is requested. There are toilets fitted with the NKS lock at the Fishguard and Holyhead terminals.

Information & advice

Irish Wheelchair Association
Áras Chúchulainn, Blackheath Drive, Clontarf, Dublin 3.
☎ +353 (0)1 818 6400
✉ info@iwa.ie
🌐 www.iwa.ie
Voluntary organisation of people with physical disabilities. Operate an Information Resource Centre which has some information on accessible holidays in Ireland and elsewhere. It also has a holiday and respite centre in Roscommon, a small holiday centre in Kilkenny, and a respite centre in Dublin.

Equipment hire

SHOPMOBILITY
The National Federation of Shopmobility UK (NFSUK), PO Box 6641, Christchurch BH23 9DQ.
☎ 0844 41 41 850
✉ info@shopmobilityuk.org
🌐 www.shopmobilityuk.org
Hire manual and powered wheelchairs and scooters. Have a range of branches around the UK. You can find the nearest Shopmobility schemes to you on their on-line Directory. Access is obtained by clicking on the 'Shopmobility Directory' button on the top of the row to the left of their website and using the search criteria. You will need to contact a specific Shopmobility Scheme in order to make equipment bookings or find out detailed information. General and contact information is contained in their Directory.

Advance Electrical Mobility
4 Crumlin Village, Dublin 12, Ireland.
☎ +353 1 455 3168
✉ info@aemobility.com
🌐 www.aemobility.com
Supply and maintain a wide range of
mobility and other equipment with
powered scooters and wheelchairs available
for rent.

BOC Medispeed
BOC Home Care, Blyry Business Park,
Athlone County West Meath, Ireland.
☎ 00 800 220 20202
✉ medispeed@bocgascs.ie
   healthcareinfo.ie@boc.com
🌐 www.boconline.ie
   www.bochealthcare.ie

The major supplier of medical oxygen
in Ireland can provide both domestic
and ambulatory oxygen for tourists with
advanced notice on arrival in the country or
at their final destination.

MMS Medical Ltd
51 Eastgate Drive, Little Island, Cork,
Ireland.
☎ +353 21 461 8000
✉ info@mmsmedical.ie
🌐 www.mmsmedical.ie
Company, with additional centres in Dublin
and Galway, that can hire and sell a wide
range of mobility and other equipment.

Motability Ireland Ltd
The Irish Mobility Centre, Unit 21,
Ashbourne Industrial Park, Ashbourne, Co
Meath, Ireland.
☎ +353 1 835 9173
✉ sales@motabilityireland.com
🌐 www.motabilityireland.com
Family-owned company with long
experience of carrying out vehicle
adaptations for disabled people. They have
a fleet of hire cars including wheelchair
accessible vehicles and automatic cars fitted
with hand controls.

McElmeel Mobility Services
15 Ballyscandal Road, Armagh BT61 8BL.
☎ 028 3752 5333
✉ info@mobility-services.com
🌐 www.mobility-services.com
Vehicle adaption company that also hires
out cars fitted with hand controls and cars
that can carry passengers in wheelchairs.

Accommodation

Trident Holiday Homes

E8 Network Enterprise Park Kilcoole, Co. Wicklow.

- ☎ +353 (0)1 201 8440
- ✉ reservations@tridentholidayhomes.ie
- 🌐 www.tridentholidayhomes.ie

Represent a range of self-catering accommodation in many parts of Ireland. Their brochure indicates those that have some facilities for disabled people.

DONAMON, Co. Roscommon

Cuisle

Donamon, Co. Roscommon.

- ☎ +353 (0)90 666 2277
- ✉ cuisle@iwa.ie
- 🌐 www.cuisle.com

A fully accessible holiday centre owned by the Irish Wheelchair Association. Located within the magnificent 50 acre site of Donamon Castle, a short drive from the quaint town of Roscommon. Highly-trained staff specialise in providing accessible and supported holidays and breaks to people with disabilities.

DUBLIN

Carmel Fallon Respite Centre

Blackheath Drive, Clontarf, Dublin 3.

- ☎ +353 (0)1 818 6458
- ✉ karen.cronin@iwa.ie
- 🌐 www.iwa.ie

Holiday and respite centre in grounds of Irish Wheelchair Association headquarters, near the coast and public transport north of City Centre.

KNOCK, Co. Mayo

Knock House Hotel

Ballyhaunis Road, Knock, Co. Mayo.

- ☎ +352 (0)94 93 88088
- ✉ info@knockhousehotel.ie
- 🌐 www.knockhousehotel.ie

Modern hotel located in the village of Knock, Co. Mayo. Minutes from the famous Knock Shrine, this hotel is in the heart of the unspoilt countryside, beside 100 acres of Shrine grounds. 20 minutes from 'Ireland West Airport Knock' and 10 minutes from Claremorris Train Station. The hotel provides a 13-seater courtesy coach pick up & drop off service. The hotel has 68 comfortable, non-smoking bedrooms, of which six have been specially designed to cater for wheelchair users. Many of the rooms enjoy views of the countryside county Mayo has to offer.

"

Guernsey is a special place, a thriving community that welcomes its visitors and leaves a lasting impression on all who set foot there.

"

Channel Islands

> *There are no cars, giving Sark an enchantment which is quite unique; its spell draws visitors back for their holidays, year after year.*

Visit Channel Islands

Welcome to the Channel Islands, where British and French influences meet and where an unexpected mix of stunning scenery, rich heritage and varied lifestyles are waiting to be discovered.

Jersey

With its unspoiled landscape and unique blend of British and French influences, Jersey really is a place where you can get away from it all, lose yourself in the Island's winding lanes or on its breath-taking coast. English is spoken and sterling is the currency – yet the streets are named in French. Jersey is reassuringly familiar to visitors from both sides of the Channel.
www.jersey.com

Guernsey

A heady mix of stunning scenery and the best of contemporary living, Guernsey is the perfect destination. Inspiring walks along the cliff paths, or lazy days on the island's beautiful beaches, Guernsey has it all.

St Peter Port, the island's capital, is a bustling harbour town, a tapestry of architectural styles that tell the story of the region's changing fortunes. Ask anyone who's been here. Guernsey is a special place, a thriving community that welcomes its visitors and leaves a lasting impression on all who set foot there.
www.visitguernsey.com

Alderney

Alderney, the third largest of the Channel Islands invites you to travel to and discover one of the few unspoiled, peaceful and natural British Isles. The island enjoys a mild climate and independence, with its own government and a fledgling off-shore finance and E-commerce sector. Despite being only 8 miles from mainland France and 30 miles from Jersey, Alderney has avoided mainstream tourism.

Visit Alderney and you will discover an oasis with an ancient and varied history, an abundance of flora and fauna, beautiful beaches, an enviable lifestyle with that unique, contagious phenomenon known as 'the Alderney Feeling'.

www.visitalderney.com

Herm

Herm is 3 miles from the coast of Guernsey and the perfect place to stay for a truly relaxing island holiday; ideal for families and anyone wanting to "get away from it all". Enjoy our beautiful unspoilt beaches and safe, clean pollution-free environment. There are no cars, no crowds and definitely no stress.

You can visit Herm for the day or choose to stay on the Island where we can offer a variety of accommodation to suit all tastes. You could stay in one of our comfortable self catering cottages or be pampered at The White House Hotel, the only hotel on the Island, where there are no telephones, televisions or clocks. You can also camp with glorious views across the French coast.

www.herm.com

Sark

Sark is the smallest of the four main Channel Islands, located 80 miles off the south coast of England. It boasts 40 miles of what must be one of the most picturesque coastlines anywhere in the world. There are no cars, giving Sark an enchantment which is quite unique; its spell draws visitors back for their holidays, year after year.

www.sark-tourism.com

Find out more information about the Channel Islands at:

www.visitchannelislands.com

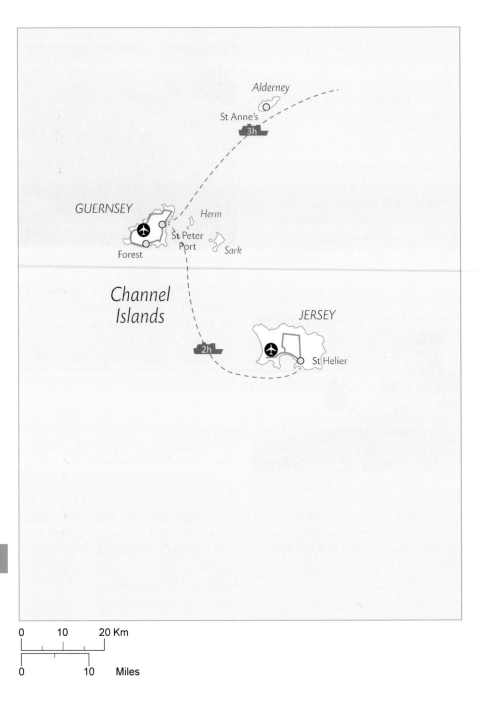

Alderney

St Anne's

3h

GUERNSEY

Herm

St Peter Port

Sark

Forest

Channel
Islands

JERSEY

2h

St Helier

0   10   20 Km

0   10   Miles

Resources

ALL ISLANDS

Tourism

Visit Channel Islands
Ⓦ www.visitchannelislands.com
You can find information about Jersey, Guernsey, Alderny, Herm and Sark on the Channel Islands tourist board website.

Transport

There are flights to both Jersey and Guernsey from many airports and regular inter-Island flights. Consult your travel agent and request assistance in advance.

Airlines offering scheduled services include:
Aer Arann
Ⓣ 0800 587 2324
Ⓦ www.aerarann.com

Aer Lingus
Ⓣ 0870 876 5000
Ⓦ www.aerlingus.com

Aurigny Air Services
Ⓣ 01481 822886
Ⓦ www.aurigny.com

Blue Islands
Ⓣ +44 (0)8456 20 21 22
Ⓦ www.blueislands.com

BmiBaby
Ⓣ 0905 8282828
Ⓦ www.bmibaby.com
(Calls cost 65p per minute from a BT Landline. Calls from mobiles and other networks will be considerably more.)

British Airways
Ⓣ 0844 493 0787
Ⓦ www.britishairways.com

British Midland
Ⓣ 0844 8484 888
Ⓦ www.flybmi.com

FlyBE
Ⓣ 0871 700 0535
Ⓦ www.flybe.com

Thomsonfly
Ⓣ 0871 231 4787
Ⓦ www.thomsonfly.com

Condor Ferries
Ⓔ reservations@condorferries.co.uk
Ⓦ www.condorferries.co.uk
Operate fast car ferry services to Guernsey, Jersey and France all year from Weymouth and from Poole from spring to October. A traditional ferry service is also operated all year from Portsmouth. Fast ferry services also operate between Jersey and Guernsey and to St Malo both from the Channel Islands and UK. There is lift between the car deck and the main passenger facilities. Disabled passengers should ask for any assistance that may be required when booking.

For port enquiries contact

Weymouth	Ⓣ	01305 763003
Poole	Ⓣ	01202 207215
Guernsey	Ⓣ	01481 729666
Jersey	Ⓣ	01534 601000

JERSEY

Tourism

Jersey Tourism

Liberation Square, St Helier, Jersey JE1 1BB.
- 📞 01534 500777
- ✉ info@jersey.com
- 🌐 www.jersey.com

Jersey Tourism supplies general tourist material and can provide information on accessible accommodation, attractions, transport, equipment hire and facilities.

Sea fishing
- 📞 01534 858046
- 🌐 www.tarkaseatrips.com

A boat, 'Theseus II', designed to carry wheelchair users can be chartered for fishing trips.

Transport

Bus services
- 📞 01534 877772
- 🌐 www.mybus.je

There are a number of low-floor vehicles that can carry passengers in wheelchairs. These are in use on most routes. For further information contact St Helier Bus Station Information Office.

Taxis

In addition to accessible taxis that can be hired from taxi ranks, the following have private hire cars that can carry wheelchair users:

Luxicabs
- 📞 01534 888333
- 📞 01534 887000

Citicabs
- 📞 01534 499999

Equipment hire

Channings Mobility
- 📞 01534 743982

Toilet, walking and mobility equipment are available.

Guardian Nursing Services
- 📞 01534 732335

Wheelchairs and bathing equipment are available for hire.

Jersey Cheshire Home

Rope Walk, St Helier JE2 4UU.
- 📞 01534 285858
- ✉ jersey.cheshire@jerseymail.co.uk

The hydrotherapy pool and gymnasium at the Jersey Cheshire Home on the outskirts of St Helier may be booked by disabled visitors when not otherwise in use.

The Hire Shop
- 📞 01534 873699

Manual wheelchairs are available to hire.

Technicare
- 📞 01534 888975

Scooters, wheelchairs, hoists and other equipment are all available to hire.

SHOPMOBILITY

The National Federation of Shopmobility UK (NFSUK), PO Box 6641, Christchurch BH23 9DQ.
- 📞 0844 41 41 850
- ✉ info@shopmobilityuk.org
- 🌐 www.shopmobilityuk.org

Hire manual and powered wheelchairs and scooters. Have a range of branches around the UK. You can find the nearest Shopmobility schemes to you on their on-line Directory. Access is obtained by clicking on the 'Shopmobility Directory' button on the top of the row to the left of their website and using the search criteria. You will need to contact a specific Shopmobility Scheme in order to make equipment bookings or find out detailed information. General and contact information is contained in their Directory.

Publications

A Guide to Jersey for the Disabled

W jersey.com/english/aboutjersey/disabledinformation

This guide has been compiled in association with the Jersey Access Group to assist disabled visitors to the Island. It includes a listing of accessible toilets and details of local activities. It can be found in the Disabled Information area of the About Jersey section of the tourist board website.

Gentle Wanders: Access to Nature in Jersey

Gives details of 15 wildlife sites that can be accessed by wheelchair users is available from Jersey Tourism (see contact details at the beginning of this section).

GUERNSEY

Tourism

VisitGuernsey

Information & Accommodation Services, PO Box 23, St Peter Port, Guernsey GY1 3AN.

T 01481 723552
E enquiries@visitguernsey.com
W www.visitguernsey.com

Provide general information about Guernsey and also assist with finding accommodation suitable for disabled visitors.

Guernsey Information Centre

North Esplanade, St Peter Port, Guernsey, GY1 2LQ

T +44 1481 723552
E info.centre@cultureleisure.gov.gg
W www.visitguernsey.com

Transport

Island Coachways

The Tramshed s, Les Banques, St Peter Port, Guernsey GY1 2HZ

T 01481 720210
W www.icw.gg

This company operates bus services on Guernsey and is introducing new low floor vehicles with ramps and space for a wheelchair user. Contact the company for information on routes and schedules.

Information & advice

DIAL

Offer free, impartial and confidential information and advice by telephone to disabled people, their relatives and professionals. Local branches of DIAL are constantly changing but at the time of writing, the following groups were members of DIAL UK and may be able to help visitors in their areas. Please call before travelling to check whether the service and organisation is still available.

Guernsey Information Exchange
☎ 01481 707470

A member of DIAL, GIE offers a free, impartial and confidential service of information and advice by telephone to disabled people, their relatives and professionals.

Equipment hire

St John Ambulance & Rescue Service
Healthcare Equipment Centre, Rohais, St Peter Port, Guernsey GY1 1YN.
☎ 01481 729268

The Centre has a range of equipment, including wheelchairs, for sale or hire. Early booking of hired equipment is recommended. Spare parts are stocked and repairs can be carried out.

ALDERNEY

Tourism

Information on Alderney is available from The Guernsey Tourist Board or the Alderney Tourism Office:
☎ 01481 822811
🌐 www.visitalderney.com

Alderney Information Exchange
☎ 01483 824823

A member of DIAL UK, offering a free, impartial and confidential service of information and advice by telephone to disabled people, their relatives and professionals.

Accommodation

JERSEY

Jersey Cheshire Home
Eric Young House, Rope Walk, St Helier JE2 4UU.
☎ 01534 285858
✉ welcome@jerseycheshirehome.je
🌐 www.jerseycheshirehome.je

The Leonard Matchan Suite is a respite unit attached to a purpose-built residential / nursing home for disabled people.

Maison Des Landes Hotel
St Ouen, Jersey JE3 2AA.
☎ 01534 481683
✉ contact@maisondeslandes.co.uk
🌐 www.maisondeslandes.co.uk

Maison des Landes is a charitable Trust set up by the Lions Club of Jersey to provide holidays in Jersey specifically for disabled people. The Hotel caters for disabled guests and their families or escorts, in accommodation which has been specially designed to meet the needs of disabled people. The hotel is situated nine miles from St. Helier on the gorse and heather covered headlands of Les Landes, with panoramic views of St. Ouen's Bay and the Atlantic. The hotel has a large heated indoor pool, with special wheelchairs and ramped sides for easy access. Hotel staff are on hand to assist guests into the pool.

"

The long history of the Isle has much to show. Ancient stone-age monuments such as Cashtal Yn Ard, abound.

"

Isle of Man

> *Sometimes, the best discoveries are right under your nose. Lying right at the heart of the British Isles, the Isle of Man is both familiar and a world apart.*

About Isle of Man

The Isle of Man is as lovely as it is odd. Sitting in the middle of the Irish Sea, it has a unique culture and landscape, sometimes similar to the countries that surround it, sometimes completely different.

For starters, it is a separate nation (it isn't even in the European Union!). It has its own language, the engaging Manx, an ancient Celtic tongue. It has its own government: the Tynwald, which has ruled continuously for a thousand years (longer than any other). The cats have no tails and the sheep have got four horns. It is home to the hugely popular and wonderfully dangerous TT races.

The landscape is surprisingly dramatic for such a small place. High hills rise up along the length of the island. The highest is Snaefell; best climbed in the comfort of a Victorian tram. From the top you can see six kingdoms (heaven included!); on a good day you can easily make out the mountaintops in the countries edging the Irish Sea. Where

the mountains of the island meet the sea to the west, great sea cliffs rise up. The landscape has an Irish feel (it stood in for Ireland in the comedy film 'Waking Ned'). Where the island's streams and becks meet the coast, verdant glens are formed, thick with ferns.

The long history of the Isle has much to show. Ancient stone-age monuments such as Cashtal Yn Ard, abound. Celtic and Viking crosses can be found in churchyards across the island. It has two wonderful castles, Castle Rushen in the old capital Castletown is one of Europe's best preserved, Peel Castle on its own island, one of the most romantic. The Victorian age has given it elegant resorts such as Douglas, and the world's largest waterwheel at Laxey.

The food is rather good too. Kippers, a Manx specialty. And queen scallops or 'queenies'. The seagulls at Peel like queenies too, dropping them onto the cliffs to smash them and get at their succulent flesh!

Explore the Isle of Man
Sometimes, the best discoveries are right under your nose. Lying right at the heart of the British Isles, the Isle of Man is both familiar and a world apart. Timelessly beautiful, with a character and spirit all of its own.

Explore the Isle of Man and you will find a place full of beguiling contrasts and character. Many people fall under its spell and return year after year – perhaps you will be next.

"I can't tell you how brilliant it was – it is so pretty, the pace so chilled and relaxed, and everyone was so friendly and helpful. I'm definitely going back".

Find out more information about the Isle of Man at:
www.visitisleofman.com
www.gov.im/tourism

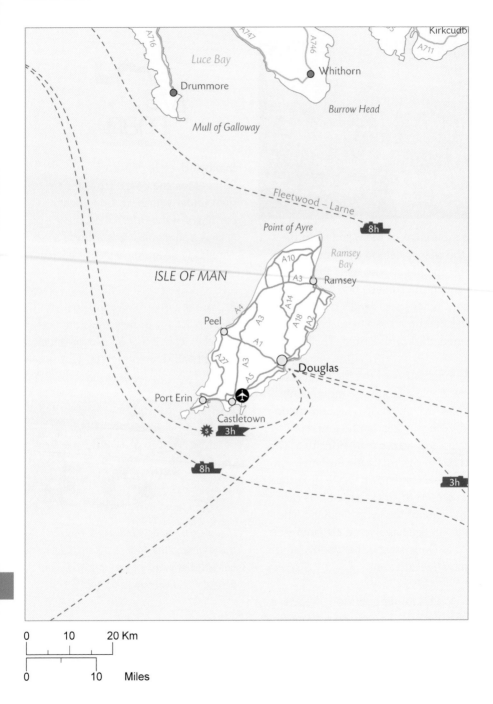

Resources

Tourism

Isle of Man Department of Tourism & Leisure

Sea Terminal Buildings, Douglas IM1 2RG.
- ☎ 01624 686766
- ✉ tourism@gov.im
- 🌐 www.visitisleofman.com

The annual holiday guide to the Isle of Man gives details of accommodation, events and attractions. An accessible accommodation leaflet lists a number of serviced and self-catering places to stay meeting the criteria of the Isle of Man Accessible Scheme.

Transport

AIR SERVICES

There are flights to the Isle of Man from many mainland airports. Consult your travel agent and request assistance in advance. Among the airlines offering scheduled services are:

Aer Arann
- ☎ 0800 587 2324
- 🌐 www.aerarann.com

Blue Islands
- ☎ 08456 20 21 2
- 🌐 www.blueislands.com

Eastern Airways
- ☎ 08703 669100
- 🌐 www.easternairways.com

FlyBE
- ☎ 0871 522 6100
- 🌐 www.flybe.com

Loganair
- ☎ 0871 700 2000
- 🌐 www.loganair.co.uk

Manx2
- ☎ 0871 200 0440
- 🌐 www.manx2.com

FERRY SERVICES

Isle of Man Steam Packet Co.
Imperial Buildings, Douglas, Isle of Man IM1 2BY.
- ☎ 08722 992 992
- 🌐 www.steam-packet.com

Operate services to Douglas from Heysham all year and Liverpool, seasonally, and from Belfast and Dublin from late March to September. The 'Ben-my-Chree' ferry on the Heysham route has a lift to all decks and two cabins adapted for disabled passengers. The winter weekend service from Liverpool, which increases to a twice daily schedule in summer, and the seasonal Belfast and Dublin services use a fast Superseacat which is adapted for disabled passengers. When making a reservation notify the company of any assistance that may be required.

BUS SERVICES

Bus services run between the airport and Douglas and other major towns. Low floor buses are being introduced and information on these, and on arrangements for disabled passengers on their railways, can be obtained from:

Isle of Man Transport
Banks Circus, Douglas IM1 5PT.
- ☎ 01624 662525
- ✉ info@busandrail.dtl.gov.im
- 🌐 www.iombusandrail.info

Space donated by

Roger Harper
Isle of Man

Children First

A guide for everyone involved in the care and support of disabled children. It covers a wide range of topics including health, play, children's services, school and benefits.

Available from Radar's online shop
www.radar-shop.org.uk

Doing Sport Differently

Available early 2012, this guide will support and encourage people with lived experience of disability or health conditions to participate in or become involved in fitness and sport.

Available from Radar's online shop
www.radar-shop.org.uk

Doing Transport Differently

Due out in 2012, this guide includes information and travellers' tales to help and inspire people with lived experience of disability or health conditions to use public transport.

Available from Radar's online shop
www.radar-shop.org.uk

Information & advice

Crossroads Care, Accessibilty Office
Masham Court, Victoria Avenue, Douglas,
Isle of Man IM2 4AW.
- 01624 628926
- mail@crossroadsiom.org
- www.connect2.im/crossroads

Accommodation

You can search for accessible
accommodation on the Isle of Man
Department of Tourism & Leisure's
website:
- www.visitisleofman.com

You will also find accessible accommodation
and facilities throughout the Isle of Man on:
- www.disabledgo.com
- www.openbritain.net

Index of advertisers

Disability Rights UK thanks all its advertisers their support.

The affordable way to enjoy a luxury British break

At 26 locations across the UK, our modern hotels provide style, comfort and top facilities; everything you need to unwind before setting off to explore. And you know you'll be returning to chic surroundings, good food and state-of-the-art health and fitness facilities.

EAT DRINK SLEEP PARTY CHILL SWEAT MEET

www.village-hotels.co.uk

Welcome to more

ACCOMMODATION & RATING

							EXCEPTIONAL	EXCEPTIONAL	1	2	1	2
LONDON												
Best Western Bromley Court Hotel, Bromley	●	●	●	●			●		●			
Meininger Hotel London Hyde Park, South Kensington	●											
Radisson Edwardian Providence Wharf, Providence Wharf	●	●	●									
SACO London – Holborn, London	●						●		●			
Tune Hotels.com – Westminster, Westminster	●								●			
YHA London Central, London	●											
YHA London Thameside, London	●											
SOUTH EAST ENGLAND												
Alconbury Guest House, Royal Tunbridge Wells	●								●			
Bardown Farm, Wadhurst					●		●		●			
Best Western York House Hotel, Eastbourne	●											
Bishop Otter Campus – University Of Chichester, Chichester	●	●		●								
Chichester Park Hotel, Chichester	●											
Eastmere House, Chichester	●											
George Bell House, Chichester	●	●										
Hay Barn & Straw Barn, Chiddingstone	●											
Heath Farm, Plumpton Green	●	●										
Heron Cottage, Biddenden	●											
High Wray, Farnham	●	●										
Honywood At Curtis Farm, Headcorn	●											
Hydro Hotel, Eastbourne	●											
Little Haven, Peacehaven	●											
Little Silver Country Hotel, Tenterden	●	●										
Myhotel Brighton, Brighton	●	●										
Seaspray, Hastings	●						●		●			
Shuttlesfield Barn, Folkestone	●	●										
The Brew House Hotel, Tunbridge Wells	●											
The Jolly Drover, Liss	●											
The Old Dairy, Eastry	●											
The Stanwell, Stanwell	●	●					●		●			
Village Maidstone, Maidstone	●	●										
West Marsden Farm, West Marden	●											
SOUTHERN ENGLAND												
Abbey Guest House, Abingdon	●	●					●		●			
Borthwood Cottages, Borthwood	●	●										

ACCOMMODATION & RATING

Accommodation	Mobility 1	Mobility 2	Mobility 3	Wheelchair	Wheelchair Exceptional	Wheelchair Exceptional	Hearing 1	Hearing 2	Visual 1	Visual 2
Doranes, Ryde	●								●	
Fort Holiday Park, Sandown	●								●	
Granny Anne's, Marlow	●									
Holiday Inn Maidenhead, Maidenhead	●									
Mulberry Rest, Newchurch, near Sandown	●									
Olympic Lodge, Stoke Mandeville	●	●		●						
Sandown Bay Holiday Park, Sandown	●									
South Lodge, Milton Keynes	●	●								
Sunny Bay Apartments, Shanklin	●									
Swallows Nest, Cogges		●								
The Blue House, Gurnard	●									
The Marine Villa, Shanklin	●	●								
The Nurse's Cottage Restaurant with Rooms, Sway	●						●		●	
Weatherhead Farm, Leckhampstead	●									
Yafford Mill Barn, Brighstone	●	●	●	●						
YHA Oxford, Oxford	●									

WEST COUNTRY

Accommodation	Mobility 1	Mobility 2	Mobility 3	Wheelchair	Wheelchair Exceptional	Wheelchair Exceptional	Hearing 1	Hearing 2	Visual 1	Visual 2
2 Danby Cottages, Nr Lydney		●								
Aquila Heights, Dorchester	●	●								
Best Western Mayfield House Hotel, Malmesbury	●	●								
Birchcroft, Ferndown	●	●					●		●	
BOD, Bournemouth	●	●	●				●		●	
Bookham Court, Bookham, Alton Pancras	●	●								
Buzzard Heights B & B, Stawell	●									
Carfax Hotel, Bath	●	●								
Character Farm Cottages, Langton Herring/Rodden	●	●								
Church Farm Country Cottages, Winsley	●	●								
Deerhurst Cottages, Gloucester	●									
Double-Gate Farm, Godney	●	●	●	●						
Ellwood Cottages, Woolland	●	●	●	●						
Gateway and Woodland Cottages, Poole	●	●								
Gorwell Farm Cottages, Gorwell	●	●								
Greyfield Farm Cottages, High Littleton	●									
Half Moon Inn, Horsington	●	●	●				●		●	
Holly Farm Cottages, Taunton	●	●								
Jubilee View Apartment, Weymouth	●									
Lakeview Holiday Cottages, Huntworth	●	●								
Lancombes House, West Milton	●									
Leadon View Barn, Newent		●								

ACCOMMODATION & RATING

	1	2	3	4	5 EXCEPTIONAL	6 EXCEPTIONAL	7 (1)	8 (2)	9 (1)	10 (2)
Lewesdon Farm Holidays, Stoke Abbott	•	•								
Lime Kiln Farm Cottages, Faulkland	•									
Malago Bed and Breakfast, Bristol	•	•	•							
Millspring, Upwey	•									
Mortons House Hotel, Corfe Castle	•	•		•					•	
Norburton Hall, Burton Bradstock	•									
Orchard Barn & Meadow Byre, Littledean	•									•
Priory Cottages, Awre Near Newnham on Severn	•									
SACO Bath, Bath	•						•		•	
South Lytchett Manor Caravan & Camping Park, Lytchett Minster	•								•	
Spreyton House, Weston Super Mare	•									
St Marys Lodge, Croscombe, Wells	•	•	•							
Stable Cottage, Beaminster	•	•								
Stables Cottage, Long Bredy	•	•								
Tamarack Lodge, Chard	•	•								
The Fountain Inn & Lodge, Parkend	•									
The Garden House, Radstock	•	•								
The Lighthouse, Tytherington	•	•								
The Lodge, Lydney, Gloucestershire	•	•								
The Lugger Inn, Chickerell	•	•								
The New Beehive Hotel, Poole	•									
The Royal Hotel, Weston Super Mare	•	•		•					•	
The Stables, South Barrow	•									
Tidmoor Self Catering Cottages, Chickerell	•	•								
Tincleton Lodge and Rose Cottage, Tincleton			•							
Walkers Farm Cottages, Stathe	•	•								
Westermill Farm, Exford	•									
Winford Manor Hotel, Winford	•	•		•						
Woodcombe Lodges, Minehead	•	•								
YHA Cheddar, Cheddar	•									

DEVON & CORNWALL

	1	2	3	4	5	6	7	8	9	10
A Little Bit Of Heaven, St Veep	•	•		•						
Arum House, Padstow	•									
Arvor Holidays, Porthtowan	•									
Ashridge Farm, Sandford	•	•	•							
Atlantis Holiday Apartments, Torquay	•	•					•		•	
Badgers Den, Budleigh Salterton	•	•								
Beer Farm, Okehampton	•	•								

341

ACCOMMODATION & RATING

Accommodation	1	2	3	4	5 (Exceptional)	6 (Exceptional)	7	8	9	10
Berrio Mill, Golberdon, near Callington	•									
Bocaddon Holiday Cottages, Lanreath, Looe	•		•							
Brean Park, Lostwithiel	•	•	•							
Bucklawren Farm, St Martins	•	•								
Budleigh Farm, Moretonhampstead	•									
Chark Country Holidays, Redmoor	•	•	•							
Country Ways, High Bickington, N.Devon		•								
Creedy Manor, Nr Crediton		•								
Crown Lodge, Torquay	•	•		•						
Forda Lodges & Cottages, Kilkhampton	•	•	•	•						
Goodlands, Axminster	•									
Gwel an Mor Lodges, Portreath			•							
Hartswell Farm, Lostwithiel	•	•			•	•				
Higher Laity Farm, Redruth		•								
Hotel Penzance, Penzance	•									
Hue's Piece, Exeter	•	•								
Isles of Scilly Country Guest House, St Marys	•									
Kernock Cottages, Pillaton			•							
Lanhydrock Hotel and Golf Club, Bodmin	•	•								
Lesquite, Looe	•	•	•							
Manna Place, Polzeath	•	•								
Mullacott Farm, Ilfracombe	•									
Mylor Yacht Harbour – Admiralty Apartments, Mylor	•									
Oak Lodge Bed and Breakfast, Stratton, Bude	•	•								
Pendragon Country House, Davidstow	•									
Penquite Farm, Golant	•	•								
Phoenix Retreat, Braunton			•							
Pollaughan Cottages, Portscatho	•	•								
Reddivallen Farmhouse, Boscastle	•									
Ropers Walk Barns, Mount Hawke	•	•	•	•						
Rose Hill Lodges, Porthtowan	•									
Rowan Barn, Hayle		•								
Smallicombe Farm, Colyton	•	•								
Smallicombe Farm, Northleigh	•	•								
South Torfrey Farm, Golant	•	•	•							
Ta Mill, St Clether		•								
The Atlantic, St Mary's	•	•								
The Old Coach House, Boscastle	•	•								
The Olde House, Chapel Amble	•									
The Park, Newquay	•	•								

ACCOMMODATION & RATING

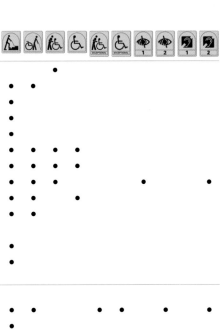

Accommodation & Rating	1	2	3	4	5	6	7	8	9	10	11	12
Todsworthy Farm Holidays, Gunnislake			•									
Tolraggott Farm Cottages, St Endellion	•	•										
Tredinney Farm Holiday Cottage, Crows-An-Wray	•											
Trelagossick Farm, Ruan High Lanes	•											
Trenona Farm Holidays, Ruan High Lanes	•											
Tudor Lodges, Morval	•	•	•	•								
West Hele, Buckland Brewer	•	•	•	•								
West Pitt Farm, Whitnage	•	•	•				•			•		
Whipcott Water Cottages, Holcombe Rogus	•	•		•								
Wooder Manor Holiday Homes, Widecombe-in-the-Moor	•	•										
Yellow Sands Cottages, Harlyn Bay	•											
YHA Lizard Point, Lizard	•											

EASTERN ENGLAND

Accommodation & Rating	1	2	3	4	5	6	7	8	9	10	11	12
Berwick Cottage, East Harling	•	•			•	•		•		•		
Boswell House Hotel, Chelmsford	•											
Boundary Stables, Happisburgh	•	•										
Break-O-Day, South Walsham		•										
Bufo Villae Guest House, Walton-on-the-Naze	•	•										
Caley Hall Hotel, Old Hunstanton		•										
Castaways Holiday Park, Bacton-on Sea.	•								•			
Church Farm Barns, Happisburgh	•	•										
Damerons Farm Holidays, Henley	•	•		•								
Foxgloves Cottage, Hunstanton	•	•										
Fritton Lake Lodges, Fritton	•											
Gladwins Farm, Nayland	•	•										
Greenbanks and Three Palms Leisure Pool, Wendling, Near Dereham	•	•										
Hill Farm Holiday Cottages, Ashdon	•											
Holmdene Farm, Beeston	•	•										
Incleborough House, Cromer	•	•										
Ivy House Country Hotel, Carlton Colville			•									
Ivy House Farm, Wortham		•										
Jack Bridge Cottage @ Jack Bridge Farm, Great Finborough	•											
Jayes Holiday Cottages, Wattisfield	•	•	•									
Jex Farm Barn and Stable, Little Snoring	•	•										
King Line Cottages, Horning	•	•										
Lee Wick Farm Holiday Cottages, Saint Osyth		•										

ACCOMMODATION & RATING

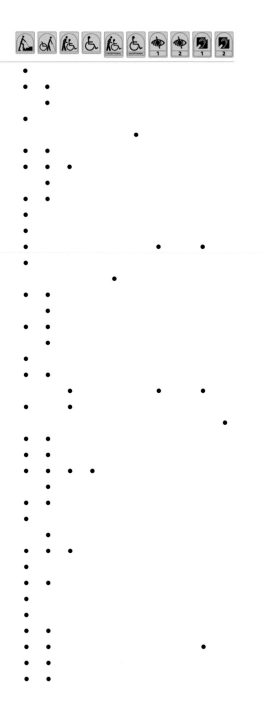

Accommodation & Rating	M1	M2	W-a	W-i	W-E1	W-E2	H1	H2	V1	V2
Leys Farmhouse Annexe, Middlewood Green	•									
Lifehouse Country Spa Resort, Thorpe-le-Soken	•	•								
Lower Wood Farm Country Cottages, Mautby		•								
Moor Farm Stable Cottages, Foxley Wood	•									
Newlands Country House, Reydon, Southwold						•				
Next Door' at Magdalen House, Methwold	•	•								
Norfolk Cottages Malthouse Farm, Gissing	•	•	•							
Oakhill, Heacham		•								
Orwell View Barns, Shotley	•	•								
Overcliff Lodge, Mundesley	•									
Oyster House, West Rudham	•									
Pakefield Caravan Park, Pakefield	•						•		•	
Park Farm Sibton, Sibton	•									
Park House Hotel, Sandringham					•					
Primrose Cottage, Bacton	•	•								
Read Hall Cottage, Mickfield		•								
Red House Farm, Haughley	•	•								
Roman Camp Inn, Aylmerton		•								
School Farm Cottages, Cratfield	•									
Sherbourne Lodge Cottages, Boxford	•	•								
Sheringham Cottages, Sheringham			•				•		•	
Spixworth Hall Cottages, Norwich	•		•							
Swilland Mill, Swilland										•
The Brudenell Hotel, Aldeburgh	•	•								
The Elm Tree Inn, Elm	•	•								
The Lodge, Beccles	•	•	•	•						
The Old Stables, Wissett Lodge, Wissett		•								
The Pheasant Hotel, Kelling	•	•								
The White Horse Inn, Hitcham	•									
Titchwell Manor Hotel, Titchwell		•								
Vine Park Cottage, Great Snoring	•	•	•							
Wattisham Hall Holiday Cottages, Wattisham	•									
Waveney River Centre, Burgh St Peter	•	•								
Wood Farm Cottages, Edgefield	•									
Wood Fen Lodge, Little Downham	•									
Woodland Leisure Park, Trimingham	•	•								
Wylene, Great Barton	•	•							•	
YHA Blaxhall, Blaxhall	•	•								
YHA Sheringham, Sheringham	•	•								

ACCOMMODATION & RATING

Accommodation	♿1	♿2	♿3	♿4	Exc.1	Exc.2	Hearing 1	Hearing 2	Sign 1	Sign 2
YHA Wells-next-the-Sea Youth Hostel, Wells-next-the-Sea	•	•								

EAST MIDLANDS

Accommodation	♿1	♿2	♿3	♿4	Exc.1	Exc.2	Hearing 1	Hearing 2	Sign 1	Sign 2
Alpine Lodge Guest House, Buxton									•	
Ash Tree Cottage – PK763, Hartington	•									
Bainfield Lodge, Burgh on Bain									•	
Bay Tree Cottage, Goulceby, Louth	•									
Belmont Hotel, Leicester	•									
Best Western Admiral Rodney Hotel, Horncastle	•									
Black Swan Guest House, Marton	•									
Blyton Ponds, Blyton	•									
Brackenborough Hall Coach House Holidays, Louth	•						•		•	
Browns, Worksop	•									
Canal Farm Cottages, Grainthorpe	•									
Chatsworth, Skegness	•									
Chestnut Cottage and Willow Cottage, Old Brampton	•									
Church View Barn, Swepstone									•	
Cliff Farm Cottage, North Carlton				•						
Clumber Park Hotel & Spa, Clumber Park, Worksop	•									
Colours Guest House, Mablethorpe	•									
Coton Lodge, Guilsborough	•									
Crewyard Cottages, Leverton, Nr Boston	•									
Dairy Cottage, Newark	•									
Elms Farm Cottages, Hubberts Bridge, Nr Boston	•	•					•		•	
Forest Lodges, Swadlincote		•								
Grange Farm Holiday Cottages, Salmonby	•									
Greenfield Farm, Minting	•									
Greystones Guest Accommodation, South Scarle	•									
Half Moon Hotel and Restaurant, Alford	•									
Hall Farm Hotel & Restaurant, Ashby-cum-Fenby		•								
Helsey House Cottages, Helsey, Nr Hogsthorpe	•									
Hoe Grange Holidays, Brassington	•	•	•				•		•	
Horseshoe Cottage Farm, Hallgates, Cropston	•								•	
Imago at Burleigh Court, Loughborough	•	•		•			•		•	
Ingoldale Park, Ingoldmells			•							
Ings Barn, Thorpe St Peter	•									
Kents Farm Cottages, Grainthorpe	•									
Lady Gate Guest House, Diseworth							•			
Ladybower Apartments, Bamford										•

ACCOMMODATION & RATING

Accommodation	1	2	3	4	5	6	7	8	9	10
Leys Guest House, Loughborough									•	
Lodge Trust Country Park, Oakham	•	•								
Meridian Retreats, Hareby	•									
Nene Valley Cottages, Wigsthorpe		•								
Nursery Cottage, The Granary, Millhouse & The Stables, Louth	•	•								
Oaklands Country Lodges, Church Broughton	•	•								
Old Barn Inn Ltd, Glooston									•	
Old House Farm Cottages, Newhaven	•	•								
Oundle Cottage Breaks, Oundle	•									
Petwood Hotel, Woodhall Spa	•									
Rural Roosts, Stainfield	•									
Sketchley Grange Hotel, Hinckley	•									
Spring Cottage, Castle Donnington									•	
Stennetts Farm Cottages, Holbeach	•									
Stonepits Farm Bed & Breakfast, Wycomb									•	
Supreme Inns, Bicker	•									
The Angel Hotel & Restaurant, Market Harborough									•	
The Courtyard at Hodsock Priory, Blyth		•								
The Fox Inn, Wilbarston									•	
The Grange Holiday Cottages, East Barkwith	•									
The Manor House Stables, Martin	•									
The Old Dairy Cottage, North Willingham			•							
The Old Stables, Harpswell	•									
The Red Lion Inn, Partney, Nr Spilsby	•	•								
The Thomas Centre, Covenham St Bartholomew		•								
Thorganby Hall Farm Cottages, Little Walk and Marris, Thorganby	•									
Tudor Terrace Guest House, Cleethorpes	•									
Village Limits Country Pub, Restaurant and Motel, Woodhall Spa	•									
Walton Thorns Farm Cottages, Thrussington										•
Wheeldon Trees Farm, Earl Sterndale		•								
Whitton Lodge, Hardstoft	•	•								
Wiggonlea Stable and Fletchers Barn, Alderwasley	•									
YHA National Forest, Moira	•	•								
YHA Sherwood Forest, Edwinstowe, Nottinghamshire	•									
Yorkshire Bridge Inn, Bamford									•	

ACCOMMODATION & RATING

ACCOMMODATION & RATING

NORTH WEST ENGLAND

Accommodation	1	2	3	4	5 (Exc.)	6 (Exc.)	Hearing 1	Hearing 2	Visual 1	Visual 2
4 The Croft (Ground Floor Apartment), Caton		•					•			
Ashley Victoria, Blackpool		•								
Ashton Hall Cottages, Ashton with Stodday	•									
Atrium Apartments by Bridge Street Worldwide, Manchester	•						•		•	
Avondale, Lytham St Annes	•									
Avondale, Staveley	•									
Bannerdale, Mungrisdale	•									
Barnacre Cottages, Garstang	•									
Beachwood Guest House, Blackpool	•									
Bessiestown Farm Country Guesthouse, Catlowdy, Longtown	•	•								
Best Western Mytton Fold Hotel and Golf Complex, Langho		•								
Bewleys Hotel, Manchester Airport, Manchester		•								
Big Blue Hotel, Blackpool	•									
Bleasdale Cottages s/c, Lower Fairsnape Farm, Bleasdale	•	•								
Brookside Hotel, Chester	•									
Cleveley Mere Boutique Lodges, Scorton	•									
Clough Head Farm, Edgworth		•								
Coast Apartments, Blackpool	•									
Cross Farm Cottages, Downholland	•									
Eden Vale Luxury Holiday Flats, Morecambe	•									
Fernhill B&B, Rochdale	•									
Grosvenor Pulford Hotel and Spa, Pulford		•					•		•	
Hawksmoor Guest House, Windermere	•									
Herons Well, West Kirby		•								
Hilton Manchester Deansgate, Manchester				•					•	
Holmsdale, Blackpool	•									
Howscales, Kirkoswald	•	•								
Ibis Hotel, Liverpool		•								
Kerridge End Holiday Cottages, Rainow	•		•							
Knotts Farm Holiday Cottages, Quernmore, Lancaster	•	•								
Ladderstile Retreat, Near Congleton	•	•								
Lake District Disabled Holidays, Crook					•					
Lancashire County Cricket Club & Old Trafford Lodge, Manchester		•					•		•	
Linskeldfield Tarn Holiday Cottages, Isel, Cockermouth	•									

ACCOMMODATION & RATING

ACCOMMODATION & RATING

Accommodation	Mobility 1	Mobility 2	Mobility 3	Mobility 4	Access Exceptional	Access Exceptional	Visual Impairment 1	Visual Impairment 2	Hearing Impairment 1	Hearing Impairment 2
Tottergill Farm Cottages, Castle Carrock, Brampton	●									
Wall Hill Farm Guest House, Acton Bridge		●								
Willowbank Holiday Home and Touring Park, Ainsdale, Southport		●					●			
YHA Arnside, Arnside	●	●								
YHA Borrowdale, Longthwaite, Borrowdale	●	●	●	●						
YHA Liverpool, Liverpool	●									
YHA Manchester, Castlefield, Manchester	●	●								

Accommodation	Mobility 1	Mobility 2	Mobility 3	Mobility 4	Access Exceptional	Access Exceptional	Visual Impairment 1	Visual Impairment 2	Hearing Impairment 1	Hearing Impairment 2
5 Leys Holiday Accommodation, Filey			●							
9 Dalegarth and Heron Ghyll, Buckden	●	●								
Beech Farm Cottages, Wrelton	●									
Best Western Monkbar Hotel, York		●								
Brimham Rocks Cottages, Fellbeck		●								
Captain Cook's Haven, Whitby		●								
Cow Pasture Cottage & Swallowtail Cottage, Ebberston		●								
Dale House Farm Cottages, Staithes		●								
Eastgate Cottages, Pickering		●								
Field House Farm Cottages, Sewerby		●								
Flamborough Rock Cottages, Flamborough		●								
Groves Dyke, Whitby	●									
Helme Pasture, Summerbridge		●								
Ilkley Moor Cottages and Apartments at Westwood Lodge, Ilkley	●	●								
Inglenook Guest House, Scarborough	●									
Keld Head Farm Cottages, Pickering	●									
Little Weghill Farm, Preston, Hull	●									
Lovesome Hill Farm, Lovesome Hill	●									
Marina Holiday Apartments, Bridlington		●								
Mel House Cottages, Newton-on-Rawcliffe	●	●	●	●						
Partridge Cottage, Kirkbymoorside				●						
Pound Cottage, Copper Cottage & Crown Cottage, Riccall, York	●	●	●							
Pride-N-Joy, Bridlington			●							
Providence Place, Bridlington	●	●								
Rawcliffe House Farm, Stape			●							
Rudstone Walk Country Accommodation, Brough	●									
Sandsend Bay Cottages, Sandsend		●								
Scarborough Travel and Holiday Lodge, Scarborough	●									

ACCOMMODATION & RATING

Accommodation & Rating	1	2	3	4	5 EXC	6 EXC	7	8	9	10
Sunset Cottage, Newton on Rawcliffe, Pickering	•									
The Cart Shed, Stannington	•									
The Cornmill, Kirkbymoorside	•									
The Courtyard & Ruxpin Cottage, High Catton, Stamford Brigde	•	•								
The Dovecote Barns York, Kelfield	•	•	•							
The Ellerby, Ellerby	•	•								
The Grainary, Harwood Dale				•						
The Hawthornes Lodges, Middleton, Pickering	•									
The Lodge at Birkby Hall, Baliff Bridge, Brighouse	•	•								
The Old Post Office, Thorpe Bassett	•									
Thornton Lodge Farm, Easingwold		•								
Tower House Executive Guest House, Pontefract	•									
Walnut Garth, Swinton, Malton	•									
Weetwood Hall, Leeds		•								
Whitby Holiday Park, Whitby	•								•	
Wolds View Holiday Cottages, Yapham	•									
YHA Helmsley, Helmsley		•					•			
YHA Lockton, Lockton		•								
YHA Whitby, Whitby	•	•					•		•	

NORTH EAST ENGLAND

North East England	1	2	3	4	5 EXC	6 EXC	7	8	9	10
Alwent Mill Cottage, Winston	•									
Beacon Hill Farm, Longhorsley		•								
Brownrigg Lodges, Bellingham	•	•								
Burradon Farm Cottages and Houses, Cramlington, Northumberland	•	•		•			•		•	
Calvert Trust Kielder, Kielder	•	•	•	•				•		•
Carr Edge Farm, Newbrough, Hexham	•	•								
Clover Hill Cottage, Lambley, Near Brampton	•									
Coach House B&B, Bardon Mill	•	•								
Cornriggs Cottages, Cornriggs, Cowshill			•						•	
Craster Pine Lodges, Craster	•	•								
Crookhouse, Kirknewton	•	•								
Doxford Cottages, Northumberland		•								
Doxford Hall Hotel & Spa, Chathill, Northumberland		•							•	
East Greystone Farm Cottages, Gainford		•								
Elwick Farm Cottages, Belford	•									
Euro Hostel Newcastle, Newcastle upon Tyne	•	•					•		•	
Falstone Barns, Falstone	•									

ACCOMMODATION & RATING

Accommodation	1	2	3	4	5	6	7	8	9	10
Fenham Farm, Coastal Bed & Breakfast, Berwick-upon-Tweed	●									
Fenton Hill Farm Cottages, Wooler	●									
Grindon Cartshed, Haydon Bridge	●	●								
Hadrian & Derwent Country Escapes, Ruffside Village			●							
Hamsteels Hall Cottages, Quebec, Durham	●									
Hedley Hall Country Cottages, Sunniside, Nr Newcastle upon Tyne	●	●	●				●		●	
Hilton Newcastle Gateshead, Newcastle upon Tyne		●					●		●	
Linden Hall Golf & Country Club, Longhorsley	●	●								
Little Owl Lodge, Butterknowle	●	●								
Lucker Hall Steading, Lucker, Northumberland		●								
Lumbylaw Cottages, Edlingham	●									
Meadow Hill Guest House, Berwick-upon-Tweed	●									
Mellwaters Barn, Bowes	●	●	●	●					●	
Mill Granary Cottages, Ingleton	●	●								
Old High Shield, Bardon Mill	●									
Outchester & Ross Farm Cottages, Bamburgh	●									
Redesdale Arms, Rochester, Nr Otterburn	●									
River Cottage, Darlington									●	
Shaftoe's, Haydon Bridge	●									
Skylark Cottage, Thornton, Berwick-upon-Tweed									●	
Stable Court, Eggleston	●									
Stonecroft and Swallows Nest, Cockfield, Bishop Auckland			●							
The Collingwood Arms Hotel, Cornhill on Tweed	●									
The Hytte, Bingfield, Hexham	●	●			●	●	●		●	
The Old Byre (Rye Hill Farm), Slaley, nr Hexham		●								
The Old Farmhouse, Grindon Farm, Haydon Bridge	●	●			●	●				
The Reading Rooms, North Charlton	●	●							●	
The Ship Inn, High Hesleden		●								
Village Farm, Shilbottle	●									
West Ord Holiday Cottages, Berwick-upon-Tweed	●									